New Literacies

New Literacies
Third edition

COLIN LANKSHEAR and
MICHELE KNOBEL

Open University Press

Open University Press
McGraw-Hill Education
McGraw-Hill House
Shoppenhangers Road
Maidenhead
Berkshire
England
SL6 2QL

email: enquiries@openup.co.uk
world wide web: www.openup.co.uk

and Two Penn Plaza, New York, NY 10121-2289, USA

First published 2011

A catalogue record of this book is available from the British Library

ISBN-13: 978-0-33-524216-0 (pb)
eISBN: 978-0-33-524217-7

Library of Congress Cataloging-in-Publication Data
CIP data applied for

Typeset by RefineCatch Limited, Bungay, Suffolk
Printed in Great Britain by Ball and Bain Ltd, Glasgow

Fictitious names of companies, products, people, characters and/or data that may
be used herein (in case studies or in examples) are not intended to represent any
real individual, company, product or event.

The McGraw·Hill Companies

To JPG
colleague, compañero, friend

Contents

Foreword

In *New Literacies: Everyday Practices and Social Learning*, Colin Lankshear and Michele Knobel invite readers to participate fully in coming to grips with why the *new* in new literacies will be with us for some time to come. Not *new*, as in a replacement metaphor, but new in the sense that social, economic, cultural, intellectual, and institutional changes are continually at work, even as I write. It is this perceived permanency of the new that is destined, in my opinion, to make a difference in how educators view and respond to new literacies in relation to everyday social practices and classroom learning.

But I am getting ahead of myself. Let me back up and recount some of the ways in which the authors invite us, as readers, to experience new literacies first hand, regardless of where we are on our personal learning trajectories. If grounding in new literacies is what we need, it is readily available. The authors provide the most accessible account of the evolution of new literacies that I have read anywhere. Not satisfied with words alone, Lankshear and Knobel point us to websites that exemplify the very points they are making, and in a timely fashion. This modelling of just-in-time learning is effective, to say the least. What is more, the websites they have chosen typically invite us to interact with content in ways that makes concepts such as *participatory culture, collaboration,* and *distributed expertise* meaningful, and above all useful, especially when dealing with the demands and constraints that are part of teaching and learning in today's schools at every level, including post-secondary institutions.

This third edition of *New Literacies* invites us to go beyond merely imagining how advances in technology and a rapidly ascending social paradigm are affecting our ways of being, both professionally and in our spare time. It does so by taking us behind the scenes to witness first-hand how the authors use new literacies in applying contemporary principles of social learning, (e.g., 'performance before competence') to their own work as teacher educators. An up-to-date account of how these same literacies and principles apply to curriculum and learning in an urban public school serving grades 6 through 12 is but another indicator of the authors' attention to existing examples of the concepts they explore.

Like the two earlier editions of *New Literacies*, this third edition offers an abundance of state-of-the-art content. It has the added advantage, however, of making its appearance at a time that coincides with a sea change of reform-minded initiatives driven in part by well-known international evaluations, such as PISA (Program for International Student Assessment), which compares countries globally on the basis of their 15-year-olds' scholastic performance in the domains of reading, mathematical, and scientific literacy. PISA, unlike most nationally administered large-scale assessments, offers countries a choice in terms of whether or not their students will be assessed using e-texts. This choice seems particularly cogent given that PISA evaluates young people's acquisition of skills deemed essential for full participation in a global society. Moreover, it is a choice that is in direct alignment with the goals and purposes of *New Literacies: Everyday Practices and Social Learning*.

Finally, and most importantly for the first time, in this third edition of a universally respected text, Colin Lankshear and Michele Knobel put their scholarly credentials to work in ways that afford unique and practical insights into how current approaches to formal schooling stand to benefit from incorporating new literacies embedded in a social learning framework. Time has never been more urgent. Any lingering notions that expertise is limited and scarce are outdated and potentially damaging in a world where new literacies hitched to ever advancing technologies are fast determining who will (and will not) be available to interact in a participatory culture – a way of living and being that values collaboration, collective intelligence, and the means for mobilizing distributed expertise.

Donna Alvermann
University of Georgia

Preface to the third edition

When the Open University Press negotiated a third edition of *New Literacies*, we welcomed the opportunity to revise and update our previous work. When we produced the second edition, Facebook was in its infancy, Twitter had not yet been launched, 'apps' were but a twinkle in the 'i' of the smart phone, and social learning was still almost entirely thought about in relation to non-formal or informal learning contexts. The White Paper, *Confronting the Challenge of Participatory Culture: Media Education for the 21st Century* (Jenkins et al. 2006) was not yet published, and John Seely Brown and Richard Adler's (2008) call to address social learning within formal education was two years away.

As people worldwide flooded to social networking and microblogging services, as 'mashing up' serviceware applications became a routine pastime, and as educators interested in serious reform advanced the case for restructuring formal learning along 'participatory' cultural lines, it was time to rethink our ideas about new literacies in relation to education.

This edition builds further on our conception of new literacies in terms of new technical and new ethos 'stuff' from the previous edition, and extends our account of literacy in theory, policy, and practice from 'reading' to the 'new literacies'. The bulk of the book, however, comprises new content. Our accounts of blogging and digital remix have been seriously reframed in order to build on our attempt to put more punch into our thinking about literacy in terms of 'practice theory'. We pay careful attention to the relationship between Web 2.0 as a business model and the affordances of the Read/Write web for participatory culture, and make a concerted effort to address qualitative aspects of participation and collaboration within a range of popular everyday pursuits. The influential argument about the strength of weak ties and the trend toward networked individualism is taken up within the context of discussing online social networking and the significance of network awareness in terms of new literacies.

Part 3 of the book, on social learning, is entirely new. In Chapter 7, we discuss concepts, research, and ideologies pertaining to far-reaching changes that have occurred during recent decades, and some of their potential implications for and applications to formal learning. These include the concepts of 'learning to be', 'collaboration platforms' for learning, 'push' and 'pull' paradigms for mobilizing and allocating learning resources, and the significance currently attached to innovation and productiveness. In Chapter 8, we address some empirical attempts to pursue ideals of social learning within formal learning contexts at school and university levels. We expect to see a rapid growth in theory, research and experimental practices in this broad area during the coming decade.

As always, the chapters that follow are but points on our personal learning trajectories. We believe there is vastly more to be thought and said about new literacies in the current conjuncture than we could ever think or say, let alone say *now*. At the same time, we are hopeful that readers will find something in this book that may be helpful in taking them from where they presently are to where they might want to go in their reflection and practice at the interfaces among literacies, technologies and everyday social engagements.

Colin Lankshear and Michele Knobel
Mexico City
30 May 2011

Acknowledgements

This book has been encouraged and supported in diverse ways by many people to whom we are indebted. We want to acknowledge their support and generosity here.

We have drawn heavily on inspiration from friends and colleagues with whom we work in different ways and in different contexts. We owe much to Donna Alvermann, Chris Barrus, Chris Bigum, Rebecca Black, Bill Cope, Julia Davies, Betty Hayes, Erik Jacobson, Henry Jenkins, Mary Kalantzis, Kevin Leander, Matt Lewis, Guy Merchant, Leonie Rowan, Angela Thomas and, as always, James Paul Gee. In their individual ways, they exemplify the critical, inquiring, progressive spirit that seeks to maximize human well-being using the material and non-material resources available to us. Long may they run.

We want to acknowledge the inspiration we have drawn from work by dana boyd, John Seely Brown, Mimi Ito, Lawrence Lessig, Tim O'Reilly, Andreas Reckwitz, Howard Rheingold and Katie Salen. Their perspectives are absolutely integral to how we think about new literacies, everyday practices and social learning.

Donna Alvermann and Donald Leu have done much to help us understand more clearly who we are trying to write for and why. They have supported our work in the most generous and unobtrusive ways, while at the same time continuing their own tireless and selfless work in the name of better education for all, and especially for those who have received less than their due share of social benefits from the systems within which they are constrained to live. Despite already having more than enough tasks to complete, Donna generously accepted our invitation to write the Foreword for this book. We know what this kind of unsolicited added pressure involves, and treasure the collegiality woven into her text. Don invited us to present the opening Plenary Address at the 2004 National Reading Conference annual meeting in San Antonio, which provided an important motivational opportunity for us to develop material that has been further refined for this book. With Julie Coiro, Don has also extended our range of interest in new literacies through our collaboration in an edited *Handbook of New Literacies Research*.

As always, we appreciate greatly the support of Shona Mullen and our other colleagues at the Open University Press – in particular, Fiona Richman, Umar Masood, James Bishop, Kiera Jamison, Richard Townrow, and Zen Mian. We also thank Susan Dunsmore for her careful copyediting. They are a wonderful team to work with, and we hope that our efforts in this book are enough to repay their continuing faith in our work.

Some chapters in this book build on work that has been published in journals and conference proceedings. We have benefited from the opportunities we have had to rehearse ideas in other places. Thanks are due here to the *International Journal of Learning*, the *Journal of Adolescent and Adult Literacy*, *The 54th Yearbook of the National Reading Conference* and Peter Lang (USA).

During the period in which this book has been conceived and written we have enjoyed strong support from friends, colleagues, and institutions in México, Spain, Australia and Canada. Without this, our work during the past four years simply would not have been possible. We want to thank Angela Guzmán, Hilario Rivera Rodríguez, Ma. del Pilar Avila Guzmán, Gustavo Cabrera López, Gabriel Arreguín Cervantes, Toni Chao, Guadalupe López Bonilla, Alma Carrasco, Pep Aparicio Guadas, Neil Anderson, Ruth Ann Brown, Andrew Manning, the Faculties of Education at Montclair State University, Mount Saint Vincent University, McGill University, and the School of Education at James Cook University.

We want to thank those students who have kindly given us permission to use their work, and the many cohorts of students who, since 2004, have 'come along for the ride' as we have conjointly explored ways of learning that have been new and different for all of us so far as formal educational contexts are concerned. In particular, we want to thank Shannon Donovan, Susan Whitty, Jenny Hawley, Karey Lee Donovan, Marie Barry, Rhonda Currie, Patricia Donovan, Janice Ciavaglia, Holly Stone, Ann Landry, Sonja Beck, Carolyn Coley, Krista Conway, Deborah Hoven, Paula Maynard, Tanya Hunt, Sherry Healey-Jennings, Joy Seaward, Michelle Patey, Anne Payne, Michele Dawson, Dara Best-Pinsent, Robyn Hillier, Lori Deeley, Heather Wood, Donna Powers-Toms and Rosena Dunphy for graciously allowing us to make explicit reference to their work.

We appreciate the work of those anonymous reviewers of the previous edition of this book who responded to invitations by the Open University Press to provide feedback to guide this new edition, and also thank the authors of published reviews of the previous editions for their constructive critical feedback and the boost they gave the previous editions of our book in the marketplace. We'd also like to thank people within the blogosphere who have discussed different chapters and ideas from previous editions, and who have helped us to think more closely about what we mean by 'new literacies'.

Finally, we simply could not survive in our everyday and professional lives without the kinds of resource support provided by Google and Wikipedia, and know we are not alone here.

PART 1

New Literacies: Concepts and Theory

CHAPTER 1

From 'reading' to 'new' literacies

Introduction

During the period from the early 1970s to the early 1990s the profile and status of literacy changed dramatically across many modern education systems, particularly in economically developed Anglo-American countries. This process has intensified since then, with the mass availability and take-up of sophisticated and powerful digital technologies and electronic networks.

Prior to the 1970s in countries like the USA, Canada, Britain, Australia and New Zealand, the word 'literacy' scarcely featured in formal educational discourse. Instead, there was a well-established academic field of reading research, mainly grounded in psycholinguistics, and a range of time-honoured instructional methods for teaching pupils how to decode, encode and comprehend printed alphabetic texts. Seen as the prior condition for getting on with the real business of school learning, teaching reading and writing was 'got out of the way' as quickly as possible following entry to school. It was generally assumed that students at large would master reading and writing well enough to serve them during their school years and beyond. Some, of course, would learn to read and write more quickly than others, and would read and write with greater sophistication and comprehension than others. Some learners would struggle. But to all intents and purposes, the great majority of students would learn to read and write sufficiently well to make their ways into the adult world.

At this time 'literacy' was used generally in relation to non-formal educational settings, and, in particular, in relation to adults who were deemed to be *illiterate*. 'Literacy' was the name given to programmes of non-formal instruction – not associated with formal educational institutions like schools – that were offered to illiterate adults to help them acquire basic abilities to read and write. In Britain, North America, and Australasia, official statistics obtained for census measures indicated near-zero levels of adult illiteracy. Such adult literacy initiatives as existed in these countries were small-scale, largely voluntary endeavours involving adult literacy tutors working with individuals or small groups of learners. Indeed, within First World English-speaking societies, 'literacy teaching' was the name of marginal spaces of non-formal education work intended to provide a 'second chance' for those whose illiteracy was often seen as directly associated with other debilitating or dysfunctional conditions and circumstances. These included 'conditions' like unemployment, imprisonment, drug and alcohol abuse, teenage pregnancy, inferior physical and psychic health, and so on. There was no perception that learning to read and write presented an educational problem or concern on any significant scale.

Literacy to the forefront

By the end of the 1970s, this comfortable viewpoint had been turned upside down throughout modern Anglophone societies. By 1980, literacy had moved from its relatively marginal position within English-language educational discourse, and from its primary association with non-formal adult education initiatives, to the very forefront of educational policy, practice and research. Numerous reasons have been linked to this change, five of which seem to us especially interesting:

1 Paulo Freire and the radical education movement;
2 The 1970s literacy crisis;
3 Literacy, economic growth and social well-being;
4 Literacy, accountability, efficiency and quality;
5 The growth of sociocultural theory.

Paulo Freire and the radical education movement

The rise to prominence of Paulo Freire's work within the larger context of the radical education movement of the late 1960s and early 1970s (see Freire 1972, 1973; Freire and Macedo 1987) was a key factor in bringing the term 'literacy' to the foreground as a key concept in contemporary educational theory and research throughout the English-speaking world. Shortly after his work on education as a practice of freedom was published in Portuguese, Freire was offered a visiting professorship at Harvard University (1969), and his *Cultural Action for Freedom* was published as a *Harvard Education Review* monograph in 1970. His classic work, *Pedagogy of the Oppressed*, was published the same year. Resonant with social justice concerns and a rising tide of critical theory scholarship, Freire's approach to non-formal literacy education captured the imagination, respect, and support of many academics and political activists in First World countries – particularly, in North America – and was adopted as the philosophical basis for national and regional adult literacy programmes in a number of Third World countries. It provided the theoretical underpinning for the development of critical pedagogy, including critical literacy, in the USA during the 1980s. In the years immediately following the publication of Freire's early works, 'literacy' became an important focal concept within emergent sociocultural theory (e.g., Scribner and Cole 1981), and within educational research and theory and teacher education more widely.

Freire's work with peasant groups in Brazil and Chile provided an example of how literacy work could be central to radical approaches to education aimed at building critical social praxis. His concept of literacy as 'reading the word and the world' involved much more than merely the ideas of decoding and encoding print. Far from being the sole objective of literacy education, learning how to encode and decode alphabetic print was integrated into an expansive pedagogy in which groups of learners collaboratively pursued critical consciousness of their world via a reflexive or 'cyclical' process of reflection and action. Through their efforts to act on the world, and to analyse and understand the results of their action, people can come to know the world better: more 'deeply' and 'critically'.

From this perspective, 'illiteracy' is seen as a consequence of unjust social processes and relations that have been created historically and become 'woven' (or, as we might say today, 'hard-wired') into the social structure. Yet, insofar as these unjust social arrangements have been created and are sustained through human activity, they can equally be *changed* through human action. Before such 'transformative cultural action' can occur, however, it is necessary to understand the nature and origins of social oppression.

In Freire's pedagogy, learning to write and read *words* became a focus for adults in pursuing critical awareness of how oppressive practices and relations operated in everyday life. Words that were highly charged with meaning for them – words that expressed their fears, hopes, troubles and their dreams for a better life – provided the vocabulary by which they learned to write and read. These words were discussed intensively in order to explore how the world 'worked'. In the context of this oral discussion, the *written* forms of these words, as well as of other words that could be built out of their syllables and phonemes, were introduced. In the context of discussing and thinking about these words, participants learned what they 'looked like' as text, and how to write and read them.

Within Freire's approach to promoting literacy, then, the process of learning literally to read and write words was an integral part of learning to understand how the world operates socially and culturally in ways that produce unequal opportunities and outcomes for different groups of people. Ultimately, this analysis was to provide a starting point for participants to take action on the world in an attempt to change it in ways that would create social processes and relations that were more just. Groups would undertake cultural action for change in the world in the light of their analysis of their circumstances. They would then analyze and evaluate the results of their action in order to take the next step in cultural action. This *praxis* of reflection and action was the means of knowing the world more deeply and accurately, since it involved 'testing' it to see how it works in the light of concepts and theories developed collaboratively in discussion of experiences and beliefs. Freirean literacy education was, then, an integral component of a radical, politicized pedagogy purposefully designed to stimulate action for change.

The 1970s literacy crisis

A second factor in the development of 'literacy' as a widely used concept in education was the dramatic discovery – many called it an *invention* – of widespread functional illiteracy among adults in the USA during the early 1970s. This was not a measure of 'absolute literacy' but, rather, of the extent to which members of a population could be said to be reading and writing at a level deemed to be the minimal requirement for being able to manage the kinds of texts they would have to deal with on a day-to-day survival basis.

Following its announcement in the USA, culminating in the classic 1983 policy statement *A Nation at Risk* (NCEE 1983), the 'literacy crisis' quickly spread to other emerging post-industrial societies. Whether it was in Britain, the USA, Canada, Australia or New Zealand, much the same storyline emerged: schools were failing to ensure that all learners became literate to the extent required to live 'effectively' under contemporary conditions. Research and reports commissioned by governments claimed relentlessly that standards were falling, that far-reaching educational reform was needed, and that curriculum and pedagogy had to be overhauled in order to ensure that all students would acquire at the very least a functional level of literacy.

Depending on the criteria used to define 'functionality', estimates of functional illiteracy varied. Figures cited for the USA during the 1970s and 1980s ranged from around 10 per cent to almost one-third of the population. British estimates were as high as 6–8 million, or around 15% of the adult population, and Australian estimates suggested that 10% of the adult population might have had serious difficulties with reading and writing. Figures produced for New Zealand in 1977 indicated that 50,000–100,000 people aged 15 and over (5–10% of the adult population at the time) read and wrote below a reading age of $9\frac{1}{2}$ years on standardized PAT tests.

This alleged literacy *crisis* coincided with early awareness of profound structural change in the economy, as the USA moved toward becoming a post-industrial society. Post-industrialism entailed far-reaching restructuring of the labour market and employment as well as deep changes in major organizations and institutions of daily life. Large numbers of people were seen as poorly prepared for these changes. In calls for urgent action to pre-empt an impending disaster, 'Literacy' emerged as the key word.

Literacy, economic growth and social well-being

During the 1950s and 1960s, and again in the 1990s, it became fashionable among development theorists to associate a country's 'readiness' for 'economic take-off' with attainment of a certain level of adult literacy across the nation. For example, during the 1960s, it was widely argued by development theorists that having at least a large minority of the male population achieve literacy was a precondition for underdeveloped nations to 'take off' economically (Anderson 1966). A figure of at least 40 per cent of adults (especially males) deemed literate in a population was seen as the threshold for economic development. This became a rationale for promoting adult literacy campaigns throughout many Third World countries in Africa, Asia, and Latin America as a strategic component of economic and social development policies. Illiteracy was seen as a major impediment to economic development, and literacy campaigns were prescribed as cost-effective measures for developing the minimal levels of 'manpower' needed to give a country a chance for economic take-off. These campaigns were usually undertaken as non-formal programmes aimed at adults – although children often participated – conducted outside the education *system* as such.

1960s versions of human capital theory explained the relationship between literacy levels and economic take-off in terms of the importance of literacy for the emergence of cognitive and personal qualities that are in turn conducive to economic development. Oxenham (1980) argues that the association of literacy with 'a modernization syndrome' and the development of such attitudes and dispositions as 'flexibility', 'adaptability', 'willingness to accept change', and 'proneness to accept innovations', were guiding assumptions driving literacy campaigns in Third World countries following World War II (see Street 1984: 185). Similarly, Hägerstrand claims that the demand for education is at times an innovation that must be introduced in order to open a society up to further innovation. Literacy and other new skills, says Hägerstrand (1966: 244), eventually transform social communications and resistance into patterns more susceptible to innovation and associated progress.

Parallel arguments to those advanced for Third World countries earlier were advanced for so-called 'developed' economies during the 1990s within the context of widespread changes in the conditions of work, key factors impacting on economic and social life, and in the *modus operandi* of public institutions. The OECD spearheaded research, assessment, and policy development work predicated on the perceived relationship between literacy levels, economic growth and labour market viability, and a range of non-market benefits (e.g., OECD 1991; OECD and Human Resources Development Canada 1997). With respect to literacy and economic growth and well-being, it was increasingly believed that the average literacy level of a country's population is a better indicator of economic growth than is educational achievement as measured by credentials (cf. Coulombe et al. 2004). Evidence was advanced that countries with greater inequalities in literacy levels have greater inequalities in income distribution. Emphasis was given to the role of globalization and technological change in generating greater labour market competition, upping the ante for literacy skills in order to compete for better paid work opportunities. Moreover, in many countries, loss of manufacturing and economic restructuring during the

1980s and 1990s had resulted in radically changed conditions of work within companies, where everyday routines like total quality management and devolved responsibility to frontline workers required greater interaction with a range of printed forms and documents on the part of workers who were often migrants in the process of learning the local language (Gee et al. 1996). Reduced levels of welfare support within many countries, and changes in bureaucratic structures increased demands on individuals for independence and 'responsibilization' which, in many cases, meant wrestling with diverse and complex genres of print information. Claims for associations between high literacy and better health outcomes, and between literacy proficiency and public and civic participation, long maintained for developing countries, became increasingly common across the entire range of OECD countries (OECD Directorate of Education 2000: xv).

Literacy, accountability, efficiency and quality

During the 1980s and 1990s, literacy emerged as an 'arch indicator' for the professional accountability of schools and teachers and for the political legitimacy of public education systems, policies and administrations. Education systems increasingly moved to a model based on national- or state-level curricula and curriculum standards or outcome levels, and reporting based on student performance assessed on a regular basis, particularly in literacy and numeracy. This 'standards–testing–accountability–performance' model of education reform is defended politically with a range of familiar justifications. These include greater transparency of school performance, improved student performance on what the tests measure, greater accountability of schools to their communities, better value for the taxpayer, and quality assurance.

As an institutionalized activity of the state, education is seen to be legitimated through the principle of performativity (Lyotard 1984). This is the principle of optimizing the overall performance of social institutions (like schools) according to the criterion of efficiency: the 'endless optimization of the cost/benefit (input/output) ratio' (Lyotard 1993: 25). Specific institutions are legitimated by their contribution to maximizing the performance of the state or corporate systems of which they are a part. Governments and administrations report their successes to political constituencies. For example, rejecting the charge that the UK's National Reading Strategy had had minimal impact on reading standards, Schools Minister Andrew Adonis claimed: 'This is not an opinion: it is fact. 2007 results in reading show that 84 per cent of 11-year-olds achieved the expected level – up 17 percentage points since 1997' (BBC 2007).

In a classic statement of school/teacher accountability, the 1998 Australian government policy paper *Literacy for All* (DEETYA 1998) described a National Plan for literacy based on beginning literacy assessment as early as possible, with agreed benchmarks for grades 3, 5, 7 and 9. All states were to assess against the benchmarks, as a basis for national reporting. Teachers were to be provided with professional development to support the Plan, and early intervention strategies were introduced. The first principle underlying the Plan was 'better educational accountability through improved assessment and reporting', involving collection of information of 'real use' to schools, teachers, parents, and governments.

Most recently, in June 2010, a statement of K-12 Common Core State Standards for English Language Arts & Literacy in History/Social Studies, Science, and Technical Subjects produced on behalf of 48 states, two territories, and the District of Columbia was published in the USA (Common Core Standards Initiative 2010). Led by the Council of Chief State School Officers and the National Governors Association, the initiative has built on work conducted over recent decades by US states to establish high-quality education standards. The Common Core State Standards have been developed to help ensure that all students 'are college and career ready in literacy no later than the end of high school' (ibid.: Introduction). They provide grade-specific standards for K-12 in reading, writing, speaking, listening and language, which 'lay out a vision of what it means to be a literate person' under current conditions. States can incorporate the standards into their existing subject standards or, alternatively, adopt them as content area literacy standards (ibid.). By September 2010, 35 US states and the District of Columbia had already adopted the standards as a basis for future curriculum development and assessment purposes.

The growth of sociocultural theory

The final reason to be identified here as being associated with literacy moving to the forefront of educational agendas from the 1970s was the increasing development and popularity of a *sociocultural* perspective within studies of language and the social sciences (Gee 1996: Ch. 3; Gee et al. 1996: Ch. 1). During the 1980s and 1990s this impacted strongly on conceptual and theoretical understandings of practices involving texts. Early influential works drew on theory and research from different but broadly compatible fields. Gee (1996: Ch. 1) documents these very nicely. For example, Harvey Graff's (1979) book, *The Literacy Myth*, drew on revisionist history. Silvia Scribner and Michael Cole's *The Psychology of Literacy* (1981) drew on concepts and instrumentation that reflected pioneering work in social cognition by Vygotsky and Luria, and developed a concept of 'practice' that has evolved into a key construct within sociocultural approaches to literacy. Ron and Suzanne Scollon's *Narrative, Literacy and Face in Interethnic Communication* (1981) worked at complex interfaces between linguistics, anthropology and epistemology to explore relationships among social practices, worldviews, orality and literacy. Shirley Brice Heath (1983) explored the ways literacy is embedded in cultural contexts over an extended period using an ethnographic design and research methods in her major study, *Ways with Words*. Brian Street's *Literacy in Theory and in Practice* (1984) was strongly grounded in anthropology. Together with even earlier work done by scholars in history and cultural studies in Britain, like Robert K. Webb's *The British Working Class Reader* (1955) and Richard Hoggart's *The Uses of Literacy: Aspects of Working Class Life* (1957), among many others (see Lankshear 1999), these studies provided a strong base informed by research from which to challenge established approaches to teaching reading and writing in schools and the growing emphasis on 'literacy basics' and 'functional literacy' fuelled by the alleged literacy crisis.

Reflection and discussion

- What do you think it means to say that unequal literacy outcomes among people are 'hard-wired' into the social structure? What kinds of data might provide evidence for and against the claim?

- Why do you think some critics regarded the discovery in the 1970s of large-scale illiteracy in North America as an *invention*? What evidence can you find for and against this position?

- Many people believe that literacy levels are directly related to a country's economic prosperity and growth. Do you agree with this view? If so, why? If not, why not? If you believe there is a direct relationship, what kind of relationship is it?

- What is meant by 'accountability'? To what extent and on what grounds do you consider literacy outcomes based on standardized tests to be a valid accountability measure for educators?

- What do you understand by 'a sociocultural approach' to literacy? What are some of the ways it differs from, say, a psycholinguistic approach?

A brilliant career: five contemporary literacy trends

Within this broad historical context, as a concept and social phenomenon alike, 'literacy' emerged quickly and decisively as a key focus of education policy, educational research and publishing, and of pedagogical effort within formal education. For many politicians, policymakers and administrators, it came to comprise *the* key focus. Legislation like the *Literacy for All* national literacy plan in Australia (1998) and the *No Child Left Behind Act* passed in 2001 in the USA enshrined literacy as the new 'bottom line' and the new 'centre of gravity' for school education. With hindsight, this dramatic emergence of *literacy* as an educational focus can be viewed from several angles: (1) 'literacy' displaced 'reading' and 'writing' in educational language; (2) literacy became a considerable industry; (3) literacy assumed a loftier status in the eyes of educationists; (4) 'literacy' came to apply to an ever increasing variety of practices; and (5) literacy is now being defined with the word 'new'. We will discuss each of these in turn in the remainder of this chapter.

'Literacy' in educational language

The *educational language* associated with the development of competence with text changed, as we have already noted, from the language of 'reading' and 'writing' to the language of 'literacy'. The term began to figure prominently in school timetables and programme descriptions. The names of professional journals changed. For example, the *Australian Journal of Reading* became the *Australian Journal of Language and Literacy*, the *Journal of Reading* became the *Journal of Adolescent and Adult Literacy*, and the *Journal of Reading Behavior* became the *Journal of Literacy Research*. Likewise, areas of focus for professional and resource development were renamed. For example, 'emergent literacy' subsumed the conventional coverall term, 'reading readiness', and the then new label, 'writing readiness'; 'literacy development' was used in place of reading or writing development; 'literacy studies' instead of 'language arts research' and the like.

The name change did not always count for much, since in many cases people continued doing in the name of 'literacy' much the same as they had always done as 'reading' teachers or researchers. The point is, however, that whereas 'reading' has traditionally been conceived in *psychological* terms, 'literacy' has always been much more a *sociological* concept. For example, 'illiteracy' and 'illiterate' usually carried social class or social group connotations. Being illiterate tended to be associated with being poor, being of marginal status, and so on. In addition, the sociocultural approach to literacy overtly rejects the idea that textual practices are even largely, let alone solely, a matter of processes that 'go on in the head', or that essentially involve heads communicating with each other by means of graphic signs. From a sociocultural perspective, literacy is a matter of social practices. Literacies are bound up with social, institutional and cultural relationships, and can be understood only when they are situated within their social, cultural and historical contexts (Gee et al. 1996: xii). Moreover, they are always connected to social identities – to being particular kinds of people. Literacies are always embedded in Discourses (Gee 2000). From around 1992 Gee has distinguished between Discourse (with a capital D) and discourse. The former is the notion of ways of being in the world that integrate identities, and the latter refers to the language bits, or language uses, of Discourses (see the discussion of 'powerful literacy' on pp. 19–21.) Texts are integral parts of innumerable everyday *'lived, talked, enacted, value-and-belief-laden* practices' that are 'carried out in specific places and at specific times' (Gee et al. 1996: 3; emphasis in original). Reading and writing are not the same things in a youth zine (pronounced 'zeen') culture, an online chat space, a school classroom, a feminist reading group, or in different kinds of religious ceremonies. People read and write differently out of different social practices, and these different ways with words are part of different ways of being persons and different ways and facets of doing life.

This has important implications. From a sociocultural perspective, it is impossible to separate out from text-mediated social practices the 'bits' concerned with reading or writing (or any other sense of 'literacy') and to treat them independently of all the 'non-print' bits, like values and gestures, context and meaning, actions and objects, talk and interaction, tools and spaces. They are all non-subtractable parts of integrated wholes. 'Literacy bits' do not exist apart from the social practices in which they are embedded and within which they are acquired. If, in some trivial sense they *can* be said to exist (e.g., as code), they do not *mean* anything. Hence, they cannot meaningfully be taught and learned as separate from the rest of the practice (Gee 1996).

By adopting and developing 'literacy' as their key word, socioculturally oriented theorists, researchers, and educators sought, among other things, to bypass the psychological reductionism inscribed on more than a century of educational activity associated with 'reading'. They wanted to keep *the social* to the forefront, and to keep the 'embeddedness' of literacy within larger social practices in clear view. This was often subverted, however, when reading specialists and experts simply adopted the term 'literacy' without taking up its substance.

Literacy as an industry

The scope and amount of *formal* educational activity in the name of literacy that was funded and sanctioned by official government policy, guidelines and directives reached impressive levels. Literacy quickly became a considerable *industry*, involving public and private providers of diverse goods and services at different rungs on the education ladder. Adult and workplace literacy programmes received formal recognition, funding, and credentialling in a manner previously unknown. Funding to providers was usually pegged to achievement outcomes and accountability procedures. In countries like Australia, national and state-level policies actually factored workplace literacy competencies into the awards and remuneration system, providing incentives for workers to participate in work-related and work-based literacy programmes, many of which were conducted during company time. Adults and workers whose language backgrounds were not in the dominant/official language of the country were often specially targeted.

Resource and professional development activities mushroomed. Literacy educators and literacy programme providers sought curriculum resources, pedagogical approaches, and specialized training for their work. Armies of literacy consultants, resource developers, and professional development experts quickly emerged to meet the market for literacy goods and services. In keeping with the tradition of formal education, the belief that such work should be grounded in research was also officially recognized and, to a greater or lesser extent, funded. Literacy soon emerged as a major focus within educational research. Once again, the Australian case ranks among the most complex and carefully staged responses to the belief that high levels of functional and work-related literacy on the part of all members of a nation's population is a precondition of successful transition to becoming a post-industrial economy and a knowledge society. At the end of the 1980s, the Australian Language and Literacy Policy legislated for competitive research funding to support a national level research programme in the area of Child Literacy. During the 1990s, the National Children's Literacy Projects programme allocated on a highly competitive basis millions of research dollars for targeted projects addressing diverse aspects of school-age children's literacy. These funds counted toward the research quantum of individual universities, which in turn determined the level of government funding they received for general research activity. Research Centres and Schools or Departments specializing in (language and) literacy education became key planks in Education Faculty structures, and often emerged among the top research income earners within their faculties.

Two massive international literacy measurement and comparison initiatives involving the OECD and collaborating governments and institutions have unfolded since the mid-1990s, namely the International Adult Literacy Survey (IALS) and the OECD Programme for International Student Assessment (PISA).

The IALS involves collaborating governments, research institutions, national statistical agencies and the OECD. The first round, in 1994, involved nine countries (Canada, France, Germany, Ireland, the Netherlands, Poland, Sweden, Switzerland, and the United States). In 1996, Australia, Flemish Belgium, New Zealand and the UK (England, Northern Ireland, Scotland, and Wales) participated in a second round, and in 1998 Chile, the Czech Republic, Denmark, Finland, Hungary, Italy, Norway, Slovenia, and the Italian-speaking region of Switzerland participated in a third round. Five levels of literacy were distinguished, with Level 3 being considered 'a suitable minimum for coping with the demands of everyday life and work in a complex, advanced society' (OECD Directorate of Education 2010). The final report from the survey, *Literacy in the Information Age*, was published by the OECD and Statistics Canada in 2000, and subsequent statistically based reports have appeared on an occasional basis – including the influential *Literacy Scores, Human Capital and Growth across Fourteen OECD Countries* (Coulombe et al. 2004).

PISA is an internationally standardized assessment of reading literacy, mathematical literacy (numeracy) and scientific literacy, instigated in 1997 and occurring in three-year cycles between 2000 and 2015. The assessment was jointly developed by participating countries and is administered to between 4,500 and 10,000 students in each participating country. Reading literacy was first assessed in 2000, followed by mathematical literacy and problem solving in 2003, and scientific literacy in 2006. A second round of reading literacy assessment, with an optional component on reading electronic texts, was undertaken in 2009. A total of 43 countries participated in the first cycle, 41 in the second, 57 in the third, and 67 in the fourth. Participants are 15-year-old students, since the assessment is designed to yield cross-country comparisons among learners nearing the end of their compulsory education. A statistically rigorous sampling design is employed to produce as near representative results as possible, and 'stringent quality assurance mechanisms' are applied in translation and data collection (OECD 2009: 13). Attempts are made to ensure 'cultural and linguistic breadth and balance in the assessment materials' (ibid.). Besides student scores, data are collected on students, families, and institutional factors with a view to helping explain differences in performance. The tests assess content knowledge as well as the ability to apply knowledge and information to 'real life' tasks and challenges. A key aim of the initiative is to identify conditions associated with success on the tests to help guide education policy development among participating OECD and partner countries.

According to the *PISA 2009 Assessment Framework* (OECD 2009: 13), policymakers around the world use PISA findings:

> [to] gauge the knowledge and skills of students in their own country in comparison with those of the other participating countries; establish benchmarks for educational improvement, for example, in terms of the mean scores achieved by other countries or their capacity to provide high levels of equity in educational outcomes and opportunities; and understand relative strengths and weaknesses of their education systems.

A 'loftier' status for literacy

As literacy began taking up more space within the recognized role and scope of formal education, it also began to assume a *loftier* status in terms of how it was defined and understood by educationists, policymakers and social commentators. It was as if those who believed education should involve and count for much more than was usually implied by the term 'literacy' responded by building more (and more) into their conceptions of literacy in order to defend and preserve more expansive educational purposes and standards.

(a) This trend began with the announcement of the literacy crisis. The issue was not mere 'basic literacy' but, rather, *functional* literacy. For all its instrumental connotations, functional literacy was not to be reduced to some demeaning bottom line. Hence, for example, Jonathan Kozol (1985: 56) cited one expert's view from the early 1980s that anyone who didn't have 'at least a twelfth grade reading, writing and calculating level' would be 'absolutely lost' by the 1990s. The speed-up in the rate of change meant that even *functional* literacy had to be defined expansively.

(b) From the standpoint of cultural cohesion, the urgent interest shown, especially in the USA, in relation to cultural literacy in the late 1980s and early 1990s was concerned with the kind of knowledge young people were thought to need in order to participate effectively in social life as active and informed citizens. Advocates of cultural literacy addressed the kinds of approaches and programmes schools should provide to this end. The association of cultural knowledge with literacy was, perhaps, made most clearly by E. D. Hirsch, Jr in his highly influential book *Cultural Literacy: What Every American Needs to Know* (1987). Hirsch argued that students need to be familiar with a cultural canon in order to be able to negotiate their social context effectively. This canon comprises relevant cultural information that has high status in the public sphere. It is assumed that all members of society share this knowledge as part of their cultural heritage. Hirsch discerned cultural *illiteracy* among growing numbers of students who could not contextualize information or communicate with their fellows within the context of a larger national culture because they lacked the common cultural stock presumed to make such communication and meaning-making possible. Hirsch regards 'literate Americans' as those who possess a particular body of cultural knowledge, which he has itemized and updated throughout numerous books.

(c) Through its PISA assessment initiative, the OECD (2009: 9) advances a concept of literacy that combines knowledge/information with cognitive skills/processes and personal dispositions/attitudes integral to 'doing well in life', by being able to apply what one knows successfully to everyday tasks and challenges across a range of domains – across work, leisure, community/civic and domestic pursuits. This concept of literacy is 'based on a dynamic model of lifelong learning in which new knowledge and skills necessary for successful adaptation to a changing world are continuously acquired throughout life' (ibid.). The 'literacy' assessed by PISA does not simply tap students' knowledge but, also, their abilities 'to reflect, and to apply their knowledge and experience to real-life issues' (ibid.). The idea is that students who do well on the test – who have high reading, mathematical and science literacy – are the kinds of people who will likely know how to do the kinds of things they will need to be able to do in the future, because they know how to apply what they have learned – and not merely to reproduce content. They are the kinds of people likely 'to continue learning throughout their lives by applying what they learn in school to non-school environments, evaluating their choices and making decisions' (ibid.). Consequently, this conception of literacy encapsulates what the OECD sees as the ideal outcome of school education. From the OECD's perspective, its ideal of literacy is a key goal, if not *the* key goal, of formal education: to know how to apply one's learning effectively across the range of everyday contexts and situations, and to have the requisite qualities for 'going on' as a learner throughout life.

(d) An interesting account that builds on a sociocultural perspective to develop a robust conception of literacy can be found in a 'three-dimensional' model (Green 1988, 1997). This view argues that literacy should be seen as having three interlocking dimensions of learning and practice: the operational, the cultural and the critical. These dimensions bring together language, meaning and context (Green 1988), and no one dimension has any priority over the others. In an integrated view of literate practice and literacy pedagogy, all dimensions need to be taken into account simultaneously. The *operational* dimension focuses on the language aspect of literacy. It includes but also goes beyond competence with the tools, procedures and techniques involved in being able to handle the written language system proficiently. It includes being able to read and write/key in a range of contexts in an appropriate and adequate manner. The *cultural* dimension involves competence with the meaning system of a social practice; knowing how to make and grasp meanings appropriately within the practice – in short, it focuses on understanding texts in relation to contexts. This means knowing what it is about given contexts of practice that makes for appropriateness or inappropriateness of particular ways of reading and writing. The *critical* dimension involves awareness that all social practices, and thus all literacies, are socially constructed and 'selective': they include some representations and classifications – values, purposes, rules, standards, and perspectives – and exclude others. To participate effectively and productively in any literate practice, people must be socialized into it. But if individuals are socialized into a social practice without realizing that it is socially constructed and selective, and that it can be acted on and transformed, they cannot play an active role in changing it. The critical dimension of literacy is the basis for ensuring that individuals are not merely able to participate in some existing literacy and make meanings within it, but also that, in various ways, they are able to transform and actively produce it (Green 1988; Gee et al. 1996). Hence, rather than focusing on the 'how to' knowledge of literacy, the 3D model of literacy complements and supplements operational or technical competence by contextualizing literacy with due regard for matters of culture, history and power.

(e) Some educationists working from a sociocultural perspective have focused on how cultural and linguistic diversity and the burgeoning impact of new communications technologies are changing demands on learners in terms of what we have identified here as the operational and cultural dimensions of literacies. Learners need new operational and cultural 'knowledges' in order to acquire new languages that provide access to new forms of work, civic, and private practices in their everyday lives. At the same time, learners need to develop strengths in the critical dimension of literacy as well. Mary Kalantzis and Bill Cope (1997) make this clear with respect to literacy demands in relation to work. They note that with a new work life comes a new language, with much of it attributable to new technologies like 'iconographic, text and screen-based modes of interacting with automated machinery' and to changes in the social relations of work (Kalantzis and Cope 1997: 5). This new work life can be even more highly exploitative and unjust than its predecessor. Accordingly, Kalantzis and Cope claim that when responding to radical contemporary changes in working life, literacy educators need to walk a fine line. On one side of the line, educators must ensure that learners 'have the opportunity to develop skills for access to new forms of work through learning the new language of work'. On the other side of the line, the fact remains that 'as teachers, our role is not simply to be technocrats'. The role of educators is not to produce 'docile, compliant workers', either. Rather, students need to develop the skills 'to speak up, to negotiate and to be able to engage critically with the conditions of their working lives' (ibid.: 6).

Conceived from a sociocultural standpoint, literacies entail deep and extensive knowledge. Being literate involves much more than simply knowing *how* to operate the language system. The cultural and critical facets of knowledge integral to being literate are demanding, particularly given the new and changing knowledge components of literacies under contemporary social, economic, cultural, political and civic conditions. Being literate in any of the myriad forms literacies take presupposes complex amalgams of propositional, procedural and 'performative' forms of knowledge. Making meaning is knowledge-intensive, and much of the knowledge that school-based learning is required to develop and mobilize is knowledge involved in meaning making.

(f) The idea that literacies can be more or less 'powerful' has been developed in an interesting way by James Gee (1990). For Gee (1990), a powerful literacy is not a specific literacy *per se* but, rather, a way of using a literacy. He defines being literate as having control, or fluent mastery, of language uses within what he calls secondary Discourses. Gee defines Discourses as 'ways of being in the world', which integrate words, acts, gestures, attitudes, beliefs, purposes, clothes, bodily movements and positions, and so on. Discourses also integrate *identities*, in the sense that through their participation in Discourses individuals are identified and identifiable as members of socially meaningful groups or networks and players of socially meaningful roles (ibid.: 142–3). Language is integral to Discourses, but Discourses are always much more than language alone. Language uses – or what Gee calls the 'language bits' of Discourses – are 'connected stretches of language that make sense', that are meaningful within a Discourse (ibid.: 143). Language uses vary from Discourse to Discourse, but well-known examples include 'conversations, stories, reports, arguments, essays', as well as explanations, commands, interviews, ways of eliciting information, and so on (ibid.: 143).

Gee distinguishes between a person's primary Discourse and its distinctive language use (which he mostly refers to as 'discourse' (with a small 'd'), and their secondary Discourses and their respective language uses. Our primary Discourse involves 'face to face communication with intimates', and is the Discourse of our immediate group (ibid.: 143). Primary Discourses differ from social group to social group (by social class, ethnicity, etc.). We each belong to just one primary Discourse, which shapes who and what we initially are as persons. Members of all social groups that extend beyond immediate, face-to-face encounters also encounter secondary Discourses through their participation in secondary institutions, such as schools, churches, sports clubs, community groups, workplaces, and so on. These secondary Discourses have their own more or less distinctive language uses and they shape our identities in particular ways – as we take on their beliefs, purposes, ways of speaking and acting, moving, dressing, and so on. According to Gee, then, since there are multiple secondary Discourses, and since literacy and being literate are defined in terms of controlling secondary language uses, there are multiple – indeed, *many* – literacies and ways of being literate. In all cases, however, being literate means being able to use the 'right' language in the 'right' ways within a Discourse. This corresponds roughly to command of the 'operational' and 'cultural' dimensions of literacy previously mentioned.

On the basis of these ideas, Gee defines *powerful* literacy in terms of employing a secondary language use as a 'metalanguage' for understanding, analysing and critiquing other Discourses and the way they constitute us as persons and situate us within society (ibid.: 153; see also Gee 1991: 8–9). By a metalanguage, he means, 'a set of meta-words, meta-values [and] meta-beliefs' (Gee 1990: 153). Practising a powerful literacy, so defined, can provide the basis for reconstituting our selves/identities and resituating ourselves within society.

To understand and critique a particular Discourse using a powerful literacy derived from some other Discourse requires understanding both

Discourses *as Discourses*: what they are, how they operate, what values and ways of being in the world they promote, how their 'language bits' reflect and enable this. This is metalevel knowledge. In powerful literacy we draw on such knowledge to provide us with a reason, a basis, and an alternative in terms of which we can decide to opt out of another Discourse or work to change it.

From the standpoint of such perspectives, it was considered very important to ensure that literacy agendas be expansive. Because literacy was being prioritized within education policy, it was important to resist the potential for sectional interests to 'steer' literacy along narrow and/ or minimal lines.

The radical 'multiplicity' of literacy

Since the 1980s and, especially, the 1990s, the term 'literacy' has been applied to an ever-increasing variety of practices. It has reached the point today where it seems that almost any knowledge and learning deemed educationally valuable can somehow or other be conceived as a literacy.

Sometimes this involves 'literacy' becoming a metaphor for 'competence', 'proficiency' or 'being functional'. Concepts like 'being computer literate' or being 'technologically literate' are sometimes used simply to mean that someone is more or less proficient with a computer or some other device like a video recorder: they can 'make sense of' and 'use' computers, or can program their video player or mobile phone. In this sense, talk of being computer literate or technologically literate has become everyday terminology. This is actually an index for just how focal literacy has become as a social issue and an educational ideal during the past two or three decades.

Getting closer to more literal associations with language *per se*, we nowadays hear frequent references to 'oral literacy', 'visual literacy', 'information literacy', 'media literacy', 'science literacy' and even 'emotional literacy'. These uses foreground the notion of being able to communicate or make meaning – as a producer or receiver – using signs, signals, codes, graphic images. In cases like 'science literacy', the concept implies being able to read and write meaningfully the language and literature of science. It is close to the idea advanced in the 1970s by philosophers like Paul Hirst (1974) with respect to knowledge and the academic disciplines. Hirst spoke of 'forms and fields of knowledge' – systematic ways of understanding the world, epitomized by academic disciplines – as having their own discrete 'languages and literatures'. To 'be on the inside' of a form or field of knowledge meant being able to 'speak' its language and 'read and write its literature'. The language comprised the procedures, techniques, standards, methods used by expert practitioners. The literature comprised the products generated by faithful and competent practitioners who spoke the language in question.

In the case of ideas like 'media literacy' or 'information literacy', we sometimes find implications that we need to learn to 'read' media or information sources in specialized ways in order to 'get what is really there' and/or to avoid being 'taken in'. This is the idea that there are ways of deciphering media and information more or less *wittingly* or *critically* as an 'insider' or, at least, as an effective receiver or producer within the media spaces in question. To some extent, this implies the ability to identify strategies and techniques being used to produce particular kinds of effects on what we think, believe, or desire.

An example here is provided by David Sholle and Stan Denski's (1993) account of television within their treatment of critical media literacy. They observe that television can be seen as 'a *pedagogical machine*' that operates to construct discourses 'that function primarily in the locus of a mode of transmission where "culture becomes defined solely by markets for culture"' (1993: 309; original emphasis; the quotation is from Wexler 1988: 98). Sholle and Denski argue that if teachers are to educate learners to become media literate,

> we must attend to the multiple references and codes that position them [the learners]. This means paying attention to the manner in which popular culture texts are constructed by and construct various discursive codes, but also how such texts express various contradictory ideological interests and how these texts might be taken up in a way that creates possibilities for different constructions of cultural and political life.
>
> (1993: 309)

'Digital literacy' and 'twenty-first-century literacies' are two especially high-profile literacies at present. Since the mid-1990s, digital literacy has emerged in many education policy documents as a core educational goal – often associated with fears about the emergence of a 'digital divide' between those who are digitally literate and those who are not. Conceptions of digital literacy have tended to be of two main kinds, neatly distinguished by Paul Gilster (in Pool 1997: 6) in terms of 'mastering ideas' versus 'mastering keystrokes'. The former is described by David Bawden (2008: 19) as a 'special kind of mindset or thinking' – a substantive *way* of being literate in the sense of engaging with meanings within intensified digital environments – and the latter typically involves sets of skills, tasks and performances seen as necessary for technical proficiency with digital tools. Allan Martin broaches (2008: 156) this dichotomy with his concept of 'literacies of the digital'. Most of these literacies originated prior to the prevalence of digital technologies, but have been seen as ways of helping understand phenomena that 'have become more significant or even transformed in digital contexts' (ibid.). Literacies of the digital include 'computer/IT/ICT literacy', 'technological literacy', 'information literacy', 'media literacy', 'visual literacy' and 'communication literacy' (ibid.: 156–64). Hence, for example, concepts of computer literacy began as ideas of mastery of computing basics (to the mid-1980s), evolved into ideas of how to apply software applications in work, home, education and leisure pursuits (mid-1980s to late 1990s), and since the late 1990s have entered a reflective phase that pays increased attention to evaluative, innovative, and metalevel issues and approaches (ibid.: 156–7). Similarly, technological literacy has involved 'an uneasy marriage' between 'a skills-based vocational approach' and 'a critical, action-oriented "academic" approach' (ibid.: 158).

Gilster (1997; in Pool 1997) defined 'digital literacy' as 'the ability to understand and use information in multiple formats from a wide variety of sources when it is presented via computers' and, particularly, through the medium of the internet (Gilster, in Pool 1997: 6). Digital literacy involves 'adapting our skills to an evocative new medium, [and] our experience of the Internet will be determined by how we master its core competencies' (ibid.), which are not merely 'operational' or 'technical' competencies but, rather, complex performances of knowledge assembly, evaluating information content, searching the internet, and navigating hypertext – which comprise epistemic as well as more 'operational' elements. Gilster claims we need to teach and learn 'how to use the Web properly and how to be critical' (Gilster, in Pool 1997: 8). Citing the familiar image of students using the internet to find information that they simply cut and paste into a 'cobbled-together collection of quotes or multimedia items', Gilster argues that we need to teach students 'how to assimilate the information, evaluate it, and then reintegrate it' (in Pool 1997: 9). This involves particular attitudes, dispositions and qualities of mind as well as more technical operations.

As indicated earlier, David Bawden (2008) and Allan Martin (2008) have recently advanced state-of-the-art accounts of digital literacy that build on previous accounts of 'literacies of the digital' and, particularly, on the kind of broad conception advanced by writers like Gilster, but go beyond them in helpful ways.

Bawden conceives of digital literacy as an essential requirement for life in a digital age in terms of four constitutive components: underpinnings, background knowledge, central competencies, and attitudes and perspectives. Underpinnings comprise literacy *per se* and core computing skills, without which there can be no digital literacy. Background knowledge of the world of information and the nature of information resources affords understanding of how digital and non-digital information is created and communicated and of resulting information sources. Central competencies include knowing how to read and understand digital and non-digital formats and to create and communicate information, as well as how to assemble knowledge, and how to 'pull' and 'push' information. Attitudes and perspectives of independent learning and of moral and social literacy reflect the importance of digital literacy for helping us learn what we need for our particular situations and for understanding sensible and appropriate conduct within digital environments (Bawden 2008: 28–30). To the extent that these components are in place, we are digitally literate in a sense that honours the importance of understanding, meaning, and context within human lives. In a similar vein, Martin (2008: 167) proposes that we understand digital literacy as

> the awareness, attitude and ability of individuals to appropriately use digital tools and facilities to identify, access, manage, integrate, evaluate, analyze and synthesize digital resources, construct new knowledge, create media expressions, and communicate with others, in the context of specific life situations, in order to enable constructive social action; and to reflect upon this process.

Talk of twenty-first-century literacies emerged from the mid-1990s, but has flourished in conjunction with concepts like twenty-first-century skills (Jenkins et al. 2006) in recent years. In 2007, the US National Council of Teachers of English published a policy research brief urging the importance of re-orienting English Language Arts education in response to changes impacting on everyday social practices wrought by 'global economies, new technologies, and exponential growth in information' (NCTE 2007: 1). Helping prepare students for a changed world means that English Language Arts teachers must increasingly focus on 'problem solving, collaboration, and analysis', as well as on 'skills with word processing, hypertext, LCDs, Web cams, digital streaming podcasts, smartboards, and social networking software', all of which are 'central to individual and community success' (ibid.) Hence, twenty-first-century literacies are not simply about technologies, although proficiency with new technologies is now as integral to being literate as proficiency with conventional literacy tools has been in the past.

In 2008, the NCTE formally adopted a position on twenty-first-century literacies, asserting that contemporary life 'demands that a literate person possess a wide range of abilities and competencies, many literacies' (NCTE 2008: n.p.). These literacies are 'multiple, dynamic, and malleable', and range from 'reading online newspapers to participating in virtual classrooms' (ibid.). The Council's policy position proposes that today's and tomorrow's readers and writers must:

- Develop proficiency with the tools of technology;
- Build relationships with others to pose and solve problems collaboratively and cross-culturally;
- Design and share information for global communities to meet a variety of purposes;
- Manage, analyze, and synthesize multiple streams of simultaneous information;
- Create, critique, analyze, and evaluate multi-media texts;
- Attend to the ethical responsibilities required by these complex environments (ibid.).

Howard Rheingold (2009a, 2009b) provides a highly generative and evocative account of twenty-first-century literacies based on social media and beginning from a conception of literacy as 'skills plus community' (Rheingold 2009a). In many ways this puts dynamic substance into the NCTE's list of constitutive elements of twenty-first-century literacies, although Rheingold questions the extent to which his ideal of twenty-first-century literacies might be realized within schools operating under their current purposes. He emphasizes five 'literacies', which he calls 'attention', 'participation', 'cooperation' (or 'collaboration' or 'collective action'), 'critical consumption' (or 'crap detection') and 'net(work) awareness', respectively. None of these is self-standing, although Rheingold sees 'attention' as 'a fundamental particle' of the others. Rather, they overlap and are contiguous, and fluency involves being able to put them together as required by particular purposes and situations.

The literacy of attention involves mindfulness about where we put our attention and how to exercise our attention: who and what to attend to, and how to attend, when and why (Rheingold 2009c). The reason why some people can multitask effectively and others cannot is because some know better how to 'sample flows', rather than working their way through 'queues' (Rheingold 2009a), and how to focus attention effectively on multiple particulars simultaneously. Becoming literate in this sense involves learning how to exercise our attention, which, of course, means knowing what is *worth* attending to in terms of quality, relevance, and the like (Rheingold 2009c). This, in turn, relates to 'critical consumption' and is pertinent to effective participation and co-operation. The literacy of 'critical consumption' is predicated on the fact that knowing how to pose questions to a search engine for seeking information must be buttressed with knowing how to evaluate the quality of the results (Rheingold 2009d). This begins from estimating the authority or reputation of sources, which in turn involves understanding how networks mediate and assess authority and reputation. Social media (in the sense of Web 2.0 resources) enable participation by their very nature, and Rheingold agrees with people like Yochai Benkler and Henry Jenkins that merely participating gives us 'a sense of being in the world'. At the same time, mere participation is just a beginning, as endless 'boring' online artifacts and interactions attest. The literacy of participation involves being able to participate in ways that benefit others as well as ourselves and, hence, will garner attention and reputation. Social media enable our capacity to do things together that give us more power than by doing things alone, and this underpins the literacy of co-operation: knowing how to organize collective action and, ideally, how to build (mash up) platforms that facilitate the kind of collective action or collaboration required in particular situations. At the same time, co-operating involves judgements of knowing who and what are worth

---

Reflection and discussion

- To what extent do you think a good case can be made for talking about a literacy *industry*?

- Why do you think some policymakers, politicians, research organizations, and business leaders take international literacy rankings and comparisons so seriously?

- If you had to compile a list of the top ten cultural knowledge items you think all people in your country should know, what would they be? Compare your list with those compiled by two other people. Discuss these three lists in terms of what they include and exclude, individually and collectively. What do you consider most significant in your findings?

- To what extent do you think that literacy has a 'lofty' status at present? Do you think its status is 'too lofty', 'not lofty enough', or 'about right'? What are the reasons for you viewpoint?

- Has literacy become *too* 'multiple' to be a useful educational construct? What reasons might be advanced for and against the judgement that is has become '*too* multiple'?

co-operating with and through, which draws upon social capital as 'the capacity to get things done with other people without going through official channels' (Rheingold 2009a). Building, nurturing and sustaining social capital is the province of the literacy of net(work) awareness (Rheingold 2009e), to which understanding the increasing importance of reputation online and the role of diffuse reciprocity is fundamental. Knowing that and why a few high-quality connections in different places and spaces can constitute a powerful basis for achieving purposes and getting things done is central to net(work) awareness literacy. So is knowing who to trust to be an authority or expert on some aspect and recruiting them to one's personal network. This involves judgement about who to allow into one's attention, completing the circle of integration among these literacies. Fundamental to all of this, for Rheingold, is the fact that while mere 'use' of social media, and 'mere participation' in and through social media is not enough, it is nonetheless the starting point. The task for educators is to explore how best to draw upon the pervasive reality of 'networked publics' to support educational ends generally, and proficient acquisition of twenty-first-century literacies in particular.

'New' literacies

Nowadays, literacy scholars and researchers commonly use the word 'new' in association with 'literacy' and 'literacies'. This occurs in two main ways, which we call *paradigmatic* and *ontological* respectively.

The *paradigmatic* sense of 'new' occurs in talk of the 'New Literacy Studies' (Street 1993; Gee 1996, 2000). This refers to a particular sociocultural approach to understanding and researching literacy. The 'New Literacy Studies' can be seen as a new theoretical and research *paradigm* for looking at literacy: a new alternative to the previously established paradigm that was based on psycholinguistics. The use of 'new' here parallels that which is involved in names for initiatives or movements such as the New School of Social Research, the New Science, the New Criticism (and New Critics). In all such cases, the proponents think of their project as comprising a new and different paradigm relative to an existing orthodoxy or dominant approach.

This paradigmatic sense of 'new' in relation to literacy is not concerned with new literacies as such but, rather, with a new approach to thinking about literacy as a social phenomenon. As it happens, numerous scholars who are associated with the New Literacy Studies paradigm are researching and writing about the kinds of practices we are calling new literacies. But that is simply a contingency. The 'New' of New Literacy Studies and the 'new' of new literacies in the sense we are discussing here are quite distinct ideas. By the same token, and for reasons we hope will become apparent in this book, we think that new literacies in the way we understand and describe them here can really only be researched effectively from a sociocultural perspective, of which the New Literacy Studies is an example.

Our idea of the *ontological* sense of 'new' is intended to relate directly to new literacies of the kinds under discussion here. The terms 'ontological' and 'ontology' are being used in multiple ways in the context of talk about new technologies and new social practices involving new technologies, so it is necessary that we spell out what we mean by our use of 'ontological'. In simple language, we are using 'ontological' here to refer to the 'nature' or 'stuff' of new literacies. To say that 'new' literacies are ontologically new is to say that they consist of a different kind of 'stuff' from conventional literacies we have known in the past. It is the idea that changes have occurred in the character and substance of literacies that are associated with larger changes in technology, institutions, media and the economy, and with the rapid movement toward global scale in manufacture, finance, communications, and so on. As we see things, this idea can be broken down into two parts.

The first part has to do with the rise of digital-electronic technologies and, with this, the emergence of 'post-typographic' forms of texts and text production. It is the idea that 'new' literacies are different kinds of phenomena – are made of different stuff, or are significantly different in their nature – from 'conventional' print-based literacies. The argument is that contemporary changes have impacted on social practices in all the main areas of everyday life within modern societies: in work, at leisure, in the home, in education, in the community, and in the public sphere. Established social practices have been transformed, and new forms of social practice have emerged and continue to emerge at a rapid rate. Many of these new and changing social practices involve new and changing ways of producing, distributing, exchanging, and receiving texts by *electronic* means. These include the production and exchange of multimodal forms of texts that can arrive via digital code as sound, text, images, video, animations, and any combination of these.

In the ontological sense of 'new', the category of 'new literacies' refers to practices that are mediated by 'post-typographic' forms of texts. 'Ontologically new' literacies involve things like using and constructing hyperlinks between documents and/or images, sounds, movies, etc.; text messaging on a mobile phone; using digital semiotic languages (such as those used by the characters in the online episodic game *Banja*, or emoticons used in email, online chat space or in instant messaging); manipulating a mouse to move around within a text; reading file extensions and identifying what software will 'read' each file; navigating three-dimensional worlds online; uploading images from a camera or digital phone to a computer or to the internet; inserting text into a digital image or animation, attaching sound to an image; building multimedia role-play universes online; choosing, building or customizing a blog template.

The second part of the idea of new literacies as ontologically new is a little more complex, and will be discussed at length in Chapter 3. Let's think of the points made in the previous paragraph as having mainly to do with ontologically new literacies involving a different kind of *technical stuff* from conventional literacies: for example, screens and pixels rather than paper and type, digital code rather than material print (whether printed by hand, typewriter or press), seamlessly multimodal rather than involving distinct processes for distinct modes (text, image, sound), and so on, transmittable via electronic networks and in real time, rather than via printing, hard copy publishing, and post, etc. In addition to being made of different 'technical' stuff from conventional literacies, new literacies are *also* made of what we might call different *'ethos* stuff' from what we typically associate with conventional literacies. For example, they are often more 'participatory', more 'collaborative', and more 'distributed'; less 'published', less 'individuated', and less 'author-centric' than conventional literacies. New literacies involve a significantly different *configuration of values* from conventional literacies. They involve different kinds of social and cultural *relations*, they flow out of different kinds of priorities and values, and so on. At least, they do so up to an extent that makes it plausible to distinguish between conventional and new literacies in a broad way. The different 'ethos' of new literacies is linked to the different 'technical' character of new literacies in complex – albeit *contingent* – ways. Hence, it is useful to separate these aspects out as two dimensions of what is *ontologically* new about new literacies.

The following chapters focus overwhelmingly on literacies that are associated with the massive growth of electronic information and communications technologies, and their increasing role and place within our everyday lives. To a large extent it is literacies in this post-typographic sense that schools have identified as their main challenge as far as incorporating 'new literacies' into their programmes and as media for learning are concerned. At the same time, the relationship between 'new literacies' and new digital electronic technologies does not seem to us to be a one-to-one relationship. We think of some literacies being 'new' *without them necessarily involving the use of new digital electronic* technologies: for example, scenario planning that is done using blackboards and butcher's paper (Lankshear and Knobel 2006: 94–7); paper-format zines (Duncombe

1997; Vale 1997; Lankshear and Knobel 2003: 27–9), and conventional text productions produced in the course of enacting fan-oriented identities around media like manga comics or TV shows (Mahiri 2001; Jenkins 2010: 235–6), popular cultural literary texts, and popular contemporary

---

Reflection and discussion

Using the discussion in this chapter as a basis for deciding, which of the following might *not* be considered 'new' literacies, and why?

- Reading any or all of Shakespeare's plays online.
- Contributing to a wiki, such as Wikipedia.org.
- Operating a mobile Twitter account.
- Accessing a portable document file (pdf) of a student assignment archived online.
- Watching digitized versions of old television shows online (e.g., use video.google.com to search for shows like *Lost in Space* or *Doctor Who*).
- Playing a massively multi-player online game, like Kingdom of Loathing (Kingdomofloathing.com).
- Using an educational CD-ROM package like the *Reader Rabbit* series to practise reading and spelling skills.
- Participating in an online social networking site (e.g., Bebo, Facebook, MySpace, Orkut).
- Creating fan-based animations that remix clips from a range of animation shows and movies.
- Blogging.
- Scanning a handwritten and self-illustrated story and posting it online.
- Using image manipulation software like *Adobe Photoshop* to alter, enhance, or spoof an image as part of contributing to a set of images similarly altered around a given idea, theme, or message.

Repeat this activity after you have read Chapters 2 and 3, and compare your later responses and reasons with those provided here.

---

card games like *Pokémon, DragonBall Z* and *Yu-Gi-Oh!* (Pahl 2002). Such practices are saturated in 'new ethos stuff' in ways that distinguish them quite dramatically from conventional literacies; particularly those that populate formal education.

In Chapter 2, we explain how we understand literacies in general, as a necessary step in the argument toward understanding *new* literacies.

Literacies: practice, Discourse, and encoded texts

Introduction

In Chapter 1, we referred to the emergence and maturation of a sociocultural approach to understanding literacy as a major factor in the development of literacy studies as a field of research and theoretical endeavour. This approach evolved from work being done across a range of disciplinary fields including social linguistics, anthropology, social cognition, cultural psychology, history, and cultural studies, among others (Gee 1990, 1996, 2008a; Alvermann 2009). This approach is what Gee (1990) first called the 'New Literacy Studies' – the name that has stuck – which seeks to understand literacy 'in its full range of cognitive, social, interactional, cultural, political, institutional, economic, moral, and historical contexts' (Gee 2008a: 2). A key tenet of the New Literacy Studies is that literacy is best understood 'as a shorthand for the social practices and conceptions of reading and writing' (Street 1984: 2). That is, 'literacy' is always and everywhere a matter of *literacies*. Hence, the task in this chapter is not to define 'literacy' as some singular phenomenon but, rather, to understand literacies as multiple.

We define literacies as 'socially recognized ways in which people generate, communicate, and negotiate meanings, as members of Discourses, through the medium of encoded texts'. As with any definition of a phenomenon whose scope is large and complex, there are a number of key ideas here that need spelling out in more detail. This is what we will do in the remainder of this chapter, beginning with a discussion of practice theory, or theories of social practice, as a distinctive and currently highly influential variant of social theory. Our aim is to provide an account of literacies that will provide a sound basis for discussing in subsequent chapters a range of new literacies in ways that are useful for educators as well as informative for others who are interested in how literacies are emerging and evolving under contemporary conditions of media/technology, popular cultural affinities, approaches to learning, and ways of being in the world.

The rise of practice theory as social theory

The idea of *socially recognized ways* of generating, communicating and negotiating meanings is essentially the technical concept of *practice* as widely used with reference to literacy as social practice(s) and, more generally, to the view of social practice as the 'smallest unit' of social theory and social analysis (Reckwitz 2002: 245, 249). While a good deal of work in literacy studies is undertaken for immediate practical and pragmatic ends, such as looking for better ways to do literacy education, the ultimate purpose of researching literacies is to contribute toward a deeper and richer understanding of how the social and cultural world 'ticks'. Literacy studies is a subset of social inquiry and social theory, committed to understanding as well as possible how social order and human agency and action are accomplished in ways that give overall 'shape' to human lives. How does life get to be 'structured' and 'arranged' in ways – for better or for worse – that we can get socialized into, such that we can go about doing and being in ways that make some kind of sense, and that 'carry over' from day to day such that on any Tuesday the world looks much the same as it did on Monday, and we know how to 'go on'?

In an interesting, accessible, and helpful discussion, Andreas Reckwitz (2002) argues that 'practice theories' or 'theories of social practice' have begun to emerge as a distinctive type of social theory. Reckwitz argues that modern social theory (dating from the late eighteenth century) has provided a range of theoretical approaches to explaining 'the social': notably, 'purpose-oriented theories of action', 'norm-oriented theories of action', and 'cultural theories'. He identifies practice theory as a form of *cultural* theory of social phenomena, based on the idea that humans share ways of making sense of or ascribing meaning to the world as the means for 'doing life together' (or 'being social'). As a particular form of cultural theory of the social, *practice theory* locates this shared knowledge in everyday social practices.

Reckwitz (2002: 250) describes a practice as a routinized type of activity that consists of several interconnected elements: namely, 'forms of bodily activities, forms of mental activities, "things" and their use, a background knowledge in the form of understanding, know how, states of emotion and motivational knowledge' (ibid.: 254). Wherever a practice exists we necessarily find all of these elements present, and connected to each other in specific and distinctive ways. A practice cannot be reduced to one or two of these elements, and differences in the ways they are interconnected constitute variations in the practice or, even, different practices. In short, practices are routinized ways of moving our bodies, handling objects and using things, understanding and describing the world, desiring and conceiving of tasks and purposes, of treating subjects, and so on (ibid.).

Taking the concrete example of playing football, Reckwitz (ibid.: 252) says that in part this involves a routinized and patterned range of bodily performances – ways of moving and manoeuvring that we instantly associate with playing football (of one code or another). At the same time these bodily performances – patterns of bodily activity – are joined to patterns of mental activity: distinctive forms of 'know-how', of interpretation (e.g., interpreting what other players are doing as a basis for anticipating and acting), of aims and purposes (e.g., winning, playing well, playing fairly), emotions, feelings, desires (e.g., a productive level of tension, feelings of excitement, elation or disappointment), and so on. For Reckwitz (ibid.: 252), these 'mental patterns' are not the private '"possession" of an individual "deep inside"' but, rather, are 'part of the social practice' in the sense that Gee (1992) refers to in terms of 'the social mind'. In addition, playing football involves using various objects or things (e.g., balls, posts, expanses of turf) in certain ways, and particular patterns of language use and discursive interaction integral to playing the game with a view to winning or, at least, playing well.

Humans, then, are bearers or carriers of practices, through which they do and be and understand. As carriers of practices, through participation in practices, individuals 'perform' their bodies and their minds, their desires and ends, their emotions and values, in particular ways. They thereby achieve identity and membership, roles and relationships, understandings and accountabilities. In doing so, their 'performances' carry the social order. They 'bear' social structure and the ongoing maintenance of social order. Social structure – the social order – is located in social practices.

It is important to recognize that while practices are *routines* and, to that extent (relatively) stable and recognizable as particular ways of doing things, they are nonetheless dynamic, mutable, and not completely monolithic. There are different versions of particular practices, more and less expert versions, and there is room for a degree of innovation and variation (and significant innovation on a noticeable scale often results in the creation of new practices). Bloggers, for example, may blog quite differently from one another – thematically and topically, or in terms of additional media and applications used, their regularity of posting, etc. – while nonetheless being recognizable as bloggers. Their mental, bodily and dispositional performances, use of tools, and so on, may vary significantly while remaining versions of blogging. The sense they respectively make of blogging may differ, as may their understandings of the blogosphere. Yet they are bloggers and engaged in blogging. The details of the 'elements' of blogging and the interconnections between these elements can vary from case to case – within recognizable limits – and it is these nuances that good social research will identify and document and explain, thereby contributing to our knowledge of the social world: of action and order.

Literacy as practice

Silvia Scribner and Michael Cole (1981) introduced a technical concept of 'practice' to literacy theory based on their research into the relationship between literacy and cognition. This research was undertaken at a time when it was common to think of literacy as a 'tool' or 'technology' – a writing system – that produces valuable outcomes when people apply it. Against this view, Scribner and Cole conceptualized literacy as *practice*.

They define 'practice' in a series of statements. A practice is:

[A] recurrent, goal-directed sequence of activities using a particular technology and a particular system of knowledge ...

[It] always refers to socially developed and patterned ways of using technology and knowledge to accomplish tasks ...

[T]asks that humans engage in constitute a social practice when they are directed to socially recognized goals and make use of a shared technology and knowledge system.

(ibid.: 236)

According to Scribner and Cole, applying knowledge to accomplish tasks in the presence of technology – where 'technology' is not confined to the digital, but includes a range of tools and techniques – always involves 'coordinated sets of actions', which they call skills. They identify such skills as part of any practice: 'A practice, then, consists of three components: technology, knowledge and skills' (ibid.: 236).

Rather than simple cause–effect relationships between a technology (e.g., literacy as writing system) and outcomes (e.g., new skills, new kinds of knowledge and thinking processes, economic and social development), a concept and theory of practice see *all* of these – technologies, knowledges, and skills – as inter-related, dynamically connected to one another, and mutually evolving in conjunction with people's changing ideas about purposes and tasks. Within broad fields or domains of practice – like education, medicine, farming, or cooking – changes in ideas about how something might be done will generate new tasks that call for refinements in knowledge (theory, concepts, etc.), skills and processes, and technologies. These in turn will act back on people's ideas about what else could be done, in what ways, and so on.

Scribner and Cole then apply this concept of practice to literacy. They approach literacy as 'a set of socially organized practices which make use of a symbol system and a technology for producing and disseminating it' (ibid.: 236). They say that literacy is not a matter of knowing how to read and write a particular kind of script but, rather, a matter of 'applying this knowledge for specific purposes in specific contexts of use' (ibid.: 236). It is true that one can sit down with, say, a page of a book and just randomly 'decode' some words without having any purpose other than sounding out letters in one's head, and with no concern for what the words signify. One *can* do that. But it is not a meaningful thing to do other, perhaps, than with the odd purpose of confirming to oneself that one can do it. Rather, engaging in literacy involves bringing technology knowledge and skills together within some context of point and purpose.

This means that literacy is really like a family of practices – literacies – that will include such 'socially evolved and patterned activities' as letter writing, keeping records and inventories, keeping a diary, writing memos, posting announcements, participating in an online social news space, and so on. These all vary to some extent from one another in terms of the technologies used (pencil, typewriter, pen, font options, the kind of surface 'written' on); the knowledge drawn upon (formatting conventions, use of register, information about the topic), and their skill requirements (hand–eye coordination, using a mouse). Their very names intimate purpose, and situate literacies within contexts of practice.

The kinds of literacy practices described by Scribner and Cole on the basis of their research among the Vai people of Liberia constitute so many *recognized ways* of generating, communicating, and negotiating meanings through the medium of encoded texts. These ways are 'recurrent' – they are socially recognized as *patterns* of activity – and are engaged in on a regular basis under these socially recognized patterned descriptions.

Since Scribner and Cole presented their account of practice and literacy practices, the concept has been reworked and refined many times (see, for example, Street 1984, 2001; Barton 1991; Prinsloo and Breier 1996; Barton and Hamilton 1998; Hull and Schultz 2001), especially in the form of *literacy as social practice*. Barton and Hamilton (1998: 6, 11) claim that the idea of literacy practices

> offers a powerful way of conceptualising the link between the activities of reading and writing and the social structures [cf. Reckwitz, above] in which they are embedded and which they help to shape ... People are active in what they do, and literacy practices are embedded in broader social goals and cultural practices ... Any study of literacy practices must therefore situate reading and writing activities in these broader contexts and motivations for use.

In this sense, literacy practices are 'what people do with literacy' (Barton and Hamilton 1998: 6), and where and how they do it; but within contexts of larger purposeful engagements and involvements – 'larger' social practices – that shape the way literacies play out in particular situations. Barton and Hamilton's well-known account employs what has become a popular conceptual frame for talking about literacy in terms of social practice: practices, events and texts. This leads to the claim that we should understand literacy as 'a set of social practices [that] can be inferred from events which are mediated by written texts' (ibid.: 8).

A key point here, as we have already seen in Reckwitz's account of practice theory, is that (literacy) practices are not wholly observable units of human activity because they involve various kinds of non-observable (although potentially inferable) elements, like values, feelings, knowledge and beliefs, attitudes, etc., including how participants think about literacy, make sense of literacy, talk about literacy, and so on (Barton and Hamilton 1998: 6). By contrast, literacy events *are* observable. They are 'observable episodes which arise from practices and are shaped by them', and where texts 'are central to the activity' (ibid.: 7) – such as where one is using a recipe book for cooking, a set of instructions for assembling something, a religious text for worshipping, cards for playing a game, and so on. From this perspective, identifying, describing, and understanding literacies as social practice(s) begins from '[analysing] events in order to learn about practices' (ibid.: 8): beginning from the observable, and 'tracking back' to discover as much as possible about, and otherwise infer as soundly as possible about, the social practice in which the literacy event is embedded.

At this juncture a number of questions and issues arise. One concerns the relationship between literacy practices and literacies. Another concerns variations among literacy practices. With respect to the former, Barton and Hamilton elect to identify literacies as 'coherent configurations of literacy practices' that are associated with 'particular aspects of cultural life' or 'domains of life' (ibid.: 9), such as academic literacy, workplace literacy, various home and community-based literacies, and so on. So, depending on how academic literacy is configured, it might include, for example, specific practices of essay writing, taking notes, annotating a text, generating spreadsheets, creating bibliographies, searching academic databases, and so on.

At the same time, there is obviously a great deal of variation between different people and different instances of these more specific practices and their respective 'configurations'. As Gee (2008a: 44–5) observes, different people read certain kinds of texts in particular ways that can vary widely from person to person. For instance, people read and act on recipes very differently, depending on their 'socialization histories' regarding the social practice of cooking. Some people follow the recipe to the letter. Others see the recipe as an approximation or a broad kind of plan or design that can be modified in appropriate ways that will still bring a good result (e.g., by varying spices, stepping the chilli up or down, substituting pork for chicken, varying amounts of ingredients). Likewise, different students read academic texts very differently, and the practices of bloggers and online social networkers can differ enormously in 'look and feel'. Gee (ibid.: 44) argues that someone learns to read texts of a given type in a particular way only if they have had 'experience in settings where texts of type X are read in way Y'. The same text – say, a bible – will be read and responded to very differently if one's religious formation has been fundamentalist, liberationist, Protestant, Catholic, etc. Moreover, school students might read history texts very differently depending on whether their experiences have emphasized remembering what is written versus using the text as one resource among many to be mobilized for acts of interpretation. In terms of talking about practice, these differences will play out at the level of know-how, reflecting differences in values and understandings, and resulting in differences in skills in the sense described by Scribner and Cole (1981). These differences involve 'unobservables' that can be tapped by probing histories of socialization (e.g., through interviewing) or by inferring on the basis of accumulated familiarity with people and their practices.

This is what, following Gee, we mean by saying that people's socially recognized ways of generating, communicating, and negotiating meanings – as acts of cultural participation and involvement in practices – are undertaken always and everywhere from the standpoint of Discourse memberships. We will return to this later. Meanwhile, it is sufficient to say that a focus on socially recognized ways of doing meaning work go far beyond literal or strictly semantic meanings alone; extending to the level of engaging in cultural activity that constitutes the stuff of *living meaningfully* – acting within and as part of an ordered social reality that one's activity carries and, to a greater or lesser extent, may modify. In any event, exploring and understanding such 'socially recognized ways' will involve cashing out, among other things, the tools/technology, knowledge, and skills dimensions of practice, as discussed by Scribner and Cole, or inferring practices from an analysis of events along lines described by latter-day proponents of the concept of literacy as social practice.

Reflection and discussion

- What do you think Reckwitz (2002: 252) means when he says that the 'mental patterns' involved in practices are not the private '"possession" of an individual "deep inside"' but, rather, are 'part of the social practice'?

- Barton and Hamilton (1998: 7) see literacy events as 'observable episodes which arise from practices and are shaped by them'. Discuss how you think you would identify and locate literacy events associated with practices of online social networking.

- Compare and discuss some of the kinds of knowledges, skills, and techniques needed to produce, make sense of, and interact with texts found on the following websites:
  - reddit.com
  - books.google.com
  - worth1000.com
  - mugglenet.com
  - boingboing.net
  - mangastream.com

To continue unpacking our definition of literacies we turn now to the idea of encodification.

Encoded texts

We have identified encoded texts as the medium through which meanings are generated, communicated, exchanged, and negotiated in and through the diverse social practices of literacy, i.e., literacies. By 'encoded texts' we mean texts that have been rendered in a form that allows them to be retrieved, worked with, and made available independently of the physical presence of another person. 'Encoded texts' are texts that have been 'frozen' or 'captured' in ways that free them from their immediate context of production so that they can 'travel' because they are 'transportable'.

Perhaps what is most important about literacy as a social phenomenon is that it enables people to do what cannot be done by orality alone. Literacy enables human beings to communicate and share meanings in ways that go beyond the use of voice within face-to-face settings (which is orality). Literacy checks in when the conditions of everyday life are such that people need more than the use of voice alone to get the meaning-making work done that needs to get done for life to go on. The bottom line for literacy is that it enables meaning-making to occur or 'travel' across space and time, mediated by systems of signs in the form of encoded texts of one kind or another. Unencoded texts like speech and hand signs 'expire' at the point of production other than to the extent that they can live on – fallibly – in the memories of whoever was there at the time. Encoded texts give (semi-) permanence and transcendence to thought and language in the sense that they can 'travel' without requiring particular people to transport them. The particular kinds of codes employed in literacy practices are varied and contingent. Literacies can involve *any* kind of codification system that 'captures' language in the sense we have described. Literacy includes 'letteracy' (i.e., within the English language, recognition and manipulation of alphabetic symbols), but in our view goes far beyond this, which puts us at odds with scholars who tie literacy to *reading* and *writing* alone. In our view, someone who 'freezes' language as a digitally encoded passage of speech and uploads it to the internet as a podcast is engaging in literacy. So, equally, is someone who photoshops an image – whether or not it includes a written text component. It is not that memory and speech alone *cannot* sustain considerable meaning-making across distance and contexts. It is just that this is exponentially enabled and facilitated by literacy as encodification, which permits all kinds of procedures and institutions and practices that would be impossible, or impossibly cumbersome, without encoded thought and language.

Meaning and texts

As we have seen, while literacies call us to generate and communicate meanings and to invite others to make meaning from our texts in turn, this can only be done by having something to make meaning *from*, namely a kind of 'potential' conveyed by the text and that is engaged through interaction with the text by its audience or recipients. Gunther Kress (2003: 37–8) makes this point in relation to alphabetic writing. He talks of readers doing 'semiotic work' when they read a written text. This is 'the work of filling the elements of writing with content' (ibid.): that is, the work of making meaning from the writing in the text. Kress argues that meaning involves two kinds of work. One is *articulation*, which is performed in the production of 'the outwardly made sign' (e.g., writing). The other is *interpretation*, which involves producing 'the inwardly made sign' in reading (see also Gee 2004: Ch. 6).

Our idea of meanings that are generated and negotiated within literacy practices is, however, wider and looser than many literacy scholars might accept. We think Gee's (1997, 2004, 2008a) Discourse approach to literacies draws attention to the complexity and richness of the relationship between literacies and 'ways of being together in the world'. So when we look at somebody's blog we might well find that much of the meaning to be made has to do with who we think the blog writer *is*: what they are like, how they want to think of themselves, and how they want us to think of them. Likewise, a particular text that someone produces might well be best understood as an expression of wanting to feel 'connected' or 'related' right now. The meaning to be 'filled in' might be much more *relational* than *literal* or, even, 'linguistic' or 'semantic' in a strict sense. It might be more about expressing solidarity or affinity with particular people.

This is an important point when it comes to understanding the internet, online practices and online 'content'. Almost anything available online becomes a resource for diverse kinds of meaning-making. In many cases the meanings that are made will not be intelligible to people at large or, in some cases, to many people at all. Some might be shared only by 'insiders' of quite small interest groups or cliques. Consider, for example, the way that eBay has been used to spoof a range of social conventions and to generate diverse kinds of quirky activity. A man auctioned his soul in 2006 and received a cash payment that came with the condition that he would spend 50 hours in church. Two sisters auctioned off a cornflake shaped like Illinois for US$1350 – spawning countless copycat auctions in return (e.g., a cornflake shaped like Hawaii, a potato chip shaped like Australia). In another case an individual auctioned a ten-year-old toasted cheese sandwich the owner said had an imprint of the Virgin Mary on it, and that had not gone mouldy or disintegrated since it was made in 1994. Moreover, she said it had brought her luck at a casino. An internet casino purchased the sandwich for $28,000 and planned to take it on tour to raise money for charity. Other sellers responded with Virgin Mary toasted sandwich makers, T-shirts, coffee mugs, etc. (BBC News 2004). An Australian – also in 2006 – listed New Zealand for sale on eBay, with a starting price of $0.01. The auction reached AU$3000 before eBay cancelled it. A similar thing happened in 2008, when Iceland was put up for sale during the nation's financial crisis – bids reached £10 million before the auction was pulled by eBay (Wikipedia 2010a). More recently, a young man tried to raise money for the Cancer Research UK foundation by auctioning off a ghost (perhaps imitating the famous 'ghost in a jar' auction on eBay in 2003), but was found to be in violation of eBay's rules for selling an intangible object (ibid.). The meanings of such actions have little to do with established practices of auctioning, and the interpretation of texts describing the items have little or nothing to do with the literal words *per se*. People may be prepared to bid/spend money just to be in solidarity with the spoof: to say, 'I get it', thereby signalling their insiderness with the practice, expressing solidarity with the seller, enacting an 'affinity' or, even, trying to save a soul.

In similar vein, after Iraqi journalist, Muntadhar Al-Zaidi, threw both of his shoes at President George Bush during a press conference that was part of Bush's 'farewell' visit to Iraq in 2008, a video of the actual event flew around the world via the internet and grabbed international attention. This in turn spawned a large number of response texts that remixed this event with popular culture texts to underscore the intended insult behind Al-Zaidi's act (e.g., remixing arcade game soundtracks and target shooting tactics with the original video; having Al-Zaidi throw a Reddit alien at Bush; remixing clips from the Three Stooges and pie-throwing with the original clip), or to suggest ways in which Bush could have responded (e.g., bending backwards to dodge the shoes as Neo bends backwards to dodge bullets in the first *Matrix* movie). Collectively, these videos and images have come to be known as the 'Iraqi Shoe Toss' meme (see Know Your Meme 2010a). Key to understanding this event, aside from being familiar with a range of popular culture texts, is understanding the war on Iraq and the outrageous number of civilian and military deaths that occurred (are occurring) as a result (Al-Zaidi cried out 'This is for the widows and orphans and all those killed in Iraq' as he threw the second shoe), and knowing that throwing shoes 'is an act of extreme disrespect' in many Arabic cultures (Wikipedia 2010b). Having no knowledge of the political, social and cultural controversy surrounding the war in Iraq would render the set of remix clips only partially or superficially interpretable.

Aside from shared experiences or knowledge of current events, meaningful content within many new literacy practices clearly requires shared interests and pleasures. Remixing anime videos or films makes this point very clearly, as we will see in Chapter 5. This practice involves, for example, splicing together – remixing – very short clips from a range of commercial anime (animated Japanese cartoons) to create an entirely new narrative set to a matching music soundtrack (see examples at Animemusicvideos.org). Anime music video remixes can be entirely in-canon; that is, they draw on only one anime series for their visual resources. Others remix clips from across a number of series depending on purpose. Anime music video remixes can be humorous, dramatic, action-packed, thought-provoking – especially when they explore characters or relationships not developed in an anime series – and even social commentaries (see Knobel et al. 2010). Anime music video remixes are likely to appeal most to existing fans of all things anime who enjoy other fans' tinkering around with original texts to create new – albeit still recognizable – anime videos. Popular culture anthropologists like Mimi Ito argue that this kind of creative work is driven largely by a push to communicate with and relate to interested others, rather than by the goal of sharing 'information' about specific anime productions or characters (Ito 2006; Ito et al. 2009).

Meaning and Discourse memberships

Jim Gee (2008a) speaks of sociocultural approaches to language and literacy as *Discourse* approaches, as mentioned in the previous chapter. Discourse can be seen as the underlying principle of meaning and meaningfulness. We 'do life' as individuals and as members of social and cultural groups – always as what Gee calls 'situated selves' – in and through Discourses, which can be understood as meaningful coordinations of human and non-human elements. Besides people themselves, the human elements of coordinations include such things as people's ways of thinking, acting, feeling, moving, dressing, speaking, gesturing, believing, and valuing, and non-human elements include such things as tools, objects, institutions, networks, places, vehicles, machines, physical spaces, buildings, and so on.

A person rushing an email (or text) message to head office as they hand their boarding pass to the airline attendant at the entrance to the aircraft boarding ramp is recognizable (to others and themselves) as a certain kind of person. In this moment she is part of a *coordination* that includes as its elements such things as the person herself, some way of thinking and feeling (maximizing time to get more done), rules (her smartphone must be switched off when the plane is leaving the gate), institutions (airports and air travel, the company they work for), tools (a phone, a network), accessories (a computer bag and compact travel bag), clothes (a suit, perhaps), language (facility with emailing concisely and accurately). These various elements all get and are got 'in sync' (Gee 2008a: 155). The various elements simultaneously coordinate the others and are coordinated by them (institutional requirements and timetables prompt the particular use of the phone during the last seconds before boarding; the email (or text) message makes a demand back on someone in the company; the meeting ahead has influenced choice of clothes – smart but comfortable, etc.). This 'in sync-ness' tells us who and what that person is (like, a business executive in the middle of a three-city day). As Gee puts it: 'Within such coordinations we humans become *recognizable* to ourselves and to others and *recognize* ourselves, other people, and things as meaningful in distinctive ways' (1997: xiv).

Humans and non-human elements move in and out of such coordinations all the time. Identities (of humans and non-humans alike) are chronicles of the trajectories of coordinations we move through, over time. Different coordinations call on us to think, act, believe, dress, feel, speak, relate in different ways to a greater or lesser extent. To know how to do this, when to do it, and that we should do it is the 'nature' of living meaningfully. Another way of saying this is to say that we get recruited to Discourses as part of our 'birthright' as social and cultural beings, and that in and through our social engagement with Discourses we each become identifiable as a particular kind of person (a trajectory and amalgam of 'situated selves' that change as our purposes, contexts, and Discourse coordinations change) and learn to be a particular kind of person. A Discourse

> is a way of 'being together in the world' for humans, their ways of thinking and feeling (etc.), and for non-human things, as well, such that coordinations of elements, and elements themselves, take on recognizable identities. 'Discourse' names the patterning of coordinations, their recognizability, as well as that of their elements.
>
> (Gee 1997: xv)

Discourses are of many kinds – classrooms, sports, friendship networks, church gatherings, clubs, gangs, academic disciplines, discussion lists, chatrooms, types of women, weddings, funerals, families. They are made up by coordinations and they make coordinations and elements recognizable. Discourses are the stuff of meaning and meaningfulness; they constitute the 'shape' and 'order' of the world. We enact them and they enact us. To be in a Discourse is to be able to coordinate elements of that Discourse competently and to be coordinated by them competently.

These ideas provide us with ways of thinking about literacies, as elements of coordinations, and as themselves coordinations that are parts of Discourses, depending on the level of specificity being operated with in a particular case. So, for example, the case of the executive *emailing/texting* a memo or request or reminder to head office while boarding a plane might be seen as an element in the enactment of a particular coordination that constitutes part of being a business executive (working on the run in a way that is recognizable as quintessential business executive *modus operandi*). From this perspective, a literacy is an element in a coordination.

At a different level we might think of a literacy practice in the sense spelled out by Scribner and Cole as a coordination among technology, knowledge and skills. The case of the business person from our earlier example who is being a letter writer, emailer, or memo writer involves coordinating an internetworked telephone with knowledge of email/memo etiquette, format,

---

Reflection and discussion

- Do you agree with the claims that 'someone who "freezes" language as a digitally encoded passage of speech and uploads it to the internet as a podcast is engaging in literacy' and so, equally, is 'someone who photoshops an image – whether or not it includes a written text component'?
  - If so, what are your reasons?
  - If not, what are your reasons?
  - If you are undecided, what are the issues you can't decide upon?

- Do you think the view of 'meaning' as related to literacy that we are advancing in this chapter is:
  - Too wide?
  - Not wide enough?
  - About right?

  What are your reasons for your viewpoint?

register, and institutional structure (who to send it to in order to get the desired result) and requisite skills (texting on the run with one hand and an eye to luggage and boarding pass with the other, all the while organizing thoughts succinctly …).

As constitutive parts of participation in or membership of a Discourse, literacies are always about much more, and involve much more, than just the production of texts. They are (also) contexts or pretexts for enacting and refining memberships of Discourses that include such dimensions as feeding back, providing support, sharing knowledge and expertise, explaining rules, sharing jokes, commiserating, doing one's job, expressing opinions, showing solidarity, enacting an affinity (Gee 2004), and so on.

What did Mark Zuckerberg do?

At the time of writing (24 September 2010) the film about Facebook co-founder Mark Zuckerberg, *The Social Network*, is premiering at the New York Film Festival. It provides us with a timely and graphic catalyst for bringing together key ideas advanced in this chapter in support of our view that literacies are 'socially recognized ways in which people generate, communicate, and negotiate meanings, as members of Discourses, through the medium of encoded texts'. We can get at this by asking the question: 'What did Mark Zuckerberg (and his collaborators Eduardo Saverin, Dustin Moskovitz, and Chris Hughes) *do* in 2004 when they designed and launched Facebook.com?'

Setting aside for our purposes the controversy surrounding the development and launch of this social networking service (see, for example, Greenspan 2008; Wikipedia 2010c), what Zuckerberg and his collaborators did, in the first instance, was to create and launch an online social media platform and service (an online architecture and space) which established a *way* (a means and a *modus operandi*) for people at large to exchange meanings and engage in a meaningful form of practice mediated by various kinds of encodifications. If we pick things up from Scribner and Cole (1981), we can see that Facebook provided a (complex and sophisticated) technology that allowed participants to employ various coordinated sets of actions ('skills') informed by particular kinds of knowledge and know-how in recurring sequences in order to get things done. This includes, for example, knowing how to set up a Facebook account and deciding what name to use (your full name, your name before you changed it, a disguised name, your nickname); typically, this means deciding which name the people who mean the most to you or with whom you plan to network know you by.

Particular navigation skills include understanding the different 'spaces' of one's Facebook profile pages, and how to navigate these via mouse clicks or key presses. This involves recognizing and understanding that the 'friend request' icon is clicked to manage requests or suggestions for 'friending' or establishing a network connection with someone (e.g., accept, ignore); that the messages icon is not the same as the notifications icon (one lists private messages sent directly to you email-style within Facebook, the other is a summary list of Facebook activity for everyone in your overall Facebook network). Other skills and knowledge include understanding the difference between the news feed (where everyone's status updates are posted) and your profile page (where accounts of your Facebook activity are posted), and how to switch between the two spaces.

Even something as seemingly straightforward as a status update that lets your friends know what you're doing, thinking about, or whatever, involves making use of a particular set of skills and understandings. This includes knowing where to type and which button to click on (in this case, the 'share' button, rather than something that says 'post' or 'publish'); perhaps knowing how to shorten long URLs of websites you're recommending using services like TinyURL.com or Bit.ly; deciding what's newsworthy for your friends or what you're comfortable making public (e.g., do you post derogatory remarks about a student or co-worker; or do you post links to pictures of cute cats, etc.?). Facebook makes it possible to attach or add different things like photos, video, or events to your status update – Facebook literacy can thus involve understanding which icon to click and how to add different media to your post. To delete a personal status post, the user needs to know that the function is hidden, and requires them to 'mouse over' it (i.e., slide the mouse-controlled cursor over a blank space to the right of the update) to reveal the 'remove' option. Responding to someone's status update means deciding between simply clicking on the 'like' hyperlink to show solidarity or appreciation, or clicking on the 'comment' hyperlink and writing something in response. As with the process for removing one's own status update, the user needs to mouse over the top right-hand corner of each status update comment to reveal the icon for deleting a comment felt to be inappropriate for others to see.

Other information associated with status updates includes the time the update was posted, and where it was posted from (e.g., a re-post of content shared by someone else within Facebook, from a mobile device). Users also need to know the difference between posting to someone's Facebook 'wall' – a public message service – and when to send messages privately, email-like. When reading wall posts, it helps to know that only half the conversation may be showing, with the other half written on the other interlocutor's wall, and that clicking on the 'wall-to-wall' hyperlink will reveal the entire conversation. This is, of course, just a surface sampling of what's entailed in Facebook literacy practices – but it does give a sense of some of the skills, tech know-how and knowledge brought into play by having an active Facebook profile and interacting with others.

When we pick things up from the perspective of Reckwitz (2002), we can see how 'facebooking' has entered and augmented the social fabric and contemporary cultural life to a massive extent and in profound ways during its short history to date. This does not merely convey the fact that some 500 million people around the globe are employing a common platform or online service and a range of 'skill sets' to do something we can all recognize as patterned routines (with varying degrees of difference and overlap from instance to instance of use). More than this, it means that we can see 'facebooking' as participation in and extensions of well- and often long-established social practices and Discourses. For example, those parts of social life that involve being a footballer, a builder, a teacher, a mother, a Labour Party or Republican activist (or, at least, voter), get 'played out' to some degree in Facebook entries. Being these kinds of things get projected into/onto, or lived out in Facebook space, and 'communities' of kindred and unlike spirits get reinforced, carried further and, perhaps, changed and refined in the process.

Similarly, being an entrepreneur is given a space to play out – for example, through the development of Facebook-embedded applications that might take off and become part of the platform's evolution and people's ways of interacting by using it. Zynga's *Farmville* game is a good example here. In a nutshell, *Farmville* – launched in June 2009 – entails managing and developing a 'farm' through planting, tending and harvesting crops, and husbanding animals. It is social in the sense that one helps to care for neighbours' plots and can 'gift' farm items to friends. It is free to play, although players can also pay real money to purchase in-game cash for purchasing up-scale buildings and accoutrements, and farm machinery. By September 2010, *Farmville* had registered over 62 million active users within Facebook (Wikipedia 2010d), and earned Zynga a reported US$145 million in its first six months of operation (Technology Talks 2010).

Importantly, Facebook and facebookers become implicated in or integrated into deep-seated practices of capital accumulation, business and economic production to a greater or lesser extent and more or less wittingly, through their very participation in the space. For instance, facebookers collectively are part of a massive network that can be accessed, leveraged, and 'played' by advertisers, marketers, commodity producers, and so on. Zynga Facebook games, for example, often reward players with in-game cash or other kinds of bonuses for signing up to other games or online and offline services, with monetary kickbacks for both Zygna *and* Facebook. Facebook literacy, it can be said, has become a visible component in the nuts and bolts of the (capitalist) information/knowledge economy, as well as in the more familiar economy of commodity production and exchange. Facebook literacy or, if we prefer, online social networking (of which 'facebooking' can be seen as the currently dominant version or variety) has rapidly become a significant and highly visible part of the threadwork of the contemporary social fabric: the social order. That is, the meanings that are made and exchanged and negotiated via Facebook.com are not simply literal meanings or, even, textual meanings. They are ultimately meanings at the deep social *structural* level of being recognizable kinds of people, playing recognizable roles, establishing and maintaining recognizable relationships within recognizable domains of cultural life, maintaining and refining recognizable routines that 'carry' a social-cultural order through time.

Equally, Facebook literacy shows us how 'things' that are always and everywhere 'common factors' in literacy practices – encodifications and ways of producing and interacting with them; kinds of knowledge and tools and skills, etc. – can get re-combined in changing and new ways. In a sense, almost everything that 'went into' Facebook.com already existed. What Zuckerberg and collaborators did was to mobilize and assemble and re-fit a complex range of purposes, interests, desires, resources, know-how, tools, and the like, in a distinctive, but now entirely recognized, way. In doing so, they created a particular 'configuration' (Barton and Hamilton 1998) of literacy practices: *a literacy*.

They also enacted a high-profile kind of *agency* within the shape of the overall social structure, and the fruits of this agency are now a conventional and established element of the current social order. Facebooking is now a part of the social apparatus through which human life as meaningful life – warts and all; for better and for worse – is carried out and, above all, continued. As we have seen, part of this process involves generating, exchanging and negotiating quite *specific* kinds of meanings, such as particular jokes, literal meanings, factual exchanges, etc. Part of it involves more *general* kinds of meanings: for example, reliving the experience and enjoyment of a good meal as something that members of Discourse communities (friends, families, colleagues, affinities, etc.) do. Ultimately, the meanings that are enacted and interacted with are the complex and diffuse meanings encapsulated by entire social practices as meaningful ways of doing things. At this level, engaging in Literacy Studies is to engage in social theory and social research: contributing to better describing and understanding 'how it all hangs together': rendering social life *meaningful* by making sense of social life as patterned and routinized activity in which and through which people *act*, and enact social and cultural *agency*.

Reflection and discussion

Discuss the proposition that to all intents and purposes in 2004 Mark Zuckerberg and his collaborators unleashed a literacy on the world.

Literacies

Hence, literacies are 'socially recognized ways in which people generate, communicate, and negotiate meanings, as members of Discourses, through the medium of encoded texts'. As such, blogging, fanfic writing, manga producing, meme-ing, photoshopping, anime music video practices, podcasting, vodcasting, and video gaming are *literacies*, along with letter writing, keeping a diary, maintaining records, running a paper-based zine, reading literary novels, note-making during conference presentations or lectures, reading bus timetables, and so on.

In Chapter 3, we look at some key trends and developments in the short history of the internet during its period of mass access over the two decades since 1990.

'New' literacies: technologies and values

Introduction: how long is 'new'?

Thinking about what is 'new' with respect to new literacies is challenging and important. It involves trying to understand how our conceptions and practices of literacy are changing in the midst of a far-reaching move away from one kind of social-economic-technological paradigm – and social order – and toward another.

It is too easy to make light of 'new literacies' by saying things like: 'Well, there are always newer ones coming along, so that MOOing is already an "old" new literacy ...'. Such remarks suggest new literacies have a similar kind of life trajectory to an automobile: new in 2009, semi-new in 2010, and old hat by 2011. Against this kind of 'that's so yesterday' perspective, we think 'new literacies' are best understood in terms of an historical period of social, cultural, institutional, economic, and intellectual change that is likely to span many decades – some of which are already behind us. We associate new literacies with an historical conjuncture and an ascending social paradigm. From this perspective the kinds of practices we currently identify as *new* literacies will cease to be 'new' once the social ways characterizing the ascending paradigm have become sufficiently established and grounded to be regarded as *conventional*.

The kind of transition we are talking about here is well recognized and spoken about in already familiar terms. These include the ideas of a transition from modern to postmodern worldviews and theories, from an industrial society and/or economy to post-industrial or information/ knowledge societies and/or economies, from a conception of societies based on the model of autonomous but related nation-states toward an increasingly global configuration, and so on.

The 'post-' concept is handy here because it reminds us that we are not talking of absolute alternatives, complete breaks, or binary distinctions. Postmodernity is not a *displacement* of modernity, a move to something completely different. It is more like a *transcendence*, in which elements of an earlier state of affairs are carried over and reshaped to become parts of new configurations. Ideas and practices evolve rather than become displaced – as the failure of many attempts at revolutionary change attest. We find revamped forms, say, of industrialism within post-industrialism. Technologies of industrial scale and type get transformed in ways that provide necessary and harmonious or coherent complements to digital-electronic computing and communications technologies, and integrated into new styles and sets of practices. We do better here to think in terms of continua between the various dimensions of the different paradigms. These paradigms are constructions out of complex phenomena. They are attempts to 'summarize' broad trends and patterns evident in different times and places under different conditions. They are 'idealized types' that do not exist in pure form, and that are always 'more or less' along their varying dimensions: more of a tendency toward this emphasis or priority here, less of an emphasis or tendency there; varying amounts and degrees occurring from case to case and instance to instance; and always with traces of the former in the 'substance' of the later, or the 'post'.

When we think about the current conjuncture in terms of a tendency away from one paradigm and more toward another, we think in terms of shifts in relative emphasis along the following kinds of continua (Table 3.1).

Under the first paradigm there is a tendency or a default toward thinking, acting, and organizing life around ideas of singularity, centredness, enclosure, individualization, and the like, whereas under the second paradigm there is a tendency toward thinking, acting, and organizing life around notions of multiplicity, flexibility, dispersion, non-linearity, and the like. This can be illustrated by reference to ways of thinking about and responding to people, to work, expertise, life trajectories, institutional roles and styles, and even about intelligence.

Table 3.1 Some dimensions of variation between paradigms

Modern/industrial paradigm	Postmodern/post-industrial/ knowledge society paradigm
Singular/Uniform	Multiple
Centred	De-centred
Monolithic	Dispersed, modular
Enclosed/Bounded	Open/Unbounded
Localized/Concentrated	Distributed
Stable/Fixed	Dynamic/Fluid/Flexible
Linear	Non-linear
'Push'-oriented	'Pull'-oriented
Individualized	Joint/Collaborative/Collective

For example, until relatively recently it was typical to think of a person – an individual – in terms of a single identity, a core 'self', a more or less stable and permanent 'personality' of a particular 'type'. While we recognized that individuals were 'complex' to some extent and in some sense, we nonetheless tended to emphasize their particularity in 'character', point of view, and so on. Today we are much more inclined to think of people as much more complex; indeed, to make a fetish of this complexity. People see the world from *many* perspectives, depending on which Discourse they are 'in' or 'operating out of' within a particular situation or context. We speak of multiple subjectivities here, and think of identities as multiple and shifting. Far from expecting people to manifest a singular abiding 'centre', we think more of people 'doing life' out of many Discourses, and of being able to move among many ways of thinking, speaking, valuing, judging, deciding, desiring, and acting. Not so long ago we thought in terms of individuals pursuing more or less linear life courses or trajectories, often within a more or less single location. The default norm was one job, one home, one family, one social class or status, etc., *for life*. For many, if not most, people living in modern (sub)urban environments this no longer holds. Increasingly, our default norm for life trajectories is complex and non-linear.

Similarly, many authors and researchers have written about the 'new' capitalism (e.g., Reich 1992) by mapping trends away from norms of production and distribution being located and organized in one place/country/site, around one core product or service, under the control or auspices of a single company, firm or corporation, with a specific infrastructure, and with stable roles, relationships, and responsibilities accompanying designated long-term positions within the workforce. The 'new' capitalism

(Gee et al. 1996) or 'post-capitalism' (Drucker 1993) is seen as organized materially around dispersed sites – often global – involving multiple companies, with workers often being hired for single projects or product runs, with flexible/shifting roles and responsibilities. The familiar norm of expertise residing in individual persons attached to different strata within the enterprise often gives way to the norm of distributed expertise and collective intelligence.

Similarly, John Hagel and John Seely Brown (2005) talk about how the different technologies associated with industrial modernity and post-modern knowledge societies respectively generate different common-sense models of how to mobilize scarce resources in order to get the things done that need to be done within societies. They talk of a shift away from a 'push' model of mobilizing resources toward more of a 'pull' model. This shift underpins very different institutional styles, as we will see in our account of social learning later in this book.

These, obviously, are not just shifts in ideas and beliefs; they entail changes in *practices*. Life gets organized differently. The social ordering of work, domesticity, and leisure are reconstituted. Changes in one sphere or dimension of life ripple into changes elsewhere. People who previously never had to worry about résumés before, let alone keeping them updated and bolstered by project portfolios, now have to. People who need to be mobile must find new ways to maintain personal relationships and communicate. Sooner or later these changes 'show up' in the things we do and how we do them – including the literacies we enact and how we perform them. Improvising occurs on the fly; resources and services get 'mashed up' as people respond to contingencies. It is in the details of such intricacies and their shifts that we find the 'new'. And this 'new' endures over decades, not least because for many people the kinds of changes we may be somewhat familiar with are still somewhere away in the future, and 'late arrivals' are part of the frame and need to be accommodated.

In the midst of these recent and ongoing shifts toward 'reconstituting' and 'reconfiguring' everyday practices in patterned and identifiable ways, and to a greater or lesser extent from setting to setting, we find emerging and evolving ways of generating, communicating, and negotiating meanings via encoded texts; ways that become socially recognized well enough and for long enough to be identified as new literacies – not simply in and of themselves, but as elements of a larger abiding 'new'. That is, 'new' is not over on an 'instance by instance basis' when, for example, MOOs give way to 3D role-playing worlds or chat palaces; or stand-alone, single-player, ascii-interface video gaming gives way to online, massively distributed, three-dimensional, avatar-based, multiplayer collaborative gaming that includes real-time text chat, voice chat, and even video/webcam chat. So far as new literacies are concerned, there will be many cameo performances as well as more enduring support roles and lead roles in this evolution. Some specific instances of new literacies may come and go quickly – playing no more than walk-on roles. Despite their short lives, they are nonetheless identifiable as new literacies. They are all historically significant as parts of a larger picture that is not fleeting. To dismiss them as 'old' new literacies bespeaks a failure of historical imagination. Alternatively, to look for what is new in specific instances of 'new' literacies may be a good way of enhancing our perspective on current trends and priorities in our approaches to teaching and learning.

Toward 'new' in theory and in practices

At the end of Chapter 1 we mentioned the idea of literacies that can be regarded as 'new' in an *ontological* sense – being composed of different kinds of 'stuff' from conventional literacies. We foreshadowed a distinction between new *technical* 'stuff' and new *ethos* 'stuff'. At the heart of the idea of new technical stuff is *digitality*: the growth and ongoing development of digital-electronic technologies and the use of programming languages (including the use of source code and binary code) for writing programs, storing and retrieving data, establishing electronic networks, collaboration platforms, and so on. At the heart of the idea of new ethos stuff is the idea of technological change aligning with a range of increasingly popular values. This chapter spells these ideas out to yield an account of new literacies that will underpin discussion in the remainder of this book.

'New technical stuff'

Much of what is important for literacy about the 'new technical stuff' is encapsulated in Mary Kalantzis' idea that 'You click for "A" and you click for "red"' (Cope et al. 2005: 200). To this we might add that you also click for 'send' and click to retrieve. Basically, programmers draw on syntactic and semantic rules for a given programming language, along with a core library of commands, to create a series of commands that ultimately is stored as binary code (combinations of 0s and 1s) and which, in turn, drives different kinds of applications (for text, sound, image, digital video, word processing, animation, communications functions, etc.) or digital-electronic apparatuses (computers, printers, games hardware, CD and MP3 player interfaces, etc.). Someone with access to a fairly standard computer or other mobile digital device and internet connection, and who has some basic knowledge of standard software applications can create a diverse range of meaningful artifacts using a strictly finite set of physical operations or techniques (keying, clicking, selecting, copying, dragging), in a relatively tiny space, with just one or two (albeit complex) 'tools'. They can, for example, create a multimodal text and send it to a person, a group, or an entire internet community in next to no time and at next to no cost, and receive feedback on this text, almost immediately. The text could be a photoshopped image posted to Flickr.com or to Worth1000.com. It could be an animated birthday card sent to a close friend. It could be a short animated film sequence using toys and objects found at home, complete with an original music soundtrack, embedded within a blog post. It could be a slide presentation of images of some event with narrated commentary, or edited video clips from a video game that spoof some aspect of popular culture or that retell some obscure literary work.

The technical stuff of new literacies is part and parcel of generating, communicating, and negotiating encoded meanings by providing a range of new or more widely accessible resource possibilities ('affordances') for making meaning. The technical dimensions of digital technologies greatly enlarge ways of *generating* encoded meanings available to people in comparison with what we might call conventional literacies. Someone who would readily acknowledge not being able to draw or paint or take photos with any artistic or other merit whatsoever can, in a relatively short amount of time, create a collage of images and text to contribute to a popular online meme, such as the Sad Keanu meme where a paparazzi shot of a seemingly dejected-looking Keanu Reeves (a movie actor) got placed in a range of other contexts in a show of solidarity with Reeves (see: Know Your Meme 2010b). Generating this kind of encoded text requires access to image editing software (such as is available at Gimp.org), some understanding of basic image editing 'moves' (like using the marquee tool by manipulating the mouse and click-and-drag actions to draw around and crop an image), using an image search engine to locate an appropriate new background image, knowing how to paste the cropped image onto a new background, using a blur or smudge tool to blend the cropped image into its new background, perhaps using the textbox function to add some text, then using a series of mouse clicks to upload the final image to a publicly shared online space. All in the space of ten minutes or so. In the past, even with access to a photography lab or printing outfit, or being extremely good with scissors and magazine images, this kind of high-quality, visually convincing collage or remix would have taken quite some time to produce and have been difficult to share with others on the scale now possible online.

Twitter practices present another example of how the technical 'stuff' of new technologies enables alternative or new ways of generating encoded meanings. Twitter is a microblogging service that constrains users to posting messages – 'tweets' – of 140 characters maximum. The technical restrictions on tweet length saw users draw on existing text-messaging abbreviations and phonetic conventions to save characters, along with a range of Twitter-specific shorthand notations in their posts to enhance what could be said and to whom, and how 'like' things could be found by others. For example, placing an '@' symbol in front of another person's Twitter username signals that one's tweet is directed at them specifically. Prefixing a word or phrase with a hashtag (#) automatically groups together all posts that include the same hashtagged word or phrase. For example, many television shows spark viewer-generated commentary on Twitter while the shows are airing. Tweeters can use the hashtag feature and the name of the show (e.g., #GhostHunters, #TopGear) to join in a conversation with others about the show. Twitter also uses these hashtags to identify topics 'trending' on the service, too (e.g., #Wikileaks, #2011predictions). Tweeters can make use of URL-shortening services, such as TinyURL.com, Bit.ly, and Goo.gl, to save character spaces when wanting to share an online site with others. And many Tweeters have installed the Twitter app on their smartphones for quick, on-the-fly access to Twitter, or have added the Twitter app to their Facebook profile, which automatically (re)posts their tweets to their Facebook wall. Understanding the technical dimensions of Twitter – the 140-character limit, the use of hashtags and other symbols to 'manage' and 'retrieve' content, the availability of targeted apps – and how to set up and maintain an active Twitter account are key tools in knowing how to use this social space effectively.

The new technical stuff of digital technologies also has greatly expanded the possibilities for *communicating* encoded meanings. Email applications mean that a single message can now be sent to hundreds of people simultaneously, especially if one is a member of a large email discussion list, or accidentally sends a message to all co-workers at a large institution. Social news sites like Reddit and Slashdot enable communicating directly with others from around the world (sometimes with the use of online translation services like Google Translate or Babelfish). To reprise an earlier example, it's now possible for a three-year-old girl to create a toy-based stop-motion animation and, with her father's help, post it to a video-sharing site like YouTube where – to date – it's been viewed over 9,000 times (see Thomas and Tufano 2010). This contrasts starkly with the conventional practice of pinning pre-schoolers' artworks to the fridge door for a few family members and friends to see. User-generated content hosting sites like YouTube (and Flickr, Panoramio, Blip.tv, Aniboom.com, Warcraftmovies.com), make it easy to share meanings across time and space, and even across languages and cultures. For example, in 2006, a self-recorded clip of a North American male lipsyncing and dancing to a Romanian pop song while remaining seated in his chair throughout caught on as a popular internet meme (Knobel and Lankshear 2007). The performer's mobile facial expressions carried much of the humour of this video, rather than anything said or sung. Countless blogs and discussion boards linked to the video – originally posted to YouTube – and it was reposted on various video hosting sites. Technically speaking, uploading to user-generated content sites is a matter of establishing an account with the service, accessing the upload function within the service, locating the file on one's computer or other digital device, and then perhaps writing some background or contextual details to accompany the uploaded file. Digital networks and hypertext markup language make it possible to link to the original video or embed it in other online spaces. In short, this kind of new technical stuff opens up myriad channels for communicating meanings across a broad spectrum of people and interests.

The technical stuff of digital technologies also facilitates new ways of *negotiating* encoded meanings. Instant messaging interfaces enable people to work synchronously across large distances to jointly produce meanings in the form of, say, dialogue-based role plays that provide the base structure for fully developed fan fiction narratives (see Thomas 2006). Social news sites with their comments, response and ratings functions enable posters to question, clarify and elaborate upon meanings. Reviewer comments on users' posted creative work (e.g., on Fanfiction.net, DeviantArt.com, Aniboom.com) often feed into changing or tweaking the work, or into subsequent productions (see, for example, Black 2007).

The shift from material inscriptions to digital coding, from analogue to digital representations, has unleashed conditions and possibilities that are massively *new*. In the case of the shift from print to the post-typographic, Bill Cope (in Cope et al. 2005) describes what this means for the visual rendering of texts. He explains that digital technologies reduce the basic unit of composition from the level of a character to a point below character level. In the case of a text on a screen, the unit of composition is reduced to pixels. This means that text and images can be rendered together seamlessly and relatively easily on the same page and, moreover, that text can be layered into images – both static and moving – (and vice versa) in ways that were very difficult, and in some respects *impossible*, to do physically with the resources of print.

Reflection and discussion

The broadcast media run seemingly endless stories about young people reading and writing less and less these days. Yet large and increasing numbers of young people devote much time and energy to projects that involve remixing practices like machinima, photoshopping and music composing, and fan practices like manga drawing and fanfiction writing, etc. These projects very often employ sophisticated and/or complex narratives (and other generic forms, such as composing procedural texts and the like).

- How do you explain all this effort?

- Why do you think such practices are not considered significant or important by broadcast media accounts of young people's reading and writing habits?

- Do you regard them as significant or important *practices*? If so, why? If not, why not?

- Do you regard them as significant or important *literacy* practices? If so, why? If not, why not?

In an old book there was a section with the plates and a section with the text ... For many hundreds of years ... text and images were quite separated, for very pragmatic reasons ... [I]n the first half of the 20th century ... photographic techniques ... moved away from letter press and plate systems [bringing text and image] together a bit more [with] film and plates, but it was still very difficult. But now the elementary manufacturing unit has changed radically. The raw materials you work with are on a screen. So when you press a key, it actually builds a visual representation out of pixels.

... [Moreover] if you go back one layer ... beyond pixels, the same compositional stuff produces sound as well. So you have got these basic things about human communication – namely, language, visuals and sound – which are all being manufactured in the same raw material on the same plane in the same platform.

(in Cope et al. 2005: 200)

'Podcasting' provides another contemporary example. Let's imagine the case of a hypothetical conference going on at this very minute. Given any necessary permissions being granted, the conference organizers or a delegate can podcast a presentation (it might be a keynote, or simply a regular paper that the person organizing the podcasts believes will be of interest to other people). The podcaster records the presentation on a suitable digital recorder (e.g., an mp3 player with recording functions, or a digital voice recorder, or even a laptop running sound-editing software with built-in recording options, like Audacity). Many of these devices record audio files in a 'wav' format, which generates a high-fidelity, easy-to-edit, but very large file. When the talk is finished, the conference delegate transfers the audio file from their recorder to their laptop, converts the file to an mp3 format using software like iTunes, Garageband or Audacity, which maintains the fidelity of the recording (although there is some micro-restructuring of the sound that audiophiles attend to), but reduces the size of the file and makes it more 'playable' using a range of software applications and audio devices. The podcaster uploads the digitally encoded audio mp3 file to a server, and embeds RSS (Really Simple Syndication) code so that subscribers to the podcast series are notified when a new podcast is available for downloading.

Technically speaking, to podcast means that one posts audio files reasonably regularly to the internet, and interested others can subscribe to the podcast and receive new audiofiles automatically. That is, podcasts are 'syndicated' (i.e., the location of the files online is 'pointed to' by 'really simple syndication' code [RSS]), and podcast aggregators can be used to 'subscribe' to all of this podcaster's posted audio files. These aggregators – like gPodder.org, Miro (GetMiro.com), Juice (Juicereceiver.sourceforge.net), or iTunes, for example – will automatically check for and download newly posted podcasts that can be transferred to portable listening devices and played when convenient. Posting audio files online doesn't necessarily require RSS feeds and syndication, however. Our conference delegate could just as easily upload a single audio file to a server, and then make a post to their weblog that contains a hyperlink to that file. From that moment, anybody who accesses the blog can immediately access the sound file of the presentation by clicking on the appropriate hyperlink (see also Shamburg 2010).

Our recorded conference presentation can be augmented in various ways, such as by the podcaster splicing a short introductory narrative into the front end of the file, or by adding an accompanying short video sequence filmed during the presentation, or an automated copy of the slideshow used by the presenter to illustrate key points. This file can be uploaded to the internet and/or burned to a CD-ROM for easy sharing, and so on. The same – or elements of the same – binary functions and programming language conventions and 'stuff' that encode sound can also be used to encode images and video, the display interfaces themselves, and any online file hosting and networking services. The net result is a seamless, clean, elegant and rapid production that has global 'reach' at close to 'real' time (for examples of conference podcasts, see Clippodcast (www.clippodcast.com) or search for 'conference' at Podcastalley.com).

The kinds of generative 'enabling' and 'sharing' involved in such examples remain quite revolutionary. Relatively unsophisticated home-based desktop publishing software can generate text and image effects that the best printers often could not manage under typographic conditions. 'Publishing' is no longer limited to print or images on paper, but can also include additional media like voice recordings, music files, 2D and 3D animation, video, photoshopped images, and scanned images of paper-based artworks. Even the concept of 'text' as understood in conventional print terms becomes a hazy concept when considering the array of expressive media now available to everyday folk. Diverse practices of 'remixing' – where a range of existing materials are copied, cut, spliced, edited, reworked, and mixed into a new creation – have become highly popular in part because of the quality of product 'ordinary people' can achieve.

Machinima animations provide a good example here. 'Machinima' is the term used to describe the process where fans use video games as a kind of movie set and game characters as actors to render new animated texts on their desktop computers. (In the recent past, such text production demanded very expensive, high-end 2D and 3D graphics and animation engines, and was largely confined to professional animators.) Creating machinima can involve using tools such as script editors that take advantage of the affordances of the game engine itself – e.g., enabling the remixer to manipulate point-of-view or camera angle options, pre-'script' or map player and non-player character movements, mod textures and objects in scenes, as well as use resources like backgrounds, themes, characters, and settings already available in the game. Alternatively, a machinima editor can take a puppeteer's (rather than a programmer's) approach, and manipulate characters and action within game-provided 'sets' in real time, recording the scene with screen capture software like CamStudio or Fraps, and then editing the footage to create a seamless whole. One can now buy, download for free, or subscribe-to-use software developed expressly for designing and editing one's own machinima using content from any video game (e.g., MovieStorm, iClone). Those new to the machinima creation process can access online tutorials and interviews with high-profile machinima makers for insider tips on how to create one's own high-quality animations, or buy any number of how-to books (e.g., Kelland et al. 2005; Hancock and Ingram 2007; Luckman and Potanin 2010).

According to Machinima.com (now defunct), a once popular how-to website and archive of machinima animations:

> You don't need any special equipment to make Machinima movies. In fact, if you've got a computer capable of playing Half-Life 2, Unreal Tournament 2004 or even Quake [all three are popular video games], you've already got virtually everything you need to set up your own movie studio inside your PC. You can produce films on your own, or you can hook up with a bunch of friends to act out your scripts live over a network. And once you're done, you can upload the films to this site and a potential audience of millions.
>
> (2006: 1)

The term 'machinima' is also used to describe the genre of animation generated by this process. These animations may be fanfics and extend a game narrative in some way, or the game may simply provide tools and resources for producing an entirely unrelated text. Machinima can achieve the highest professional standards. Animations completed in the early 2000s, like *Hardly Workin'* and *Red vs. Blue*, have won film festival awards worldwide. Machinima videos are increasingly used to focus attention on social and political issues. For example, *Drained of Life* (2009) was made by the machinima production company Strange Company, in conjunction with students from Dalkeith High School in Scotland (archive.org/details/ DrainedOfLife). This expressed student concerns with environmental issues and the need for popular action for improvement. Best known, perhaps, is eight-member Oil Tiger Machinima Team's *War of Internet Addiction* made within the massively multiplayer online game *World of Warcraft*. The Oil Tiger Machinima Team, headed up by Corndog, recruited around 100 *World of Warcraft* players inside China – all of whom donated their time, and many of whom remain unknown in person to the Team – to jointly create a 64-minute video that took about three months to complete (Corndog, in interview with Chao and Ye 2010: 1). The video protests about Chinese government restrictions on *World of Warcraft* server access that confine Chinese players to servers located within China. Corndog explains some of the technical dimensions involved in working in such a distributed manner:

> We cooperated through the Internet. For dubbing, for example, we discussed how to do it online, how to understand the emotion of characters, [then] they emailed me the audio files and I edited them. If there was a need to fix it, we would discuss by chatting online again.
>
> (Corndog, in interview with Chao and Ye 2010: 1)

The video was uploaded to Tudou.com – the largest video-sharing site in China – in January 2010, and attracted millions of viewers within days of going online. It has since been posted to myriad spaces online, including YouTube. In April 2010, *War of Internet Addiction* won the top prize at the prestigious annual Tudou Film Festival celebrating the best Chinese online films.

Similarly, game 'modding' involves using a video game's image and strategy engines to create fan-driven 'modifications' to the game. Modifications can generate a new game altogether, or remain 'true' to the game's universe (i.e., how characters can move, act, solve problems, and what kinds of challenges are put in place, etc., within the world of the game) and, say, add a new mini-adventure or quest for player characters to complete. Such additions might expand a level by adding new skills or qualities to the game, or create an entirely new level for players to complete that introduces a further layer of difficulty or complexity to the game (cf. Squire 2008; Steinkuehler 2008). Modding can also include developing original resources, like 'new items, weapons, characters, enemies, models, textures, levels, story lines, music, and game modes' (Wikipedia 2010e). Most mods require the user to own the original game in order to run the mod (ibid.). Some game mods have subsequently become more famous than the original game (e.g., *Counter-Strike*, a mod of *Half Life*), or have directly influenced and shaped subsequent titles (e.g., Trauma Studio's *Desert Combat*, which modded *Battlefield 1942*, resulted in the studio being bought up by the company that owns *Battlefield 1942* and put to work on *Battlefield II*) (all examples from Wikipedia 2010e).

Music can now be 'sampled' and 'remixed' using desktop computers and audio editing software (see Chapter 4). Software that comes bundled with most computers, or is otherwise easily downloaded from the internet, is all one needs for converting music files from a CD into a format that can be edited (e.g., wav), editing and splicing segments of different songs together, and converting the final music files back into a highly portable format (e.g., mp3) that can be uploaded to the internet for others to access, or used as background soundtracks in larger multimedia projects. The commercial sector has recognized the popularity of do-it-yourself music remixing, and music mix software packages like *MixPad*, *Cakewalk*, or *AV Music Morpher* can be acquired for the price of a video game. Programs that run on gameplaying machines, like *MTV Music Generator 3: This is the Remix* for PlayStation 2 and Xbox, are also available.

This *enabling* capacity of what essentially is binary code and associated hardware – the new technical 'stuff' – is integral to most of the new literacies that will concern us here. A lot of this enabling is by now so commonplace that we take it for granted, such as in everyday templates and interfaces. Examples include:

- blog templates and authoring tools that automate the 'look' of one's text (and make it easy to change font style, colour, size, to include images, video or hyperlinks);
- writing/publishing tools like word-processing software that make it easy to change fonts and text layout (e.g., columns, alignment, page orientation), or to insert images or figures or even sound files or live internet links, play with colours, and so on, by simply selecting a menu option;
- customizable websites that enable users to add modules or 'apps' that act as direct links to, or summary feeds of, particular news and information services, games, social media spaces, and the like;
- being able to open multiple programs – and windows or tabs within these programs – simultaneously, and move content between them using the copy-and-paste function;
- instant messaging interfaces that enable us to include iconic emoticons, attach files, and save conversation transcripts;
- email interfaces that make it easy to read and respond to email, keep copies of sent messages, store and manage messages;
- being able to complete and submit forms online due to the development of 'editable' or 'interactive' webpage interfaces;
- website interfaces that encode password and username functions that enable authorized access to particular online spaces;
- collaborative interactional spaces mediated by subscribing to email discussion lists using generally standardized subscription processes (e.g., sending an email to a listserv program that includes your full name and the command, 'subscribe');
- dedicated apps that directly access an online service without having to open a web browser;
- online forum interfaces that allow members to post, read and respond directly to comments;
- online real-time text-based chat interfaces that are now embedded in websites and no longer require downloading and installing specially developed 'client software' to participate.

These very interfaces and templates mean a lot of the complex program coding work has already been done for everyday users, which greatly enhances their opportunities to engage in and practise a range of new literacy practices.

Reflection and discussion

Some people would argue that all this 'new technical stuff' and the relative ease of making copies of texts and widely distributing them makes it too easy to blur the lines between public and private (e.g., sexting, webcam streaming of extremely private events, PowerPoint shows about sexual conquests) with often devastating consequences for people. Discuss some of the issues currently in the news to do with the private being made deliberately or inadvertently public, the moral dimensions of participating in spreading private texts publicly, and how educators might build such issues into new literacies instruction.

New technical stuff and copyright

Finally, there is a major issue associated with a feature of digitally encoded material available on the internet that introduces something profoundly new. The point in question is made by Lawrence Lessig (2004, 2008). It has to do with copyright and a fundamental difference between physical space (or what Lessig calls 'real space') and cyberspace.

Lessig (2004: 141–3) shows how copyright law in physical space distinguished three categories of use of copyrighted material: unregulated, regulated, and fair use. For example, there are various uses of a book that are not subject to copyright law and permissions because they do not involve making a copy of the text (unregulated), or because they involve only copying an amount of the book (whether by photocopying, reproducing in a citation, or whatever) or having a purpose (e.g., scholarly review and critique) that is deemed to fall within the limits of 'fair use'. So A can lend a book to B to read, and B to C, and so on, without falling foul of copyright – since no copy of the text is made. A can even resell the book. These fall within the category of unregulated uses, because to borrow and read a book or to sell it does not involve making a copy.

But the 'ontology' of material available on the internet – 'a distributed digital network' (ibid.: 143) – is different in a fundamental respect from material available in physical space. On the internet 'every use of a copyrighted work produces a copy' (ibid.). Without exception. This 'single arbitrary feature of a digital network' carries massive implications:

> Uses that before were presumptively unregulated are now presumptively regulated. No longer is there a set of presumptively unregulated uses

that define a freedom associated with a copyrighted work. Instead, each use is now subject to the copyright, because each use also makes a copy – category 1 [unregulated] gets sucked into category 2 [regulated].

(ibid.: 143)

Lessig isn't against copyright – far from it. Rather, he argues for a 'scaled' approach to copyright that enables copyright owners to set the terms by which their work can (or cannot) be reused. This includes specifying, for example, that a work can be shared, remixed, or reused with attribution to the original work, but cannot be for profit, or can be used for commercial purposes, or can be reused but the resulting work must be made available for others to reuse, and so on (for more, see CreativeCommons.org). We do not have space here to deal with the intricacies of copyright law and permissions. Instead, we urge readers who have not done so to read Lessig's books, *Free Culture* (2004) and *Remix* (2008), which reach the heart of pressing issues related to differences between paradigms distinguished earlier in this chapter and the 'worlds' to which they attach.

Lessig (2005, 2008) describes a range of digital remix practices like AMV (anime music video remixing), where people, a very large proportion of them young people, take 'found' artifacts and remix them into something new. In AMV practices, for example, participants record a series of anime cartoons and then video edit these to synchronize them with music tracks (see, for example, AnimeMusicVideos.org). Lessig discusses digital remix as a practice of cultural creativity against the background of a particular kind of approach to creative writing that has traditionally been common in North American schools. In this practice:

You read the book by Hemingway, *For Whom the Bell Tolls*, you read a book by F. Scott Fitzgerald, *Tender is the Night*, and then you take bits from each of these books and you put them together in an essay. You take and combine, and that's the writing, the creative writing, which constitutes education about writing: to take and to remix as a way of creating something new ... And in this practice of writing we have a very particular way of thinking about how we learn to write. We learn to write in one simple way, by doing it. We have a literacy that comes through the practice of writing, writing meaning taking these different objects and constructing with them.

(Lessig 2005: n.p.)

However, whereas the conventional creative writing practice as remix described by Lessig does not infringe copyright law, digital remix often does – and practitioners face the risk of legal action. Yet, says Lessig (in interview with Koman 2005: n.p.), digital remix as a practice of cultural creativity is a kind of writing. In fact, new digital media, he says, are changing what it means to write. Digital remix, of whatever kind, involving whatever media, 'is what writing is in the early 21st century' (ibid.). It involves working with a different set of tools from those we have written with in the past, says Lessig, but 'is just the same sort of stuff that we've always done with words' (2008: 82). Now, however,

> [It's] not just words, but ... images, film, and music. The technologies we give our kids give them a capacity to create that we never had. We've given them a world beyond words. This world is part of what I've called RW [read/write] culture. It is continuous with what has always been part of RW culture – the literacy of text. But it is more. It is the ability for amateurs to create in contexts that before only professionals ever knew.
>
> (ibid.: 108)

Lessig makes two further, crucial, points with respect to the new kind of writing. First, he argues that the way today's young people in societies like our own come to know their world is 'by tinkering with the expressions the world gives them in just the way that we [of earlier generations] came to know the world when we tinkered with its words' (2005: n.p.). To this Lessig adds the claim that this new writing needs the same freedoms as did the writing of the eighteenth, nineteenth and twentieth centuries. To do it well, he says, to understand how it works, to teach it, to develop it, and to practise it require freedoms that are currently outlawed. Hence, the kind of enabling potential inherent in digital tools underpinned by the ontology of digital code is a two-edged sword under current legislation conditions. On the one hand, it 'democratizes a certain creative process' (Lessig 2005: 143). On the other hand, its very nature means that the exercise of this democratized potential puts practitioners at risk under copyright law. Lessig argues that the law must change to keep safe a 'creative commons' on which everyone can draw and to which everyone can contribute, and with that we agree entirely.

'New ethos stuff'

As we will see in depth in later chapters, large and growing numbers of people are 'joining' literacies (and devoting impressive amounts of time and energy to them) that differ greatly from mainstream cultural models of literacy of the modern era (and, particularly, of literacies as they are constructed and engaged with in formal educational settings like schools). Much of the 'nature' of this difference is captured in Jim Gee's accounts of learning within affinity spaces (e.g., Gee 2004) – forms of what John Seely Brown and Richard Adler (2008) call *social* learning. While our interest here is wider than learning *per se*, many of the key features of affinity spaces that enable learning are nonetheless the very 'stuff' of how contemporary literacies are constituted and experienced more generally by people engaging in them. Gee describes affinity spaces as:

> specially designed spaces (physical and virtual) constructed to resource people [who are] tied together ... by a shared interest or endeavor ... [For example, the] many websites and publications devoted to [the video game 'Rise of Nations'] create a social space in which people can, to any degree they wish, small or large, affiliate with others to share knowledge and gain knowledge that is distributed and dispersed across many different people, places, Internet sites and modalities (magazines, chat rooms, guides, recordings).
>
> (2004: 9, 73)

Affinity spaces instantiate participation, collaboration, distribution and dispersion of expertise, and relatedness (ibid.: Ch. 6). These features are integral to the 'ethos stuff' of what we mean by 'new' literacies.

From Web 1.0 to Web 2.0

To grasp the significance of the idea of a new kind of *ethos* to the concept of new literacies, it is helpful to first get a sense of how various emphases, priorities, and values integral to the second social paradigm sketched above have come to play out in and through the very *architecture* of the web since the late 1990s. Just as the 'new' capitalism *'wrote'* values of collaboration, distributed expertise, collective intelligence, communities of practice, team orientation and the like into the very *practices* of work – and, hence, into the very *structure*, or social *order* – of many contemporary workplaces, so a number of pioneering organizations, companies, and individuals can be seen as having actively worked to develop a web architecture that supports social practices of many kinds and across many domains of everyday life grounded in these same values. The shift in web architecture captured in the familiar distinction between Web 1.0 and Web 2.0 can be seen as a specific concrete instance of the tendency toward thinking and acting, and otherwise organizing ways for doing everyday life – and, particularly, for doing literacies – around values central to the currently ascending social paradigm.

While the term 'Web 2.0' had been coined prior to the 2004 O'Reilly Media Web 2.0 conference, it was this conference, and Tim O'Reilly's (2005) subsequent account of distinct business models and web design principles operating in Web 1.0 and Web 2.0 respectively, that put 'Web 2.0' on the map. O'Reilly traces the origins of the distinction between Web 1.0 and Web 2.0 to discussions that addressed issues and ideas arising from the fall-out of the 2001 dotcom crash, including the observation that the major companies to survive the crash seemed to share some features in common. Parties to the initial discussions began assigning examples of internet applications and approaches to either a Web 1.0 list or a Web 2.0 list, and analysing their key distinguishing features. Using examples like the difference between Netscape and Google, and between Britannica Online and Wikipedia, participants focused on three key related differences. One is the difference between packaged software applications that operate on the desktop and software applications that are built and operate on the web. The second is between web products and services (packages) that are basically consumed by users and those that enable and encourage forms of interactivity between producers and consumers, owners, and users. The third is the difference in business models between using web content to make product available to consumers, on one hand, and putting interactive software applications on the web so that users can help build or create the product. In the web 1.0 business model, producers create the product and make it available. In the Web 2.0 business model, customers or users actually help build the business for the 'owner', by using the software to generate content – such as ideas, data, texts, images, video content, etc. – that creates value, and where this value brings advantage to the 'owner' of the business. The key to this business model is *leverage*.

O'Reilly (2005) uses examples like the difference between Netscape (the now extinct web browser) and Google's search engine, and the difference between Britannica Online and Wikipedia to illustrate the distinction between Web 1.0 and Web 2.0.

Netscape (the 'old' software paradigm of packaged software to be downloaded to the desktop) made its browser and in-built email, calendar, news, etc., software suite available free and updated it regularly. At the same time it produced a range of expensive server products for content producers. By making the browser freely available for download for millions of people to access web content, Netscape aimed to include default bookmarks within the software itself and/or to help drive traffic to paying customers' websites via its search engine and ads, along with providing server space for customers wanting to establish an online presence for their business. Netscape did not really survive the dotcom crash (it limped along for a few years, but by 2008 was no longer updated/supported by its parent company). The relationship between Netscape and its users was strictly one between *producer* of packaged software and services and *consumers.*

By contrast, Google, which survived the dotcom crash with bravura, initially created a powerful web search engine. There is no product to be downloaded or package to be consumed. Instead, there is an online resource that users *perform.* Google's search engine service functions as an *enabler* for users – it helps optimize our internet experience by helping us find what we are looking for in a way that maximizes the likelihood of us getting to 'the best information' as efficiently as possible. Of course, 'efficiency' here is a partnership between the efficacy of the search engine and the savviness of its users. What users get from Google.com may reflect their own efficiency in terms of identifying useful search terms, understanding the role of Boolean logic in an effective search, knowing how to conduct a natural language search, and being familiar with the full range of search functions available on Google (e.g., knowing about Scholar.google.com; tweaking search preferences; knowing that entering the following string into Google's search window enables a particular website or space to be searched: searchterm site:URL).

At the same time, there is an interesting and important *reciprocity* here. The search engine enables users to locate information, but at the same time users contribute to the value of the search engine by enhancing 'the scale and dynamism of the data it helps to manage' (O'Reilly 2005: n.p.). Google is, ultimately, a massive database and data management system, that evolves and improves and becomes more responsive the more it is used. Users *participate* in and through Google. Indeed, they actively *collaborate –* whether they are aware of it or not – with Google.com by contributing to building a continuously improved and more dynamic database that is mediated by Google's page rank system. To this extent, the information one user gets as a consequence of conducting a particular search is a function of searches that other users have completed and drawn on previously. The database is, so to speak, at any point in time a product of the *collective intelligence* of all users (as enacted through use of keywords, Boolean logic, natural language, etc., and which search return for a given query is most clicked on and, therefore, deemed most relevant, etc.). To all intents and purposes, Google's 'product' is the database that is *managed* through the software and generated through millions of users performing the software. The users are an integral part of Google's production; integral to developing its product. And the service automatically improves the more that people use it – a principle that O'Reilly identifies as inherently Web 2.0. Production in this case is based on 'leverage', 'collective participation', some degree of 'collaboration', and distributed expertise and intelligence, much more than on the manufacture of finished commodities by individuals and workteams operating in official production zones and/or drawing on concentrated expertise and intelligence within a shared physical setting. Google makes almost all of its money through its advertising programs (see the 'Google' entry at Wikipedia.org for a useful overview of how Google.com works).

Similarly, elements of Amazon.com's enterprise enable user interactivity with the company and its website. O'Reilly (2005) notes that Amazon harnesses user activity to produce better search results than its competitors. Whereas competitors typically lead with the company's own products or with sponsored results, Amazon always leads with the 'most popular' item corresponding to the search terms. The popularity index is a real-time computation based on an amalgam of sales and 'flow' around a product (e.g., how much user attention the book obtains, other books bought by customers who buy the book in question, and how these other books are selling and are rated), and so on. Second, he argues that Amazon's database for books has now become the main source for bibliographic data on books. According to O'Reilly, like its competitors, Amazon obtained its original database from R.R. Bowker, the ISBN registry provider that publishes *Books in Print*. However, Amazon outstripped and transcended this kind of data.

> [The company] relentlessly enhanced the data, adding publisher-supplied data such as cover images, table of contents, index, and sample material. Even more importantly, they harnessed their users to annotate the data, such that after ten years, Amazon, not Bowker, is the primary source for bibliographic data on books, a reference source for scholars and librarians as well as consumers ... Amazon 'embraced and extended' their data suppliers.
>
> (ibid.: n.p.)

In other words, Amazon leveraged collective intelligence in the form of reader engagement and consumer data into the number one bibliographic data source on books, providing a free service for scholars as much as consumers, while simultaneously outstripping competitors in sales. In doing so, it turned users into distributed 'experts' and 'authorities' on book data. It also transformed bibliographic data directories from centralized published sources to a collaboratively generated, freely available, and 'always on' and permanently updated searchable database in multiple languages, serving multiple countries at the disposal of anyone who has internet access.

The same can be said for more recent developments regarding Web 2.0 services that have developed one-stop applications – or 'apps' – for directly accessing the service, rather than needing an internet browser *per se*. Apps act like 'client' software that comprises a small program serving a particular and typically singular function. They run on mobile devices like smartphones and tablet devices. Many currently available apps leverage users' input to improve the program's functionality itself. (For example, Yelp relies on users' reviews of shops, restaurants, and things to do/see to develop its recommendation service.) Augmented reality apps like Wikitude and Layar use geotags and data from a range of online sources (much of it contributed by users) to compile just-in-time, just-in-place information about where you are. Other apps blend advertising/marketing with fundraising (e.g., Causeworld). Still others provide click-and-go access to established online Web 2.0 services, like Wikipedia, Facebook, and Google Search.

This speaks to a new emerging business model that aims at directing users' attention to particular services, rather than encouraging more free-ranging browsing of the internet *per se* (O'Reilly 2010). It is an interesting development in terms of shifts within Web 2.0 applications and what it might mean when the internet itself becomes a series of 'walled gardens' (via apps) and online spaces – the latter described as the 'creative' or 'open' internet by O'Reilly – where users themselves create and generate their own resources to meet their own purposes. For O'Reilly, both kinds of spaces – open and closed – are reciprocal and are important where business and the internet are concerned: 'Openness is where innovation happens; closedness is where [monetary] value is captured' (ibid.).

Reflection and discussion

Spell out what you understand by 'leverage' as it applies to a business model for the web.

- How would you respond to the claim that leverage necessarily involves some degree of *exploitation* of internet users?

- To what extent do you believe that the open and closed spaces described by O'Reilly are, indeed, *reciprocal*?

Looking beyond 'business'

Likewise, the online version of *Encyclopedia Britannica* is a classic instance of Web 1.0 principles. It is an online commodity that consumers can access with a subscription fee. It offers packaged content generated by reputed experts on a topic recruited by the company – just as in the paper version. The line between producers and consumers is hard and fast. Its business model and its business purpose are, to all intents and purposes, the same as Netscape's were.

By contrast, the free, collaboratively produced online encyclopedia, Wikipedia.org, reflects the principle of mobilizing collective intelligence by encouraging free and open participation, and trusting to the enterprise as a whole functioning as a self-correcting system. Whereas conventional encyclopedias are produced on the principle of recognized experts being contracted to write entries on designated topics, with the collected entries being formally published by a company, Wikipedia entries are written by anyone who wants to contribute their knowledge and understanding, and are edited by anyone else who thinks they can improve on what is already there. In other words, it is an encyclopedia created through *participation* rather than via publishing. While identifiable people are responsible for beginning and overseeing the initiative, the content is generated by anybody willing to do so.

The idea is that as more and more users read and edit entries online, the more the content will improve. At the same time, ideally, the content will reflect multiple perspectives; excesses and blindspots will be edited out; and by countless incremental steps the resource will become increasingly user friendly, useful, reliable, accountable, and refined. While there are some blips in this ideal – especially with respect to controversial topics that often see a page 'locked' or even removed from Wikipedia – the operating

---

Reflection and discussion

- What implications do you think Wikipedia has for 'knowledge'?

- What becomes of 'experts' and 'expertise' within spaces like Wikipedia?

- Wikipedia is often associated with the open source software principle coined by Eric Raymond that 'with enough eyeballs all bugs are shallow'. What does Raymond's principle mean? To what extent do you think it applies to the operating principle of Wikipedia?

- Do you think Raymond's principle could be applied to school-based learning? If so, how and where?

logic for this encyclopedia remains one of distributed and collective expertise. Trust is a key operating principle (which is why, for example, there is a collective uproar when politicians' offices are found to have interfered with an entry in order to paint someone in a better or worse light). The ethos is to reach out to all of the web for input, through limitless participation, rather than the more traditional belief that expertise is limited and scarce, and that the right to speak truths is confined to the 'properly credentialled'. The idea is *not* that anyone's opinion is as good as anybody else's but, rather, that anyone's opinion may stand until it is overwritten by someone who believes they have a better line. The right to exercise this belief is rarely constrained (see also Lankshear and Knobel 2006: 89–92).

Moreover, the example of Wikipedia raises an important point that we will return to later. This concerns the relationship between the concept of Web 2.0 as a *business model*, and the existence of Web 2.0 services and resources as a *platform for participatory culture* (Jenkins 1992, 2006b; Jenkins et al. 2006). Resources and services that can be seen in terms of a business model – and that were originally conceived and named in terms of a business model – can *also* be seen as generating vast resources and rich affordances for diverse forms of popular participation and collaboration based on affinities and social relationships occurring on a truly massive scale. The relationship is complex and easily blurred. It is also very important. In short, classic Web 2.0 success stories, like Google.com and Facebook. com and other vast profitable businesses, entail complex questions about ownership of content and the like. The Wikipedia website, by contrast, is managed by a not-for-profit foundation that from time to time seeks donations to keep it afloat. Authorship is distributed and can be anonymous. Nobody owns the content. Articles are 'donated' and are free content under a GNU licence. Wikipedia enacts elements of the same business model logic as does Google. In this sense we can distinguish between (1) instances of the business model operating in ways that generate (often massive) capital and profits, and that involve complex issues of content ownership, copyright, and ultimate control of content, and (2) instances where the leveraging and collective intelligence facets of the business model are implemented for sharing rather than for profit and commercial ends (Lessig 2008: 156–62). Wikipedia might be seen as operating along similar lines to the Open Source software movement (see Richard Stallman's essays in Gay 2010), which stands against proprietary software.

Recent years have witnessed a massive growth in social software development and availability, affording opportunities for popular participation and collaboration based on shared interests or affinities, and where participants collectively contribute to 'intelligence' and draw upon and contribute to distributed expertise, mentorship and the like. Typical examples include blogs, media and cultural content sharing sites, wikis, social networking sites, and application programming interfaces supporting the current 'apps' revolution. They provide endless further instances of the shift toward our second social paradigm.

The popular photo-sharing service Flickr.com provides an interesting example of the way in which user annotations of photos by means of 'tagging' contributes to the social construction of classification systems that are being developed from the bottom up, in contrast to traditional top-down, expert-driven classification systems. The 'tags' that users assign to photos on Flickr, and to other kinds of content on other sites, provide metadata for classifying online data to enable content searching – giving rise to what is commonly known as 'folksonomy' or 'tagsonomy'. The operating principle is simple. Flickr is a service that allows people to post photographs to the web after they have signed up for an account. For each photograph or set of photographs account holders upload to their site they can add a number of 'tags'. These are words they think describe their photo and that would lead other people who key the word(s) into the Flickr search engine to their photos (and there is a range of options that determine who a person permits to view their photos). Account holders can also invite or accept other people to be on their list of contacts. Contacts can then add tags to the photos posted by those people who have accepted them as contacts. The account holder, however, has the right to edit tags – their own and/or those added by contacts – as they wish. The millions of photos publicly available on Flickr become a searchable database of photos. Tags provide a basis for patterns of user interests to emerge in ways that enable communities of interest to build and for relationships to develop among members who share common interests, tastes, etc. They have enabled different interest groups to coalesce around shared image projects (e.g., the Tell a Story in Five Frames group, the Secret Life of Toys group).

The concept of 'folksonomy' was developed in juxtaposition to 'taxonomy'. Taxonomies are centralized, official, expert-based or top-down classification management systems. The operating principle of taxonomies is that people who presume – or are presumed – to understand a domain of phenomena determine how the individual components of that domain shall be organized in order to make a shared sense or meaning of the domain. The Dewey library classification system is a taxonomy of types of texts, according to which a given book is assigned a number on the basis of the kind of book it is deemed to be and where it fits into the system. By contrast, a folksonomy is a 'popular', non-expert, bottom-up classification management system, developed on the basis of how 'authors' (e.g., of photos) decide they want their works to be described or 'catalogued'.

One interesting consequence of folksonomic organization is that the tags people choose say something about *them* as well as about the tagged object (O'Reilly 2005). When a user finds a photo they would not have expected to fall under a particular tag, they might think the tagger's approach to classification is sufficiently interesting to delve further into it, for example, as a pursuit of 'the idiosyncratic', or the 'quirky', or 'of someone who might think a bit like me'. The scope for participants to make their own meanings, find collaborators who share these meanings, and build relationships based on shared perspectives opens up possibilities that are foreclosed by centralized and authoritative regimes that circumscribe norms of correctness, legitimacy, or propriety.

Back to a 'new ethos': collaboration, participation and distributed expertise in fanfiction

Interactivity, participation, collaboration, and the distribution and dispersal of expertise and intelligence are central to what we are calling the 'new ethos stuff' integral to new literacies. To date, however, we have merely glossed these concepts and, moreover, have done so with reference to a narrow range of examples. Most importantly, with the exception of the example from Flickr, we have not yet mentioned the kinds of popular cultural participation and collaboration typically associated with new literacies in Web 2.0 environments. To fill out the picture we turn now to a brief discussion of collaboration, participation, and distributed expertise in fanfiction.

Fanfiction, or fanfic (see also Chapter 4), has exploded as a popular literacy with the growth of the internet. In fanfiction 'devotees of a TV show, movie, or (less often) book write stories about its characters' (Plotz 2000: 1; see also Jenkins 1998, 2006b). Fanfic based on video game plotlines and characters is also growing in popularity. Fanfictions chronicle alternative adventures, mishaps or even invented histories or futures for main characters; relocate main characters from a series or movie to a new universe altogether; create 'prequels' for shows or movies; fill in plot holes; or realize relationships between characters that were only hinted at, if that, within the original text.

David Plotz (2000) describes fanfiction as turning writing into a communal art, wherein 'writing and reading become collaborative. We share the characters and work together to make them interesting and funny and sexy' (ibid.: 1). Other fanfic writers are equally forthcoming about the collaborative and shared nature of their writing practices. Silver Excel Fox describes how she supplied a character for another online friend's narrative:

> She liked my review for one of her stories, and I was kind of talking about one of her characters [in the review], and she was, so, 'I need another character. Do you want to be it?' And I'm like, 'Sure,' and I gave her a description of what I wanted my character to look like, and she took my character and put it into her story.

(interview, 2005, by Knobel and Lankshear)

Elsewhere, collaboration occurs when reviewers provide feedback on texts posted by authors for comment and review. This kind of dynamic exchange most often occurs via online forums and email discussion lists (see Chandler-Olcott and Mahar 2003; Black 2005a, 2008, 2009; Thomas 2007b). Authors and reviewers take the role of reviewing very seriously. Many fanfic writers, for example, make use of forums dedicated to 'beta-reading': public pre-publication forums where authors can obtain feedback on new stories before posting them to or publishing them on more formal fanfic sites (Black 2005a, 2005b). Some moderated or filtered fanfic forums expect authors to have their narratives beta-read before submitting them for consideration for publication. *The Force* (fanfic.theforce.net) suggests that a beta reading should pay attention to:

- 'Grammar and spelling errors. While a few errors are bound to make it through, too many such errors will result in a rejection.
- Plot continuity and technical errors. Your betas should let you know if there are any plot threads left unintentionally unresolved, and note places where there are internal continuity problems (e.g., you had a character leave the room on page four, and she speaks again on page five without re-entering or using a comm-link).
- Character issues. Fanfiction allows much more freedom than professional fiction in terms of character interpretations, but your betas should point it out if your characters suddenly begin to behave very oddly for no appreciable reason.
- Intangible things. Ask your betas to tell you what they got out of your story before you tell him or her what you meant. "I like this!" is a nice thing to hear, but what you need from a beta reader is to hear, "I really liked the way you showed Qui-Gon's early dissent from the Jedi Council, because it resonates with the way he behaves in his early scenes with

Shmi in TPM" (or whatever). If that's what you meant to convey, it tells you that you've succeeded. If it's not what you meant, it can mean two things. You may decide that you really like it, and want to leave it alone or even expand on it. You might also decide that you absolutely don't want to give that impression, and therefore you want to change the things that gave it.'

(Fan Fiction: The Force.net 2010: 1)

Two points are worth noting here. First, these guidelines for beta readings are a typical example of the kinds of resources users can access in affinity spaces. Other similar kinds of resources on which fanfic writers and reviewers can draw include 'fanfiction glossaries, fanfiction writing help sites, members' personal web pages, and official corporate sites that provide information on copyright laws for the various media texts that fans are drawing from, to name just a few' (Black 2007: 117–18). Additional resources include feedback discussion forums, feedback functions automatically appended to posted narratives within fanfic sites that let reviewers comment directly on a new text, and reviews sent to email discussion lists dedicated to fanfiction writing and/or fan art. Such resources typify the 'ethos' of affinity spaces generally. The beta reading guidelines resemble resources available in the games-based affinity spaces discussed by Gee (2004: 84), like 'FAQs that explain various aspects of the game and give players help with the game' and 'strategy guides and walkthroughs for "newbies" [new players]'. Artifacts like *The Force*'s beta reading guidelines can be seen as embodying several defining features of affinity spaces. These include: 'Newbies and masters and everyone else share common space'; 'Both individual and distributed knowledge are encouraged'; 'There are lots of different routes to status'; and 'Leadership is porous and leaders are resources' (ibid.: 85–7).

The second point concerns the character of fanfic peer review at the level of lived experience. This, of course, varies from case to case, but an already recurring theme in the small corpus of literature currently available is of participants approaching peer review in open, non-defensive/non-aggressive, constructive and generously supportive ways. These ways often become communicative and relational in tone and on levels that differ from the circumstances and connotations of peer review within conventional publishing (academic and non-academic) contexts. Moreover, they may spill over into learning opportunities that extend far beyond immediate fanfic purposes.

Rebecca Black (2008) presents a case of the social relations of peer review at their most expansive. An adolescent native Chinese speaker, now living in Canada, regularly begins her fanfics with an 'author's note' (which she

marks as 'A/N') that asks for readers' patience with her English, while at
the same time indicating that she is keen to improve her written English
fluency. Her following author note begins with a friendly Japanese greeting
('Konichiwa minna-san'), which translates as, 'Hello everybody'. This fanfic
author also includes manga-fied Ascii emoticons in her message (e.g., ^_^
instead of the traditional :) to indicate a smile; –;; to indicate nervousness):

> A/N: Konnichiwa minna-san! This is my new story ^_^. Please excuse
> my grammar and spelling mistakes. Because English is my second
> language. Also, I'm still trying to improve my writing skills ... so this
> story might be really sucks... .–;;

Black reports that these kinds of author notes 'provide writers with direct
access to the reader and enable authors to specifically state those elements
of the story (e.g., form or content) on which they would like readers and
reviewers to focus' (ibid.: 125). The author in Black's example indicates
tangentially that feedback on spelling and grammar would be appreciated.
Reviewers have seemingly heeded these author notes and have written
encouraging comments, including comments that the author writes much
better stories than many native English speakers, or they have made
suggestions for addressing grammar and spelling errors in the text (which,
according to Black, this particular fanfic writer always addresses when
revisiting and editing her posted narratives). At the same time, reviewer
feedback emphasizes that these errors are 'minor and do not interfere with
the effectiveness and overall message of the story' (ibid.).

Competing configurations of 'new ethos stuff'

We have reached a point where it is necessary to draw some distinctions
around the idea of 'a new ethos'. We began the chapter by talking about
an ascending paradigm that reflects a different way of thinking about
people, social practices and processes, and social phenomena like expertise
and intelligence from how such things were thought about under an
earlier paradigm. We have talked briefly about how, during recent
decades, economic activity – work – has been re-described, understood, and
re-structured along lines in which values of participation, collaboration,
distributed systems (of expertise, intelligence, team-orientation) have
been emphasized. The 'new' capitalism pursues new ways of identifying
workers and giving them new identities, in association with new ways of
organizing their activity (roles, relationships, performances), with a view to
enhancing the economic viability of enterprises and bureaucracies (Gee et

al. 1996). This is a new angle on an existing game – a new way to create economic value/profit/capital accumulation/efficiency through *leverage*, within a process of coaxing employees to take on new identities as members of a 'community' rather than as individuals who just happen to work in this place, for this boss or this company. The end game remains more or less the same, but is now played under a new kind of 'ethos': by affiliates collaborating with each other in a shared mission.

We have described how this kind of business model and 'ethos' was named for the web: as Web 2.0. A new *architecture* established the web as an interactive platform whereby enterprises could accumulate value by creating conditions and practices – *literacies*, no less – where users could generate value that companies/site proprietors could harness. This is Web 2.0 as *a business model*. At the same time, the architecture supporting this business model represents something of a shift in applied *ethos* from the more one-way, broadcast-oriented model retrospectively named Web 1.0. We worked our way through a staged sequence of selected examples, seeking to shift the focus from web-mediated collaborations and distributions grounded in leveraging user interactivity in the interests of the economic viability of an enterprise toward an emphasis on ways in which the impressive affordances of Web 2.0 as an interactive platform enable users to participate in *affinities*. These are affinities where their participation and collaboration enact relationships to/with others and their shared interests, and contribute collectively to building the affinity and a sense of membership in that affinity.

The examples we have used (among very many others that *could* have been used) bespeak rather different *configurations* of a broad ethos; different configurations of collaboration, participation, shared expertise, and the like. Some might say that it would be better to speak of distinct *ethoses* here, rather than different *configurations* of the same broad ethos. We prefer to think of different configurations, because what we believe is 'new' is bound up with the paradigm shift. The main thing, however, is to draw out what is at stake, and to consider how this might impact on how we choose to view the nature and scope of new literacies. A good place to start is with the following extended statement by Henry Jenkins (2010: 238–9), who says:

> I want to hold onto a distinction between participatory cultures, which may or may not be engaged with commercial portals, and web 2.0, which refers specifically to a set of commercial practices that seek to capture and harness the creative energies and collective intelligences of their users. 'Web 2.0' is not a theory of pedagogy; it is a business model. Unlike projects like Wikipedia that have emerged

from nonprofit organizations, the Open Courseware movement from educational institutions, and the Free Software movement from voluntary and unpaid affiliations, the web 2.0 companies follow a commercial imperative, however much they may also wish to facilitate the needs and interests of their consumer base. The more time we spend interacting with Facebook, YouTube, or LiveJournal, the clearer it becomes that there are real gaps between the interests of management and consumers. Academic theorists (Terranova, 2004; Green & Jenkins, 2009) have offered cogent critiques of what they describe as the 'free labor' provided by those who choose to contribute their time and effort to creating content which can be shared through such sites, while consumers and fans have offered their own blistering responses to shifts in the terms of service which devalue their contributions or claim ownership over the content they produced. Many Web 2.0 sites provide far less scaffolding and mentorship than offered by more grassroots forms of participatory culture. Despite a rhetoric of collaboration and community, they often still conceive of their users as autonomous individuals whose primary relationship is to the company that provides them services and not to each other.

'Proprietary', 'projective' and 'participatory' forms of the new ethos

At one level we might distinguish forms or configurations of collaboration, participation, and distribution that are, respectively, more or less 'proprietary', 'projective', and 'participatory' in nature.

By *'proprietary'* we refer to cases where some property ownership is involved that accrues value for some party/parties but not for others. This would be the case with internet searching that consolidates Google's predominance and attracts it disproportionately massive advertising revenues. It might also be the case with writing reviews and assigning ratings with Amazon, where Amazon's bibliographic database, ratings and review systems, recommendations, etc., draw people to its site by default; or with participating in Facebook, contributing to YouTube, and so on. Of course, there is a trade-off, a certain reciprocity involved here. We get the benefits of having a powerful search tool available/they get our value addition; we get to express our opinion of products, voice our preferences, develop proficiency as reviewers, build a review profile and portfolio, build up an online identity/they get our value additions. There *is* a two-way flow of benefits here, albeit different in kind and the reciprocity might be 'unfair', even 'exploitative', in many cases. At the very least, users should become aware of the extent to which, ways in which, and times at which they are implicated in proprietary collaborations and participations, and do their moral or evaluative 'mathematics'.

Projective configurations of the new ethos are found where people participating in affinity spaces are doing so under the primary motivation of creating some kind of artifact to meet a personal (or joint) purpose, rather than from the motivation of further enhancing an affinity, community of practice, fandom, or what Jenkins calls 'collaborative enterprises within networked publics' (2010: 233). A typical example might be of someone spending time in music video spaces because they want to 'capture' and 'portray' their wedding anniversary as a music video. They may spend (considerable) time in online spaces seeking advice, looking at other people's work, rating or favouriting some of it, responding to and feeding back on the results of assistance provided and, eventually, posting their artifacts online – but all the while from the standpoint of wanting to further their quest to produce a worthy artifact, or to continue over an extended period of time to produce regular and increasingly sophisticated or proficient 'renditions' of personally significant events as music videos. The patterns of contributing and interacting within an online space from this kind of standpoint are likely to differ considerably from those, for example, of bona fide *fans* of particular genres of music videos.

Participatory configurations of the new ethos are intimated in the difference between someone who wants to create, say, a podcast for some kind of personal purpose or as a personal expression, and those whose podcasting activities arise from motivations like 'an urge to create a shared space where, for example, fans can discuss their mutual interests in Severus Snape, or where church members can hold prayer circles, or where comic book buffs can interview writers and artists' (Jenkins 2010: 234). In other words, participation, collaboration, and distributed systems of expertise, knowledge/wisdom/intelligence and cultural production assume *participatory* forms within communities and networks of shared interests or affinities that have the kinds of characteristics associated with current conceptions of 'participation in affinity spaces' (Gee 2004), 'participatory cultures' (Jenkins et al. 2006), 'communities of practice' (Lave and Wenger 1991), and so on. These terms are widely used to capture the idea of networks and communities of shared interests where people associate, affiliate, and interact in kinds of 'collective enterprise' (Jenkins 2010: 233) in order to pursue and go as deeply as they wish into their 'affinities' or what they are especially interested in. Such activity involves collectively building, resourcing, and maintaining interactive spaces, whether face to face, virtual, or mixes of both, where participants can contribute to and draw upon myriad resources and means for building and enacting identities based on interests, in collaboration with others. Participants play diverse roles and learn from each other 'in the process of *working together* to achieve shared goals' (ibid.; compare Gee's account of affinity spaces on p. 68 above). From a new media literacies perspective, Jenkins and colleagues (2006: 3) define a participatory culture in terms of environments and social practices where there are

> relatively low barriers to artistic expression and civic engagement, strong support for creating and sharing one's creations, and some type of informal mentorship whereby what is known by the most experienced is passed along to novices. A participatory culture is also one in which members believe their contributions matter, and feel some degree of social connection with one another.
>
> (Jenkins et al. 2006: 3)

These defining characteristics have important implications for styles, modes, types, and degrees of collaboration, expertise sharing, and participation, which are touched on in our sketch of fanfiction above. The range here will typically be much greater and the priorities very different from those involved in engagements of a more proprietary and projective nature. This is because members of participatory cultures are involved in building and resourcing entire 'systems' and networks for developing and enacting identities (and ways of creative doing and being and making) within the very processes of pursuing and enacting these identities. They are collectively building, and developing the conditions and terrain for *their* interest-based engagements, as an entire enterprise, as distinct from participating in 'an enterprise of others' (proprietary), or drawing on established enterprises to engage in individual or personal goal-directed pursuits with no intrinsic or necessary investment in furthering the community, networks, or affinity space *per se*.

Lawrence Eng provides an illuminating glimpse of the spirit of participatory culture in *The Sasami Appreciation Society* (Capcorphq.com/ SAS.html#Sasami). In the mid-1990s, Eng, studying at Cornell University in the USA and a member of the university's Japanese Animation Society, became captivated by the 'cutest, blue-haired anime girl I had ever seen' (webpage no longer available). This was Sasami from the *Tenchi Muyo* anime. 'I eagerly waited for each instalment of TM and was never disappointed. Through all of this my devotion to Sasami only increased,' says Eng. He found a kindred spirit online and they began to build *The Sasami Appreciation Society*, with the mission 'to spread Sasami fandom in all ways possible, on the Net and otherwise'. Why? It's simple;

'it's our devotion to Sasami ... We're dedicated to bringing her the fandom that she deserves.'

In her account of literacy practices within the community of anime and manga fans, Mizuko Ito (2005a) identifies this spirit as the very heart of *otaku* culture. She speaks of anime *otaku* as 'media connoisseurs' and 'prosumer activists' who search for anime and manga content, and 'organize their social lives around viewing, interpreting, and remixing these media works' (ibid.: n.p). More than this, they invest enormous time and energy to resourcing spaces for others as well as themselves.

> [They] translate and subtitle all major anime works, they create web sites with hundreds and thousands of members, stay in touch 24/7 on hundreds of IRC channels, and create fan fiction, fan art, and anime music videos that rework the original works into sometimes brilliantly creative and often subversive alternative frames of reference ... To support their media obsessions otaku acquire challenging language skills and media production crafts of scripting, editing, animating, drawing, and writing. And they mobilize socially to create their own communities of interest and working groups to engage in collaborative media production and distribution. Otaku use visual media as their source material for crafting their own identities, and as the coin of the realm for their social networks. Engaging with and reinterpreting professionally produced media is one stepping stone towards critical media analysis and alternative media production.
>
> (ibid.)

Before drawing the components of this chapter together into an account of new literacies, it is important to make three brief points with respect to participation and collaboration in relation to 'new ethos stuff' and the interactive web.

Reflection and discussion

- To what extent are the distinctions between 'proprietary', 'projective', and 'participatory' configurations of 'new ethos stuff' helpful for considering the issues Jenkins raises about Web 2.0 in relation to education?

- Discuss the significance and implications for education of Jenkins' claim that Web 2.0 is a business model and not a theory of pedagogy.

First, what we are calling a new ethos and, particularly, *'participatory'* cultural creative forms of new ethos, did not arise with the internet, let alone the Web 2.0 platform. (Jenkins traces participatory media cultures from the nineteenth century.) The key point here is that the possibilities and nature of participatory cultures are contingently related to many factors – including *technological* factors – conducive to interacting, sharing, building networks and relationships, and so on. The brute fact is that the interactive web has enlarged the possibilities for participatory cultural engagement on a mind-blowing and escalating scale. Moreover, various kinds of new literacies emerge and evolve and are appropriated in the course of building, resourcing, and engaging in such participatory culture, as we will see at length in Part 2.

Second, while we have distinguished between proprietary, projective, and participatory configurations of 'new ethos stuff', we should note that these are not 'pure', self-contained, or mutually exclusive modes. They overlap considerably. During stretches of engagement in affinities involving new literacies, participants will almost inevitably move across moments of each – just as one moves across instrumental/intrinsic, commercial/ subsistence, exchange value/use value modes within activities like gardening and shopping with a view to putting food on the table and creating an aesthetically satisfying home environment.

Third, the 'nuts and bolts' of participation and collaboration within the kinds of social practices under discussion here are, so to speak, of many 'shapes and sizes'. For example, the 'participation' and 'collaboration' involved with Google when we use Google's various search tools will for the most part be *tacit*, if not unwitting. We don't *search* with a view to collaborating and are rarely conscious of doing so. By contrast, when someone invests the kind of effort described by Eng and Ito, and in Black's (2008) accounts of reader reviews in fanfiction, collaboration is absolutely active and witting. Collaborations may be more or less targeted – e.g., responding to particular requests for help, information, or advice – or more or less 'diffuse', 'generic', or anonymous – e.g., just putting it out there in case it will meet someone's need some time. Instances of participation might be as 'small' as giving a rating or 'retweeting'. Someone's prevalent mode of participation might (simply) be rating or favouriting videos on a site, or commenting on blog posts. Participation might be 'peripheral' for long periods until one is knowledgeable or confident enough to take on more 'elaborate' forms. The point is that if terms like 'participation', 'collaboration', 'distributed expertise', and other aspects of the new ethos are to get beyond the level of slogans and cliché, and to serve as descriptive, theoretical, and analytic categories in our understanding of new literacies, we need to make these kinds of distinctions and recognize varying degrees, kinds, and gradations.

'New' literacies: paradigm and peripheral cases

There can be no 'pure' conceptual account of 'new' literacies, any more than there can be of 'literacy' or 'literacies'. The stakes involved around competing views mean these concepts are 'essentially contested' (Gallie 1956). At best, one can make a case for a preferred view. Our preferred view involves distinguishing between paradigm (strongest possible) and more peripheral less strong or 'complete' cases of new literacies.

We argue that *paradigm* cases of new literacies involve *both* new technical stuff and new ethos stuff. Under current and foreseeable conditions, failure to address the 'participation', 'transparency', and 'ethical' gaps framed by Jenkins and colleagues (Jenkins et al. 2006) will constitute a grave dereliction of commitment to democratic values. Even beginning to address these gaps presupposes recognizing the importance of keeping 'new ethos stuff' and 'new technical stuff' together in the frame. Moreover, we believe that the closer the 'new ethos' dimension approximates to the forms of engagement, collaboration, sharing, and distributed expertise and 'authorship' that define 'participatory cultures' (ibid.), the more we should regard a literacy practice as 'new'. This involves a values stance based on an ideal of social learning that is actively undermined by existing educational arrangements and the wider social structures and arrangements they support (e.g., credentialling, differential allocation of scarce rewards, consumer commodity production, ownership and property relations, etc.). Paradigm cases of new literacies confront established social structures and relationships in ways we consider progressive, or 'better'. They are more inclusive, more egalitarian, more responsive to human needs, interests and satisfactions, and they model the ideal of people working together for collective good and benefit, rather than pitting individuals against one another in the cause of maintaining social arrangements that divide people radically along lines of success, status, wealth, and privilege. To make this argument well would require a book in itself. We hope the discussion in the remaining chapters indicates the kind of case we would ideally make.

At the same time, however, it is necessary to acknowledge the extent to which the kind of learning ideal portended by our second paradigm and championed – with variations – by diverse sociocultural and new media theorists *can* be pursued independently of 'new technical stuff' by putting the primary focus on the new ethos – even 'though the ideal is to do both' (Jenkins 2010: 241). New technical stuff can be, and typically is, introduced into classrooms without challenging the established culture of classroom education one iota (Cuban 2003; Lankshear and Knobel 2006: Ch 2; Jenkins 2010). It is impossible, however, to engage with learning from the standpoint of participatory culture without seeing how its learning model challenges 'the cultural context that surrounds contemporary formal education' (Jenkins 2010: 241).

Fanfiction face to face: a new literacy without new technology

In *Textual Poachers: Television Fans and Participatory Culture*, Jenkins (1992) provides rich examples from fieldwork undertaken prior to the time of mass internet access of fan-oriented literacy practices that exemplify new literacies as *ethos*. One example (ibid.: 153–3; see also Jenkins 2010) involved four women aficionados of female-centred science fiction based on TV shows, who met regularly to write fanfiction. They spread themselves about the room, doing their writing, reviewing source material, sharing resources, reading one another's work and commenting on it, seeking and offering advice, and so on. Jenkins observes as follows:

> Mary has introduced a southern character and consults Georgia-born Signe for advice about her background. Kate reviews her notes on Riptide, having spent the week rewatching favorite scenes so she can create ... Mary scrutinizes her collection of 'telepics' (photographs shot from the television image), trying to find the right words to capture the suggestion of a smile that flits across his face ... Kate passes around a letter she has received commenting on her recently published fanzine ... Each of the group members offers supportive comments on a scene Linda has just finished, all independently expressing glee over a particularly telling line ... Kate edits and publishes her own zines she prints on a photocopy machine she keeps in a spare bedroom and the group helps to assemble them for distribution. Linda and Kate are also fan artists who exhibit and sell their work at conventions; Mary is venturing into fan video making and gives other fans tips on how to shoot better telepics. Almost as striking is how writing becomes a social activity for these fans, functioning simultaneously as a form of personal expression and as a source of collective identity (part of what it means to be a fan). Each of them has something potentially interesting to contribute; the group encourages them to develop their talents fully, taking pride in their accomplishments, be they long-time fan writers and editors like Kate or relative novices like Signe.

Commenting on his fieldnotes 20 years later, Jenkins is struck by how fully they reflect strengths of a participatory cultural context as a site for (informal) learning. We are further struck by how fully they encapsulate an ideal of *social* learning, and a 'new' literacy practice from the standpoint of 'new ethos stuff' – particularly in relation to formal learning contexts.

> Sometimes the women are working on individual, self-defined projects and sometimes they are working together on mutual projects but always they are drawing moral support from their membership in an interest-driven network. Each plays multiple roles: sometimes the author, sometimes the reader, sometimes the teacher, sometimes the student, sometimes the editor, sometimes the researcher, some-times the illustrator. They move fluidly from role to role as needed, interrupting their own creative activity to lend skills and knowledge to someone else.
>
> (Jenkins 2010: 236)

The educationally significant differences between this as a case of a 'new' literacy and the paradigm cases of new literacies discussed in Part 2 of this book may be less than is often assumed, since these mainly involve details of technology/tool use, knowledge and skills. When they have authentic reasons for using them, everyday people like the women in this example are renowned for picking up, running with, re-purposing, and re-shaping new technologies with an ease analogous to the proverbial duck taking to water, without any need for formal instruction in technology use. Without a change of 'ethos' within education, the benefits from addressing the 'new technical stuff' will remain seriously constrained.

Photosharing on Flickr and The Secret Life of Toys: a paradigm case of new literacy

This section describes the new literacy practice of photosharing and curating (cf. Merchant 2010; Potter 2010) within the context of sharing an interest in or passion for toys.

Flickr.com, now part of the Yahoo! suite of online services, is a user-generated content website established for archiving, curating, and sharing digital photographs and 90-second videos. Participating in Flickr photosharing is straightforward. Anyone can browse photos designated 'public' regardless of whether they have a Flickr account. Only account holders, however, can post and comment on photos. Signing up simply involves clicking on the 'create your account' button on the Flickr homepage. There are two types of account. One is free, allowing members to post up to

200 images. The other requires a yearly subscription, providing unlimited account space and other added features. Here we focus on the free account.

Besides tagging, as mentioned earlier, key technical affordances and skills include being able to collate photos into sets and collections, based on organizing concepts of choice (e.g., 'Trip to Argentina', 'Blue Things'). It also includes being able to add 'contacts' or other Flickr members to an easily accessed list, and to establish or join 'groups' dedicated to particular interests or affinities (e.g., 'Black and White' – currently the largest group on Flickr; 'Flowers', 'Pavement', 'Empty Chairs'). Groups are richly collaborative spaces within Flickr. Including the name of the group as a key tag for any relevant photo enhances the strength and range of images included in that group. Groups may engage in meet-ups, where members get together in real life to socialize or to celebrate their shared interests by taking photographs together (Davies and Merchant 2009; Merchant 2010).

Members use Flickr in different ways and to different degrees. Some just use the space for storage, or join groups and comment on others' photos without posting photos themselves. At the other extreme, members actively invite others to view their photos, join groups based on a theme or interest, establish groups and recruit others to them, comment on their own and other people's photographs, participate in Flickr forums (ask/respond to questions, suggest features, report a bug) and activities, participate in group-based discussions, and build special relationships that can spill over into offsite spaces (including physical space) (Davies 2006; Davies and Merchant 2009).

While images uploaded to Flickr can include scanned hand-done drawings or paintings, Paintshop-generated cartoons, scanned collages, and short video clips, the digital photograph is by far the prevalent image-type. Besides adding tags, posting photos involves making various kinds of written contribution: notably, keying a title and a short description for each photo in provided textboxes. A function in a menu bar above each photo enables members to write notes that will appear directly on the image when a viewer scrolls the cursor over each 'note' icon. Often information about what kind of camera used to take a given image is automatically displayed alongside the image, or the account holder can add in particular technical details regarding the camera, the location and set-up of the shot. The display template also provides a space for comments, similar to a weblog. Comments cover a wide spectrum: from 'OMG I love it!', to comments on the 'processing' or techniques used (e.g., 'HDR is such a cliché – you've essentially ruined a nice shot'), through to high-end specialist advice regarding image quality, framing, depth of field, f-stop setting suggestions, and so on. Members will even invite 'constructive comments' to be added to an image.

Sharing skills and knowledge to do with taking and sharing good photographs is also supported within different groups' discussion forums. For example, a recent discussion on the 'Australia in Black and White' group's forum began with a member posing a question about which medium (film, digital) or process (e.g., manual or digital colour conversion) members of the group preferred to use. Responses were many and varied – from switching camera options to black and white on their iPhone through to carrying a number of different film and digital cameras around to match to shooting conditions. Sharing feedback (even unkind feedback) and expertise in such ways means that Flickr itself is not simply an archive site, but can be used as a resource to improve one's own photographic skills and as a space where interesting conversations about photography can take place, ideas for one's own photography can be gathered, and where people can simply enjoy an image on whatever terms they choose. There is no hierarchical ranking of photos from best to worst, and no theme or topic is banned (beyond images banned legally in the wider world). Users are expected to self-moderate their photos, by setting the 'viewing level' for images (i.e., safe, moderate, restricted).

The Flickr display template and its inbuilt prompts and functions serve several enabling purposes. It helps with managing viewer access to images, with joining groups, with bookmarking 'favourite' images posted by other members, with designating who can access each photo (e.g., everyone, or only those users marked as 'friends') and what copyrights images are assigned with regard to others using the photo in different venues. It also helps with inviting other people to join Flickr and to become a 'contact' of the user.

There are many other technical aspects to posting photos within a Flickr account beyond our scope here (the Flickr tag cloud, procedures for starting a new Flickr group, etc.). We turn now to a typical example of participating in a well-subscribed affinity on Flicker.com involving toy appreciation and 'bringing toys to life' – an affinity which, of course, long pre-dates and extends far beyond Flickr.

'The Secret Life of Toys' was established early in Flickr's life, during 2004, and at the time of writing has around 15,000 members and almost 200,000 images in its richly diverse photo pool. It has a wide charter: 'This group is about collecting photographic [and video] evidence that toys get up to things when people are not around. Well, not just that – It is also simply a space to collect good images of toys for everyone to enjoy' (Flickr 2010: n.p.). The photo pool reflects many different angles on toys and interests in toys. These include portraiture shots of Blythe dolls (large-eyed, big-headed, puny-bodied dolls that had a less-than-12-month production run in 1972 but gained a large fan base in the 2000s), Lego minifigs, Transformer toys, manga dolls, vinyl figures, and various other dolls and action figures in a range of everyday scenes (e.g., cooking dinner, working as lifesavers, working out), and multi-figure scenarios depicting epic battles or strange, slightly off-kilter scenarios, along with photos of new toy acquisitions, among many others.

Photos added to this group communicate meanings on different levels. Some are 'brag' photos to do with someone's latest addition to their toy collection. This could be a vintage robot, or, more typically, a vinyl figure that itself is part of a collectible series and part of the larger vinyl figures affinity space that is instantiated in different ways, including comic conventions, in blogs, in paper magazines, in comic shops, in collectors' online forums, on eBay, and so on. In and of themselves they're simply nice photos. They also, however, elicit wider meanings, like nostalgic memories of one's own childhood toys, or envy at someone's collection, or happiness over a new toy.

Some photos shared within the group tap into more specialized fan affinities, such as Stefan's Stormtrooper action figure series that ran from 3 April 2009 to 4 April 2010 (flickr.com/photos/st3f4n/sets/72157616350171741/) as a contribution to Flickr's popular '365 photos' project. Over 365 days Stefan posted an image each day to 'The Secret Life of Toys' and other toy affinity groups on Flickr. His project involved photographing Star Wars Stormtrooper action figures engaged in a range of real-world tasks, but in a human-scaled world. Typical images include two Stormtroopers fishing in a toilet, a Stormtrooper berating a real cat for sleeping, a Stormtrooper loading life-sized game cartridges into a Nintendo game machine, Stormtroopers break dancing, and Stormtroopers grappling with a giant Totoro doll, among many others. Each photo portrays the Stormtroopers as very much alive and engaged in some activity. At this level, suspending belief that toys are inanimate within the photos is a valued meaning within the 'Secret Life of Toys' group. At another level, fans of the Star Wars universe derive additional pleasure from these images by understanding Stormtroopers as enforcers on the wrong side of 'good' and how this plays out humorously in the photos. Additional popular culture references – break dancing, video game playing, the 'My Neighbour Totoro' anime movie – confer wider, intertextual meanings on these images for those who recognize them. The multilingual comments posted to each image include congratulatory notes, as well as additional information about how commentators are interpreting the image and what it means to them. Such negotiated meanings sometimes include responses from Stefan himself, turning the comment posts into a kind of friendly conversation. Stefan offers encouragement to others planning to undertake a '365 photos' project and advice on how to set up different shots.

Stefan's Stormtrooper series has been showcased on various blogs and on Twitter (follow: stormtrooper365). The 'Secret Life of Toys' group also has seemingly spawned a number of copycat sites, including a similar photo group hosted on Tumblr blog servers (Hellotokyo.tumblr.com) and a professional photographer's 'Secret Life of Toys' shopfront website where he sells prints of his toy photos (Thesecretlifeoftoys.com).

Finally, participating in photosharing and curating within groups like 'The Secret Life of Toys' can be seen as being involved in meaning-making at the level of 'carrying' the social order. It is to be recognizable as a participant in a 'form of life' which, along with countless other forms of life, organizes and constitutes human life and living in ways that can be understood – made sense of – engaged in, and responded to. In other words, participating in 'The Secret Life of Toys' is one of countless forms of social practice within which, and through which, *all* meaning-making – including that mediated by encoded texts – is accomplished.

Reflection and discussion

- Does our attempt to distinguish paradigm and more peripheral cases of new literacies work for you? If so, in what ways/ respects? If not, where do you see problems?

- In Chapters 2 and 3 we have aimed to distinguish points at which different 'levels' and kinds of *meaning* are involved when we participate in (new) literacy practices. What do you understand by these different levels and kinds of meaning, and to what extent do you find them useful for thinking about literacies and literacy education?

In Part 2 we present detailed discussions of some paradigm cases of currently popular new literacies.

New Literacies:
Some Everyday Practices

CHAPTER 4

New literacies and social practices of digital remixing

Introduction

As a *concept* associated with cultural practices, 'remixing' involves taking cultural artifacts and combining and manipulating them into new kinds of creative blends and products. In this very general sense, cultural remixing is nothing new – the Ancient Romans remixed Greek art forms and ideals in their own artworks; democratic forms of government remix a range of ancient and not-so-ancient forms of governance; architecture has always remixed styles and key structural forms.

As a *term* associated with contemporary cultural practices, however, the word 'remix' has until very recently been linked almost entirely with remixing *music*. 'Remix' in this sense refers to mixing together or reworking elements of different recorded songs or music tracks whereby the 'source song(s) retain their identity in some recognizable form' (Jacobson 2010: 28). Erik Jacobson (2010) points out that interpretations of songs and music by musicians and singers have always involved a form of reworking the original version into something that is new but, nonetheless, more or less recognizable or traceable to its original source music. The potential that recordings offer for remixing music in inventive ways reached new highs in the 1990s. During this period, remixed music became popular across a range of genres – notably, in hip hop, house and jungle music, as well as in mainstream pop, and rhythm and blues, and even in heavy metal music. What is perhaps most notable about turntable and digitally mediated music remixing is that it is open to 'people who cannot play any [musical] instruments themselves to rework and reshape previously existing songs' (ibid.: 28).

Most accounts date modern music remixing to Jamaican dance hall culture in the late 1960s, and the interventions of DJs and music recording producers who, for example, used twin turntables with different versions of the same song to be played together while controlling for speed (beats to the minute), or edited tapes to produce versions of songs suited to different kinds of audiences. Remixes sometimes simply provided a speedier version of a song, or a leaner, more stripped-back sound, or an elongated song to keep people dancing longer. Once digital sound became the norm, however, all manner of mixing and 'sampling' techniques were applied using different kinds of hardware devices or software on a computer (Hawkins 2004; Jacobson 2010).

From around 2004, discussions and conceptions of remix have been expanded and enriched as a result of trends clustering around the convergence of 'new ethos stuff' and 'new technical stuff' within popular cultural production and expression. As more and more people have used published/copyrighted cultural artifacts as resources for their own cultural creations – especially, although by no means only, through the use of digital technologies – sections of the 'culture industry' have sought to assert their property rights through digital rights management (DRM) codes and, as a final resort, legal action. Non-formal cultural producers, for their part, have pursued ways to access copyrighted material for their creative purposes as 'freely' and 'anonymously' as possible, and some commercial producers of popular cultural artifacts have made resources available for remixing purposes from the perspective that this will be good for their business. Notwithstanding such initiatives, tensions between the will to engage in free cultural creation and expression drawing on resources readily available in everyday environments, on one side, and the will to retain control over the use of 'owned' cultural resources, on the other, intensified to flashpoint. All-or-nothing, win-or-lose, winner-take-all polemics have created the risk of serious losses for both sides of the divide. Within this context, and the search for a fruitful resolution, 'remix' (see, especially, Lessig 2004, 2005, 2008; Lessig, in Koman 2005) has emerged as an important rallying point for reasoned discussion and understanding of what is at stake, and for seeking ways of ensuring that what is legitimate and valuable on both sides of the divide stands an optimal chance of being preserved, enhanced, and leveraged for the greater good.

For present purposes, two points emerging from recent discussions and elaborations of 'remix' and 'digital remix' are especially relevant, namely:

1. the general principle of remix as a necessary condition for a robust and democratic *culture*; and
2. the status of digital remixing as a new norm for writing.

We will briefly discuss these in turn.

Remix as a necessary condition for culture

More than any other author, Lawrence Lessig (2008) has developed and discussed the concept of remix as a necessary condition for cultural sustainability, development, enrichment, and well-being. At its most general, simple, necessary, and profound, remix is quite simply the idea 'of someone mixing things together and then someone else coming along and remixing that thing they have created' (Lessig 2005: n.p.). For example,

> You go see a movie by Michael Moore [or whoever] and then you whine to your friends about how it is the best movie you have ever seen or the worst movie ever made. What you are doing is taking Michael Moore's creativity and remixing it in your life. You are using it to ... extend your own views or criticize his views. You are taking culture and practicing this art of remixing. Indeed, every single act of reading and choosing and criticizing and praising culture is in this sense remix. And it is through this general practice that cultures get made.
>
> (ibid.)

When seen in these terms, we can say that remix is evident in every domain of cultural practice – including everyday conversations – and that 'culture is remix'. At the broadest level, remix is the general condition of cultures: no remix, no culture. Cultures have to be *made* – created – and they are made by mixing 'new' elements with 'pre-existing' elements in the manner of 'conversations'. We remix language every time we draw on it, and we remix meanings every time we take an idea or an artifact or a word and integrate it into what we are saying or doing or being at the time.

In more recent work, Lessig (2008) distinguishes between two broad types of cultural engagement; two different types of culture and cultural experience. One he calls 'Read/Only' (RO), the other 'Read/Write' (RW).

RO culture emphasizes the *consumption* of professionally produced cultural tokens or artifacts. The relative few produce cultural items for the many to view, read, listen to. As Lessig (ibid.: 28) puts it, a Read/ Only culture is a culture that is 'less practiced in performance, or amateur creativity, and more comfortable (think: couch) with simple consumption'. Read/Write culture, on the other hand, is one in which those who 'read' the resources of their culture also wish to 'add to the culture they read by creating and re-creating the culture around them ... using the same tools [e.g., certain kinds of musical instruments, image capturing and enhancing tools, writing and drawing technologies] the professional uses' (ibid.). Of course, the distinction is more one of degree than absolute. In RO culture there inevitably will be some degree of remixing on at least the lines of conversation and comment illustrated in Lessig's example of watching a movie, or in terms of sharing a cultural resource with others because someone thinks others will enjoy it, find it interesting, or see it as an instance of something they have commented on or evaluated in a particular way.

Making reference to an interesting historical example, Lessig (ibid.: 23–33) highlights some of the stakes that are under contest in any tug of war between the two cultures, such as that occurring at the present time. He describes the case of John Philip Sousa, an American conductor and composer who, in 1906, gave evidence about the inadequacy of existing copyright law to protect the interests and incentives for creative work of musicians within the context of (then) new technologies of player pianos and phonographs. Lessig says that for his time Sousa was a 'copyright extremist' seeking redress against machines that could make copies of compositions and sell them without having to compensate composers – because the copyright laws did not clearly cover the kinds of copies being made. In the course of giving evidence Sousa argued that these new machines not only infringed musicians' interests in terms of copyright, but also constituted a grave threat to a *'democratic* culture'. The new machines were, in today's parlance, 'Read/Only'. Their commodities were for mere consumption: *listening*. For Sousa, their proliferation would undermine amateur musicianship – people making their own music – at the same time as they infringed the rights of composers. They would undermine the process of people at large growing the technical development of music and musical culture, by supporting the production and take-up of musical instruments, amateur music teaching and sharing, and so on. Sousa feared that with the spread of such a RO musical culture 'the tide of amateurism [would] recede, until there will be left only the mechanical device and the professional executant' (ibid.: 26). Moreover, and crucially, Sousa did not accept that any copyright law covering public performance of another's work did or should extend to amateurs. In his view, there *had* to be sufficient Read/Write culture that permitted sufficient sharing of RO cultural resources to keep a democratic culture of amateur musical creation and development alive and thriving.

Lessig summarizes the position admirably. He says that Sousa did not fear that the 'actual quality of the music produced in a culture' would decline if RO culture displaced RW culture in music. Rather, his fear was

> that people would be less connected to, and hence less practiced in, *creating* that culture. Amateurism, to this professional, was a virtue – not because it produced great music, but because it *produced a musical culture*: a love for, and an appreciation of, the music he [and others like him] re-created, a respect for the music [people like him] played, and hence a connection to a democratic culture.
>
> (ibid.: 27, our emphases)

This is not simply about reproducing the music, since no reproduction can ever be exactly 'the same' as the original. There is always some degree of interpretation, making do, revision of, building upon, experimentation, and so on, involved in any taking up of cultural resources and tools. Learning to be a researcher, for example, presupposes taking up the concepts, theoretical components, data collection and analysis tools of others, and applying them to our purposes. The originals inevitably get remixed to some extent in the process of this kind of learning. No good researcher is ever going to resent or challenge this, if only because without others doing that kind of remixing, there will be no ongoing research community – or, at best, a *lesser* one – to perpetuate and validate the work s/he and other professional researchers and theorists do. No remix in research, then no robust and democratic research culture.

The status of digital remixing as a new norm for writing

As noted in Chapter 3, Lessig (2005) refers to a particular practice of creative writing within the school curriculum in parts of the USA. In this practice students read texts by multiple authors, take bits from each of them, and put them together in a single text. This is a process of taking and remixing 'as a way of creating something new' (ibid.: n.p.). Until recently this kind of remixing was done with paper, pencil, typewriter and the like. These same tools were used for learning to write in the most general sense, which, it can be argued, is also a practice of remix. Learners take words that are presented as text in one place or another and they use these words and texts and the tools of pen and pencil to make new texts, or to remix text. Lessig says that we learn to write 'in one simple way, by doing it' (ibid.). Hence, there is a literacy 'that comes through the practice of writing; writing [means] taking these different objects and constructing with them' (ibid.).

We now have *digital* remix enabled by computers. This includes, but goes far beyond, simply mixing music. It involves mixing digital images, texts, sounds, and animation; in short, all manner of found artifacts. Young people are picking this up on a massive scale and it is becoming increasingly central to their practices of making meaning and expressing ideas. Lessig argues that these practices constitute remix as *writing* for these legions of digital youth:

> When you say the word *writing*, for those of us over the age of 15, our conception of writing is writing with text ... But if you think about the ways kids under 15 using digital technology think about writing – you know, writing with text is just one way to write, and not even the most interesting way to write. The more interesting ways are increasingly to use images and sound and video to express ideas.
>
> (in Koman 2005: n.p.)

Lessig (2005) provides a range of examples of the kinds of digital remix practices that in his view constitute 'the more interesting ways [to write]' for young people. These include remixing clips from movies to create 'faux' trailers for hypothetical movies; setting remixed movie trailers to remixed music of choice that is synchronized with the visual action; recording a series of anime cartoons and then video editing them in synchrony with a popular music track; mixing 'found' images with original images in order to express a theme or idea (with or without text added); and mixing images, animations, and texts to create cartoons (including political cartoons and animations), to name just a few types.

Reflection and discussion

- Do you accept Lessig's extension of the concept of 'writing' to include practices like digital remix? If so, what are your reasons? If not, what are your reasons?

- Try to locate in the literature examples of literacy scholars who take a different view. If you adopt the standpoint of Lessig, what arguments and evidence would you present against the opposing view? What arguments and evidence from the opposing view would you bring against Lessig?

We accept this conceptual extension of 'writing' to include practices of producing, exchanging, and negotiating digitally remixed texts, which may employ a single medium or may be multimedia remixes. At the same time, we remember that not all popular cultural remix involves the use of digital technologies. For example, when fans dress up as their favourite anime, fantasy, or science fiction characters and engage in role play as a form of cosplay, they can often be seen as remixing cultural resources, but there is no necessary digital dimension in such in-person remixing, any more than there is when a barbershop quartet remixes a medley of popular songs by interspersing and overlaying content and/or playing with the genres. Equally, music remixers who use twin turntables and vinyl recordings, and video remixers who use magnetic video tape recordings, are engaged in analogue rather than digital forms of popular cultural remix. So are fan anime artists who create elaborate drawings and paintings using paper, canvas, pencils, acrylic paints, and so on.

Some typical examples of remix practices

As various kinds of sophisticated digital editing software and online read/write resources and spaces have become widely available and accessible, the nature and scope of digital remixing activities engaged in by everyday people and professionals alike, and that can be usefully under-stood in terms of new literacies, have grown rapidly. There are many more of them than can adequately be identified and discussed within a single chapter. To maximize coverage we have identified a selection of currently popular kinds of digital remixing activities and organized them into a large table, presented as an Appendix to this chapter (see pages 127–140 below). We briefly discuss a small sample of these practices as new literacies, and then provide more detailed and nuanced discussions of online fanfiction and anime/manga fan remix practices – which are among the most significant contexts of new literacies practices among young people.

The following remix practices are identified and summarized in the Appendix: making machinima movies, making movie trailers, creating fanfiction short movies, making music videos, creating fanfiction, photoshopping images, creating fan art, producing political remixes, remixing music, mashing up web applications, cosplaying/live action role playing, and modding video games. It is important to note again that several of these do not (necessarily) involve using digital technologies. At the same time, those that do not – like cosplaying and creating fan art – are often practised by digital remixers and integrated into their digital remixes (such as when cosplay sequences and fan art are recorded digitally and included in music videos or fanfiction short movies).

To understand these practices in terms of new literacies we have used four organizing concepts in the Appendix: 'Kinds of remixes', 'Kinds of involvement', 'Some literacy dimensions', and 'Some online spaces, sites and examples'. This is intended to help explicate the complex relationships among social practices, participation in practices, Discourse affiliations, situated literacy performances, sites and contexts of activity, roles and relationships within interest communities, and so on. For example, one might participate in a music video remix affinity/community without ever actually making or posting a music video; hence, without 'doing' many of those 'new literacy bits' that individuals who regularly create music videos from scratch engage in. Conversely, some 'full-on music video creators' may rarely engage in many of the literacy performances other aficionados prioritize – like participating in forums, contributing free resources for remixing, etc. Alternatively, a person who mashes up web applications as a business proposition is not 'doing the same thing' as someone who creates a mashup to help resource a fan interest and further build an affinity space. A certain degree of button pushing and code writing might be as much as they have in common.

To indicate how the kind of information provided in the Appendix can be cashed out for some typical digital remixing practices that are currently popular we will briefly discuss photoshopping, music remixing and creating serviceware mashups.

'Photoshopping' as image remix

Adobe's famous digital image editing software, *Photoshop*, has been appropriated as a verb for diverse practices of image editing, some of which involve remixing images (as distinct from just editing them by retouching them, changing their colour balance, etc.). With the growth of affordable image editing software and enhanced online storage capacities, and image-friendly website hosting sites and services, photoshopping quickly became a popular online practice, engaging a wide range of contributors with different levels of artistic and technical proficiency. Image remixing can take various forms. These include adding text to images, creating photo montages that mix elements from two or more images together (including prankster-type remixes that place the head of a famous person on, for example, the body of someone caught in a comprising situation), changing the image content itself in some way (e.g., removing someone's hair or body parts, adding additional legs to a moose), and changing image properties (e.g., changing the colours or image focus, fiddling with brightness levels or shading).

People engage in digital image remixing for a range of purposes and in the context of various kinds of practices and memberships in different kinds of communities and affinities. For example, organizations and artists, like Adbusters.org and Propagandaremix.com, respectively, produce and/ or invite image remixes to make political points, mobilize activity around causes, spoof advertisements for products and services they believe should be discouraged, and so on. Elsewhere, images are remixed simply for fun – to get a laugh – and/or to generate a hoax (e.g., Worth1000.com, SomethingAwful.com). Some community websites (e.g., Fark.com) invite members to comment on topical news items and other web content and, as part of this, host regular image remixing contests to tap into users' points of view (especially satirical or sardonic) on selected images. Not infrequently, images are remixed with a view to generating or participating in a meme (Knobel and Lankshear 2007: Ch. 9). In a very popular case, which became known as the Lost Frog Meme, a member of an image-sharing forum scanned a flier he had found in the street that looked like a young child's announcement of a lost pet (named Hopkin Green Frog) and uploaded it to a popular discussion forum. Features of the flier, which comprised a hand-drawn image of a frog accompanied by text, captured the imagination of other members of the forum, who quickly began using image editing software to manipulate the original. The meme caught on, and photoshoppers from all around the world weighed in with wide-ranging and often hilarious variations, frequently drawing on motifs and conceits embedded in internet culture and humour. Collectively, the contributions narrate a massive fictional citizen 'mobilization' in an ongoing search for Hopkin Green Frog. The remixed images include typical 'missing persons' announcement vehicles (e.g., broadcast media news reports, milk cartons, road signs), crowd scenes seemingly devoted to spreading the news about the lost frog (e.g., 'lost frog' banners at a street march and at a crowded soccer match), and a host of other 'remember Hopkin' scenarios (e.g., lost frog scratch-it lottery tickets, Hopkin's ID on someone's instant messaging buddy list, Hopkin as a 'not found' internet file image). References to popular culture artifacts and practices abound, and include reworked book covers, music album covers, video games, eBay auctions, and so on. Other images spoof advertising campaigns (e.g., an Absolut Vodka spread becomes 'Absolut Hopkin'; a Got Milk? advertisement becomes 'Got Frog?'). Many of the lost frog images refer to other memes as well. For example, an aeroplane pulling a lost frog announcement banner also appeared earlier in an 'All

Your Base Are Belong To Us' remixed image, as did photoshopped highway signs (see Lostfrog.org; Whybark 2004).

When we come to look at the kinds of literacy components associated with digital image remixing, we find that they are much more diverse than we might at first expect. If we just focus on what is involved in producing image remix *artifacts* we will capture only a fraction of the literacies dimension. At the level of 'skills' and tool use we may recognize such things as knowing how to use the marquee tool to crop around a portion of an image, or using the eyedropper tool to match colours, or eraser tool for getting rid of unwanted lines or items, and the like. With respect to relevant knowledge we might include knowing the kinds of content, effects, and nuances to include in our creations that are likely to be appreciated by others, and how to realize them within our remix. We might also include under the artifact production aspect such specific practices as knowing where to go for advice and how to phrase a specific query that attracts the most useful help, or where to go for exemplars and role models to emulate. This, however, is just a small part of it. When we turn to the idea of participating in remix affinities or communities of remix practitioners, we need also to include such literacy performances as sharing your photoshopped images online for feedback or providing feedback on the quality of someone else's photoshopped image (cf., Photoshopforums.com; Worth1000.com/community), practising and refining one's photoshop skills and understanding, writing a tutorial, or thanking someone for the useful tutorial they've written (e.g., Worth1000.com/tutorials), contributing to a photoshop contest or to a meme (e.g., Somethingawful.com/d/photoshop-phriday, Fark.com/contests, Knowyourmeme.com), knowing when a deliberately 'bad' photoshop will suit your purposes more effectively than a fine-tuned one (e.g., for humorous effect, to spoof newbie contributions to some communities), and so on. Different 'practitioner identities' will include different mixes of such literacy practices, and some of the most committed members of image remix communities may produce and publish/post relatively few image remixes, preferring to devote their time and energies to other membership roles and services (e.g., archiving images, passing resources on, setting up contests, helping newbies).

Music remixing

Within the world of digital remix, music currently is remixed in two main ways: in an audio-only form, and as audio accompanied by moving or/and still images. On a second dimension, music is remixed by professionals – people who do it for a living or for significant economic return – and by amateurs. Within these parameters the range and variation in music remixing are enormous: in terms of type/kind, genre, quality, purpose, cultural affinities, techniques, tools, degree of collaboration and interactivity, and so on. In this section we look briefly at pure music remix (audio-only). We will discuss a particular kind of music video remixing in the final section of this chapter, within the context of one fan's anime and music remixing.

Music remixing basically involves taking components of existing songs and recorded music and splicing them together to create something that differs to a greater or lesser extent from the original(s). Jacobson (2010: 29) identifies an important issue within music remix to do with how far remixing music can go before 'it becomes something substantially new', rather than a *remix* and, conversely, about what the minimum is that must be done – is duplicating a chorus enough, asks Jacobson – to warrant saying: 'Remixed by .....'? For some, the 'aura' of the original source(s) should always remain dominant, or at least clearly present and recognizable, for something to count as a remix (cf. Navas 2007, in ibid.: 28). For others, so long as one is working with extant recorded music, a creation is a remix even if the resulting collage buries all significant traces of the original source songs and music. Nonetheless, professional and amateur remixers alike often aim to call attention to their use of samples from originals, as part of the meaning or significance of the remix. Hence, remixers

> often expect their audiences to experience recognizing samples as part of the enjoyment and meaning making of listening. Indeed, part of the enjoyment of remixes is identifying how parts of the 'original' sound within the context of the remix (e.g., spotting the music to *Dr Who* or *Inspector Gadget* when they are remixed with other songs). This recognition often draws on a shared nostalgia ('Do you *remember* that?!') and supports a sense of connection between the remixer and the audience.
>
> (Jacobson 2010: 28–9; original emphases)

In some remixes the creators aim *both* to elicit listeners' recognition of the original aura(s) *and* to evoke listeners' judgement that this is, nonetheless, something new – a *new* song (ibid.: 30).

Remixing recorded music (NB: music can, of course, be remixed in live performances that don't involve pre-recorded samples) originally involved the use of multiple vinyl records and turntables and a 'mixer' (a machine that allowed the artist to alter the tempo, dynamics, pitch, and sequencing of songs), or access to the kind of equipment used in music studios to physically splice two-track tapes to create a single multi-track recording (Hawkins 2004). With the advent of digital audio editing capacity, however, the possibilities for and ease of remixing recorded music were greatly amplified and within the reach of many more people than previously. Today, with the ready availability of computers and software like Audacity, Cakewalk and Garageband, 'the tracks from any song, regardless of original tempo, can be digitally altered to work over a huge range of tempos and keys' (ibid.: viii), and can be mixed and remixed in countless ways.

As various authors (e.g., Lessig 2004, 2008; Jenkins 2006b; Lankshear and Knobel 2006; Bruns 2008; Burgess and Green 2009; Jacobson 2010) observe, media remixing now occurs in bedrooms, family rooms, and basements around the world (as well as in more 'professional' settings). Moreover, diverse online music remix community spaces and more specialized support sites actively encourage and promote music remix activities. Some, like ccMixter (ccMixter.org), are general music remixing community sites offering a rich blend of enabling resources and support, including forums, free access to samples and music, hosting services and archives, user profiles and social networking capacity, links to kindred sites, tutorials, etc. Others, like Overclocked Remix (Ocremix.org) specialize in particular types and genres of remix, like video game music remix. Some support sites specialize in specific services, such as hosting remix competitions (e.g., Remixfight.org), providing sound effects (e.g., Freesound.org), or providing free access music for remixing (e.g., Opsound. org) – for more detail, see Jacobson (2010).

Practices and purposes associated with music remixing are diverse, spanning 'projective' activity – where the best-known example is probably Danger Mouse's *Grey Album* – a mashup of the Beatles' *White Album* and rapper Jay-Z's *Black Album* – through to fan-based participatory cultural practices mediated by online spaces like Overclocked Remix and ccMixter. Some remixers prefer 'mashing up' two or more songs where all components are easily recognized, while others may remix music for ethical, political, motivational, or spiritual purposes by layering commentary or excerpts from speeches over music. The kinds of meanings exchanged and negotiated are likewise diverse: including sharing insider appreciations, signalling expertise or sophistication, making a joke or some kind of point, expressing a personal value or perspective, celebrating a fandom, and so on. Music remixing involves diverse kinds of literacy performances, which will vary in their mixes from person to person, depending on their kinds of involvements in music remixing communities and practices. They will range from using video editing software to splice together different elements as *seamlessly* as possible, to searching the web to find a receptive online space for sharing a remix with others (which includes such things as checking the most recent downloads to ensure the site is still sufficiently active), posting comments on other people's remixes, writing new lyrics or creating voice-overs for sections of the remix, seeking or offering advice on forums, and so on.

From the perspective we have adopted here, getting an academic sense of music remix in terms of new literacies may begin from going to a broad-based music remix community site and spending some time simply following links and seeing what is there, before exploring it in a more systematic way using frames and lenses like those we have suggested; e.g., in terms of purposes, tools, Discourse affiliations, tools, knowledge, projective/participatory orientation, types of member contributions, levels of meaning, forms and degrees of collaboration. This kind of exploration, however, will likely not convey much of a sense of the operational (technical, skill) aspects of the practice, or the experiential and 'existential' dimensions of remixing music, far less any approximation to an insider or fan perspective. This can only proceed from a personal focus or interest or passion and from 'taking up the tools' through supported hands-on involvement, and with a good introductory source to hand, such as Erik Jacobson's (2010) how-to account of music remix.

Creating serviceware mashups

The term 'mashup' (or 'mash up'), originally used in the context of music remixing, is now widely applied to the process of merging two or more application programming interfaces (APIs) with each other and/or with available databases. This creates new software or online-interface serviceware applications out of services and data that already exist, leveraging them to perform (often highly) specific tasks, or to meet particular purposes that cannot otherwise be met via extant applications and services. Mashups create innovative and useful – *purposeful* – process tools out of existing tools, to which they add value by enabling them, in combination, to do what could not previously be done. This is a form of customizing and tailoring existing resources to meet niched purposes, perhaps most commonly understood at present by reference to the emergence of apps (from 'applications') for mobile phones and tablets (as well as on the internet).

Some typical examples of established serviceware mashups include Panoramio.com, Twittervision.com and Wikipediavision. Panoramio.com combines Flickr-style photo hosting with Google Maps, so that users can find photos taken in particular places, or discover where a particular photo was taken. Twittervision mashes together the Twitter micro blogging API with Google Maps to show where in the world 'tweets' are being made in close to real time. Wikipediavision (lkozma.net/wpv) is similar. It shows, in close to real time, from where in the world changes are being made on Wikipedia.org.

Mashing up has been made relatively easy for people at large to do by the growth of the Web 2.0 platform. Writing on the cusp of the current apps-creating explosion, David Berlind (2006) compares the 'old' paradigm of applications operating on a computer desktop with the 'new' paradigm of applications operating on the 'webtop' in terms of the relative difficulty/ease in programming such applications. He observed that the emergence of Web 2.0 services and resources meant that the technical requirements threshold for being a 'developer' have been greatly reduced, and that a mashup can now be created in a matter of minutes:

> Before you had to be a pretty decent code jockey with languages like C++ or Visual Basic to turn your creativity into innovation. With mashups, much the same way blogging systems put Web publishing into the hands of millions of ordinary non-technical people, the barrier to developing applications and turning creativity into innovation is so low that there's a vacuum into which an entire new class of developers will be sucked. It's already [i.e., in 2006] happening.
>
> (Berlind 2006, n.p.)

Sites like Programmable Web (Programmableweb.com) provide a quick entree to current mashup culture. It provides how-to guides, serves as a portal to other sites providing information and tools, showcases a 'mashup of the day', maintains a categorized archive of mashups, and lists mashups most recently written for the site or otherwise submitted to it. At the time of writing (29 October 2010), Programmable Web's mashup of the day was a French innovation called 'Where is My Train?' It mixed a Mappy map with a database for French regional trains, so that by accessing the site – at Wimt.fr – users can check where their train is in close-to-real-time.

At the level of mashing up internet serviceware as a new literacy and, correspondingly, using mashups to meet one's purposes, many variables come into play. Developers may, for example, be innovating with a view to making money by creating a successful application. This will involve identifying potential user groups with which they may or may not share purposes and affinities. Alternatively, developers may create a mashup in the first instance to meet a need they themselves have and, secondarily, make it available to others who share their need or interest. This may be the case with many mashups created by fans and enthusiasts, who have no commercial interests and, instead, simply aim to develop an application that enhances the pleasures or satisfactions of people who share their interest or affinity. A typical example here is MyFavBands (Myfavbands.com), which merges iTunes, Last.fm, and Spotify meta data APIs to provide information about the latest releases and any upcoming concerts in your city for the bands whose names you enter into the service. From the standpoint of users, finding mashups is straightforward. A basic online search quickly leads to portals like Programmable Web, and from there it is simply a matter of entering a search on the site or searching by category links.

In terms of knowledge and skills, this kind of remix requires such things as identifying the need or purpose to be served by a mashup, the kinds of APIs and programming tools that will be needed, where any required data will come from – the kind of database to be added to the mix in cases where data are needed – determining the level of coding skills presupposed for building the mashup and, in the event of not having the required coding knowledge, finding out where and how to get it or, alternatively, whether there are tools that can create a component without the need for coding. In addition, developers have to ensure they have the necessary application server capacity, know what programming language is compatible with the APIs to be used, know how to get an API ID and sign up for an API where necessary, and know where to go for help where needed (e.g., Programmableweb.com; Openmashup.org).

In the remainder of this chapter we provide more detailed discussions of fanfiction and anime/manga fan practices, as two particularly popular contexts of new literacies practices among young people.

Reflection and discussion

Go to Programmableweb.com and locate a range of mashups. For each mashup, address the following questions:

- What can it be used for? What does it do?
- What might have motivated the developer to create it?
- What kinds of people are likely to use it?
- Does it 'add value' to its original components? If so, how?
- Would you use it? If so, when, why, and how often? If not, why not?
- How would you rate the significance of this mashup? On what grounds? Relative to what values?

Fanfiction: remixing words and content

Fanfiction – or 'fanfic' to its aficionados – is where devotees of some media or literary phenomenon write narratives using 'pre-existing plots, characters, and/or settings from their favorite media' (Black 2009: 10; see also Jenkins 2006b; Thomas 2007b). Most fanfic is written as narrative, although songfic and poetryfic also are popular forms and some fanfictions are carried as manga drawings and comics. Some fics incorporate (remixed) song lyrics, to underscore themes. 'Costume play' or cosplay – e.g., dressing up as favourite manga and anime characters – and live action role plays based on a favourite popular culture text are also gaining in popularity (for still more categories, see Wikipedia 2010f). Some commentators recognize forebears to contemporary fanfiction dating far back into the past; for example, to the 1400s with Robert Henryson's sequels to some of Geoffrey Chaucer's poetry (Pugh 2004). The phenomenon as we know it today, however, is usually related to the advent of serialized television shows. The *Star Trek* television series, which first aired in 1966 and rapidly gained a cult following, is credited with helping establish fanfiction as a distinct genre and social practice (Jenkins 1988, 1992). From the first episode, fans began writing their own stories set within the *Star Trek* universe and using key *Star Trek* characters. These fanfic writers mimeographed and bound their stories into handmade books or magazines and distributed them at *Star Trek* fan conventions, fan club meetings, or via mail. Since then, fanfic has become an established genre and, increasingly, a subject for academic study (see, for example, Jenkins 1992; Somogyi 2002; Black 2006; Thomas 2007b).

The most popular media inspiring fanfiction readers and writers, in order of contributions on the pre-eminent fanfiction affinity space, Fanfiction.net, are books, anime/manga, (video) games, TV shows, cartoons, movies, comics, plays/musicals. At time of writing (November 2010), books and anime/manga far outstripped the other media as popular catalysts for creation, measured by counts of fanfictions uploaded to Fanfiction.net. The *Harry Potter* books had generated around 482,000 fanfics at the time, followed by the top anime/manga item, *Naruto*, which had inspired around 255,000 fics. The most popular game stimulus, *Kingdom Hearts*, had generated 57,000 fics, and 42,500 fics were based on the most-favoured TV show, *Supernatural*. The *Teen Titans* cartoon had generated around 27,500 fics; the *Star Wars* movie, 25,500; the *X-Men* comic, 10,000; the US musical *Rent*, 7,000 fics. In the miscellaneous category, Wrestling had inspired over 24,000 fanfics. Interestingly, canonical works do not fare as well as one might expect. The Bible has generated almost 3,000 fics on

Fanfiction.net, but canonical books that are read in schools fare relatively poorly by comparison (e.g., *Pride and Prejudice* has generated fewer than 1,450 fics; *To Kill a Mockingbird*, 355; *Jane Eyre*, 220; *Catcher in the Rye*, 116; and *Moby Dick*, 3).

Early TV show catalysts, like *Doctor Who* (1963–89; 2005–present) and *Star Trek*, remain popular, but are now dwarfed in terms of popularity as fic generators by other shows, including *Supernatural*, *Buffy the Vampire Slayer*, *CSI* (all versions), *Stargate SG-1*, *House, M.D.*, *Hanna Montana*, *Law & Order*, and *X-Files*. Besides *Naruto*, the most popular anime/manga catalysts include *Inuyasha*, *Yu-Gi-Oh!*, and *Card Captor Sakura*. Among cartoons, *Avatar*, *The Last Airbender*, *X-Men Evolution*, and *South Park* span high to mid-range popularity. Besides *Star Wars*, the most popular movie generators of fanfiction include *Pirates of the Caribbean* (all titles), *High School Musical*, and *X-Men* (all titles). After these, the *Harry Potter* movie series, the *Twilight* series, and *Lord of the Rings* trilogy are among the most popular.

Fanfic writing can be classified into a number of different types, constituting different kinds and degrees of content remixing. The most common of these include 'in-canon writing', 'alternative universe stories', 'cross-overs', 'relationshipper (or shipper) narratives', and 'self-insert' fanfic:

- In-canon writing maintains the settings, characters, and types of plotlines found in the original media text as far as is possible, and simply adds new 'episodes' or events to the original text (e.g., a new 'episode' of the television show *Eureka* that maintains the characters and setting as faithfully as possible and that builds directly on the narratives and character histories and adventures already developed within the series itself). Pre-sequels and sequels are popular versions of in-canon writing.
- In alternative universe stories elements – characterization, setting – from an original media text are altered in some way to explore a 'what if' scenario within an otherwise in-canon fic (e.g., a sympathetic characterization of an evil character, changing the group of friends surrounding the main character).
- Cross-overs bring characters from two different original media texts together in a new story (e.g., characters from *Star Wars* brought together with the world of *Harry Potter*).
- Relationshipper (or 'shipper') narratives focus on establishing an intimate relationship between two (often minor) characters where none existed or was downplayed in the original text. These texts can focus on heterosexual relations (e.g., between *Star Trek*'s Admiral Kathryn

Janeway and Chakotay characters), or homoerotic/homosexual relations between characters (e.g., between *Star Trek*'s Captain Kirk and Mr Spock). The latter kind of fanfics are also referred to as 'slash fiction'.

• In self-insert fanfic, writers insert themselves as recognizable characters directly into a narrative (e.g., many young female fanfic writers write themselves into the *Harry Potter* series in place of Hermione, one of Harry's closest friends; many writers invent a character that is a mix of themselves and attributes from popular culture characters and insert this hybrid character into their text).

This classification of fanfic types provides an indication of the kinds of 'mixings' that go on within fanfiction as remix. There are almost no limits to hybridity here. The character of fanfic as remix is often most richly apparent in the writing of younger authors as they move across an array of media and cultural genres to combine their own stories and characters with existing ones in new narratives that may be complex and require the reader to have read widely and/or viewed or played a range of anime-related shows or games in order to fully appreciate the warp and weft of each story. One of our research informants, Silver Excel Fox (S.E.F.), talked about some of the direct influences on her own story writing, which include Greek mythology, the *Harry Potter* stories, the Bible, romance stories, hacker culture, thriller/adventure movies, and a range of anime and manga texts like *Inuyasha*, *Yu Yu Hakusho*, and *Sailor Moon*, among others:

S.E.F: Like in Greek mythology. They have the River Styx and they have the ferry man who will take you down to the underworld, or wherever you're going. And–

Michele: Have you done that at school?

S.E.F: I don't know. I just like Greek mythology. She [points to her mother] got me into it, and I kind of stuck with it.

Michele: It sounds like it's helped you out in terms of–

S.E.F: It has, because the girl in my story – in the original myth it would be a guy – it's a girl, and she's pretty. It's like the person who is taking you to your death is a girl, and she's ((laughs)) – like, I'm dying and *you're* taking me ((laughs)) And she rides an oar, which kind of makes sense because she's on the River Styx. You're gonna need something to get up that river! ((laughs)) And Yusuke [a character from *Yu Yu Hakusho*] goes and he meets kind of the Japanese version of Jesus.

                    (interview, 2005 by Knobel and Lankshear)

The kinds of remixing practices engaged in by fanfic writers produce unmistakably creative texts that draw on a range of content and resources. They support O'Reilly's claim that cultural 'creativity is rooted in re-use' and reinvention (in interview with McManus 2004: n.p.). Ian McDonald, himself a celebrated science fiction writer, discusses how remixing practices are very much in keeping with current times, and argues that the strong trend toward using material from a range of literary and non-literary sources is 'a product of our technological ability to surf, sample and mix' (in interview with Gevers 2001: n.p.). He goes so far as to claim that, '[a]nyone with an eye on the zeitgeist would agree that the art of the edit will be the cultural skill of the new century' (ibid.).

Fan fiction was a well-established practice before the development of the internet and a lot of fanfic activity still goes on outside of online environments (Jenkins 1992). Nonetheless, the explosion of the internet has had a massive impact on the scale and culture of fanfic. It has enabled almost infinitely more people to actively participate in contributing and critiquing fanfic than was previously possible. Prior to the internet becoming a mass medium, fanfic was circulated person to person among relatively small circles of aficionados and subjected to sustained critique. Authors received peer comments and suggestions for improving their stories usually in face-to-face encounters or, perhaps, via snail mail. Today, however, fanfic narratives in the tens of thousands are posted in open public forums on the internet, to be read and reviewed online by anyone who cares to do so. A Google.com search early in November 2010 for the term 'fan fiction' returned 17,300,000 hits, while a search using 'fanfic' as a keyword returned 5,610,000 hits, indicating a strong online presence.

The internet 'geography' of fanfic is complex. A good place to start is with Fanfiction.net, a pre-eminent online fan fiction site founded in 1998. This website has a searchable archive-plus-discussion board format and a link to open source writing software. Fanfiction.net hosts hundreds of thousands of fanfics, organized by categories. The front page provides an 'at a glance' sense of the site. Most of the page is taken up with news about recent developments on the site (e.g., forums can now have moderators, or a software glitch has been fixed). There is a simple menu bar across the top of the page. This menu can be used to find newly uploaded works, to access different fanfic communities, to search the site (by author pen name, story title, or summary), to go to discussion forums associated with each category of fanfic (in November 2010 there were almost 1800 forums for *Harry Potter* alone on Fanfiction.net), to access the site directory (organized by pen names and categories of fanfic and communities), and to open the site's online dictionary and thesaurus. Individual fanfic titles have links to their reviews.

Fanfiction reflects *par excellence* participatory culture as conceived by Jenkins and colleagues in terms of environments and social practices where there are

> relatively low barriers to artistic expression and civic engagement, strong support for creating and sharing one's creations, and some type of informal mentorship whereby what is known by the most experienced is passed along to novices. A participatory culture is also one in which members believe their contributions matter, and feel some degree of social connection with one another.
>
> (Jenkins et al. 2006: 3)

Anyone with an interest they want to read or write fanfiction about can sign up to sites like Fanfiction.net and begin writing, reviewing, discussing, and so on. The 'long tail of the web' is alive and well here, to the extent that it is easy – indeed, common – to find fans with strictly minority interests contributing the sole fic on a topic and nonetheless drawing support and encouragement. For example, one of just two authors remixing *Moby Dick* on Fanfiction.net posted a short (ten single lines, 112 words) opening chapter to a proposed fic titled *Mutiny*. The author notes accompanying the work included confessions that 'my summaries kind of suck' and 'I didn't know what genre to put it in either.' The opening chapter narrative has a crew member, Starbuck, in Ahab's cabin, while Ahab was asleep. Starbuck finds Ahab's gun and is wondering whether or not to shoot him. Among the four reviews is one from an obviously erudite contributor, 'Bleeding Heart Conservative' (3 June 2010), who offers beautifully understated constructive critique and strong encouragement to go on, saying:

> SERIOUSLY? No! Ahab's such a great character ... and if Starbuck gets him early, Moby Dick will never get his chance!

> All the same, I do wish to say that I am delighted that you chose to write about Ahab at all. It seems so few do. Thank you very much for sharing (and I second the idea of taking 'I suck at summaries' out of your summary. Even if you're absolutely convinced that something sucks, NEVER admit it!)
>
> (at Fanfiction.net/r/5603274/)

This exemplifies the overwhelmingly 'friendly' and supportive culture of reviewing within online fanfiction, previously discussed in some detail in Chapter 3 (see pp. 76–9). One of our research informants expresses, from the standpoint of a novice author, what reviews mean to her and do for her work.

Michele: The reviews that you get. Do you pay attention to them?

S.E.F: Oh, yes, I always read my reviews. I have 24 and most are for one story. And I was so happy 'cause the first time I posted it, I got two.

Michele: Perfect.

S.E.F: That was the thing. These were the people that I knew and they were complimenting my story, and I was sitting there ((her eyes widen in an expression of delighted surprise)). I actually bounced down the stairs! 'Oh my God, I got reviews! Oh my God! Oh my God! Oh my God!' And then I got even more reviews. 'Oh my God, this is cool! They're reading what I wrote. They read my stuff. Yes!'

Michele: I know reviewers sometimes make suggestions about what you should do. Do you make any changes based on what they say?

S.E.F: Yes, because there was one person who kind of commented on my spelling of somebody's name.

Michele: Ahhh.

S.E.F: Because there are two different types of Rikus in video games. There's the Riku from *Kingdom Hearts*, and that's r-i-k-u. And there's the girl Rikku from *Final Fantasy*. Now, *Kingdom Hearts* is kind of like a merge between Disney and *Final Fantasy* all by itself. That's how they kind of distinguish the material; Rikku as a girl is r-i-k-k-u, and a guy is r-i-k-u.
                                    (interview, 2005 by Knobel and Lankshear).

Fanfiction.net's forums provide aficionados of particular works and/or authors with a space to raise topics for discussion with other users sharing similar interests. The forums are often moderated by volunteers and have specific participation rules, including the requirement that all discussion, content, and language be suitable for teens. Forums are text-specific – organized around the popular text that fan writers are remixing. So, for example, within Fanfiction.net's category of movie-focused forums, there were 146 separate discussion forums associated with the *Pirates of the Caribbean* movies in November 2010. Topics and purposes addressed within these forums are wide-ranging, including discussion of the original movie and its sequels; speculations on the development of romantic relationships between different key characters; interest in pirate lore in general; ideas for role playing *Pirates of the Caribbean* fanfic; plot bunny topics (e.g., speculations on storylines should Jack Sparrow – the pirate at the heart of the movie – have a son or daughter); discussion of historical accuracy within the movie itself, as well as within relevant fanfics; listings of people willing to act as 'beta' readers, who provide feedback on narratives prior to them being posted publicly for review, and so on. Similar discussion thread purposes and uses can be found across all the forums hosted by Fanfiction.net and similar sites like Fictionalley.org, Fanfics.org, Fictionesque.com and Myfandoms.com.

Online spaces that help resource fanfic writers abound on the web. Between large-scale general showcasing sites like Fanfiction.net, these include more specific sites like *The Force* (Fanfic.theforce.net, see p. 77–8 above), *Plot Bunny 101* (Plotbunny101.tvheaven.com) and *How to Write Almost Readable Fan Fiction* (Littlecalamity.tripod.com/HowTo2.html). As we saw in Chapter 3, *The Force* provides guidelines for beta readings of works prior to final publication. It also offers writing tips posted by members, random writing contest-type events that specify story parameters to which fanfic authors must adhere, a fanfic lexicon, a submissions style guide for members, and links to email-based discussion lists, among other services. *Plot Bunny 101* is a site for fanfic writers to use to share 'plot bunnies': ideas for narratives that someone makes freely available to others for developing into their own stories. Plot bunnies can range from a 'story-starter' idea through to a full-blown plot line and set of characters for a story. Like *Plot Bunny 101*, *Plot Bunny Adoption Center* (Sg1hc.com/pbac) is an online repository of story starters and plotline sketches. *How to Write Almost Readable Fan Fiction* offers a guide to writing that includes advice on character development, guides to grammar and punctuation conventions, and general advice concerning spell-checking and proof-reading, how to avoid repetition and redundancy in stories, and so on.

Of particular relevance to language and literacy education, Rebecca Black (2008) provides a compelling account of fanfaction in relation to second-language acquisition. At age 11, Tanaka Nanako migrated to Canada as a non-English-speaking native speaker of Mandarin Chinese. When she had been learning English for just two and a half years she began writing fanfiction and posting it online. Her work became popular and attracted large amounts of feedback and, over time, thousands of reviews. Nanako's experience is a good example of how engaging in fanfiction writing practices – which includes drafting stories and posting them online for feedback, polishing them in light of readers' comments and suggestions, reviewing others' work, discussing narrative elements with others (e.g., plot development, setting details, character development), borrowing characters from existing texts and movies and creating original stories with them, to name only a few – can, over time, contribute to becoming an accomplished narrative writer. Her case also shows how social networks of interested others can serve to improve a learner's written mastery of a new language.

Reviewers provide Nanako with constructive criticism of various kinds, almost invariably in respectful, sympathetic, and appreciative ways. They generally focus on errata that undermine their enjoyment of the fiction, and introduce their criticisms in humble, disclaiming, even self-effacing, ways; for example, 'This is just an idea'. Nanako explicitly and repeatedly incorporates reviewer feedback into subsequent chapter revisions (cf., Black 2005a: 123). Black argues that while Nanako's English-language development was supported in school, reviewer feedback on the technical and literary dimensions of Nanako's fanfiction also contributes directly to enhancing Nanako's English writing proficiency (Black 2008). Nanako's spelling improved demonstrably over time, as did her subject–verb agreement within sentences and use of tenses, as reviewers pointed out these errors and modelled how to fix them.

A key dimension of fanfiction writing is staying 'true enough' to the original source narrative – in Nanako's case, to the *Card Captor Sakura* anime series for the most part – for the new narrative to be recognizable as 'fanfiction'. This requires good fanfiction writers to have a close, detailed knowledge of the texts from which they're drawing their ideas and resources. Reviewers comment, for example, on how Nanako is developing characters taken from an anime series, and the extent to which she is plausibly showing sides of them not necessarily explored in the original anime (Black 2007: 130). Nanako's use of Japanese terms (she is learning Japanese at school), along with Chinese Mandarin terms, in her English-language narratives generates special admiration from her readers. Reviewers regularly reference Nanako's expert anime knowledge, and in so doing, have the opportunity to display their own social and pop culture knowledge. This, in turn, becomes an exchange based in solidarity and affiliation that constructs a well-defined social network around Nanako's online fanfiction texts.

Multimediated anime fan practice: the case of Maguma

Matt Lewis (aka 'Maguma') is a 21-year-old African American college student, from a Jewish middle-class family, living in California. He participates in a range of anime fan practices, and is active on sites like

AnimeMusicVideos.org, DeviantArt.com, Cosplay.com, Youtube.com, and Livejournal.com. Matt contributes online under multiple aliases, including 'Maguma', 'Dynamite Breakdown', and 'Tsugasa' (and can be searched for online under these names). 'Maguma' (a giant monster character appearing in the Japanese scifi movie *Gorath*) is his favourite online alias. We will use 'Maguma' as the name for our case study of anime fan practices and new literacies, and hereafter refer to Matt as Maguma.

When we first interviewed Maguma, he was a high school student. At that time he had been formally diagnosed as having ADHD, and described himself in an email interview as 'an average student, Cs, Bs and a couple of Ds in Statistics and Economics (tricky stuff >w<)'. In his current (November 2010) profile description on Cosplay.com he describes himself as 'a college student aspiring to become a famous artist and Mangaka'. A 'mangaka' is a prominent manga artist and writer, and the term typically refers to Japanese manga artists. Maguma is currently enrolled in an art programme at a local community college.

At 15, Maguma was introduced to anime music video (AMV) remixing by a friend, who showed him a classic AMV on the internet. As noted earlier (p. 66), AMV is a popular form of remix that combines and syncs clips of anime (Japanese cartoon animations) with a chosen song. Maguma hadn't paid much attention to manga or anime before his friend showed him 'Narutrix', an AMV faux movie trailer parodying the *Matrix* movies. He told us

> The first AMV I officially saw was 'Narutrix' which is what got me into *Naruto* [the anime series] and downloading anime in general. After that I saw an AMV for *Azumanga Daioh* [another anime series] and decided to give it a shot.

Before beginning to remix his own AMVs, Maguma watched hundreds of AMVs online – accessing them via YouTube and the premium online archive and AMV network, AnimeMusicVideos.org (or AMV.org). Through watching these music videos Maguma became a fan of anime in general. He spent hundreds more hours watching series like *Naruto*, *Street Fighter Alpha*, *Tengen Toppa Gurren Lagann*, *Digimon*, *Fullmetal Alchemist*, *Tenjou Tenge*, and *Azumanga Daioh*.

When Maguma began making his own AMV remixes, early in 2005, he was initially most interested in understanding how to put them together at a technical level; 'I would produce like 1 a night, but they weren't amazing.' As he spent more time watching anime series and movies, and watching AMVs, he began to develop a stronger sense of what was valued and why in 'good' AMVs. These days Maguma will typically spend hundreds of hours remixing an AVM, particularly if he plans to submit it to a competition. He will have spent hundreds more watching anime online, downloading resource files, searching for appropriate scenes, and so on, before starting his production phase and subsequent editing iterations.

To create his AMVs, Maguma originally used the free video editing software that ships with Windows: *Windows Movie Maker*. He was aware that this software was looked down upon by many seasoned AMV remixers, but explained that by tinkering with the software and seeing what it could be pushed to do, he'd been able to 'create effects in *Movie Maker* that programs like *Adobe Premier* can do'. At the same time as he was exploring the functionality of *Movie Maker*, Maguma paid attention to how others were making their AMVs. He explains,

> I get a lot of inspiration from other videos on technical stuff and effects by watching others. Just because someone uses an effect doesn't mean you can't. Monkey See, Monkey do, or Make AMV, haha!

Key skills he developed included learning how to overlay moving images, superimpose still images over moving images, and the like. Other skills including being able to sync the clips both literally and symbolically to the music and the lyrics of the song soundtrack by manipulating clip length and transitions within *Movie Maker*. He learned early on how to rip DVDs of an anime movie or series, how to locate and download anime series episodes from file-sharing networks, and how to find, download, and convert anime clips from YouTube and other sites. He also makes use of his online networks and sometimes emails other AMV remixers and asks for copies of a particular clip they've used if he can't find it by any other means.

As time went on, Maguma was able to upgrade his software: 'I started to use Sony Vegas to get added effects. Now I export the clips I want to use and upload them into Vegas and edit there.' Maguma likes to push himself and the software with respect to the effects he's able to achieve in his video editing, and is prepared to spend large amounts of time mastering new effects. In his video 'Frontlines' (Youtube.com/user/maguma#p/u/30/FHZj7nxSygg), Maguma talks about 'finally' getting the chance to 'experiment with masking'. He translated this masking effect into lay terms as 'that big chomp that happens about two-thirds of the way into the video and transfers to the more heavy instrumental section'. The 'chomp' comprises an overlaid animation of a large mecha or robot mouth closing around the viewing area; the effect appears for less than a second in the video. According to Maguma, this masking effect alone 'took 2 hours to edit @_@'.

Maguma began creating and posting AMVs as a member of AnimeMusicVideos.org under the alias 'Dynamite Breakdown' (and can be looked for there under that name). His account currently contains 45 AMVs. Each comprises hundreds of short video clips taken from across an entire season of an animation series on television, or from across an anime movie and its sequels. These clips are painstakingly reassembled into a sequence that may summarize an entire season, explore under-developed or absent relationships within a series or movie, examine a range of concepts like 'belonging' or 'triumph of the underdog', and so on. Transitions between certain clips and video effects applied to clips also play an important role in AMV, and decisions about which options to use are made carefully. The overall sequence is synced with an appropriate song. Upon finding that many of his AMVs had been posted by others to YouTube without acknowledgement that he was the original remixer, Maguma opened a YouTube account. He did this reluctantly, because at the time YouTube didn't support high-resolution videos (unlike AnimeMusicVideos.org). Despite his initial reluctance, Maguma has become an active and engaged user of YouTube – uploading his AMVs, along with videos from cosplay events and video soliloquies, and subscribing to other users' accounts. Maguma's AMVs are widely viewed and he responds to most people who leave comments, by advising how he achieved a certain effect, providing information about a given series or movie, and suchlike. He likewise offers supportive and constructive criticism on other people's uploaded AMVs.

For Maguma, creating a new AMV is a recursive process. Sometimes a song he hears strikes him as eminently 'AVM-able'. Other times, he has an idea that has grown out of an anime series he would like to explore, and which he keeps on the backburner until he hears a suitable song. The match between the selected song and the anime used in conjunction with the song is very important to Maguma: 'If you use a Linkin Park song with shows like *Azumanga Daioh*, it's totally pointless.' (Linkin Park is a hard rock band, while *Azumanga Daioh* is a light-hearted, humorous anime.) He explains:

> Once I get the song I listen to it over and over again so I can get a sense of the song and am able to work with the clips without having to play the song at the same time, which makes it very hectic [i.e., listening to the song and editing clips simultaneously can be hectic].

Maguma mostly makes in-canon fan videos – fully situated within a single anime universe like *Naruto* rather than built from clips taken from different series. He typically uses the *Naruto* series and movies as the anime source for video clips, although he also makes in-canon AMVs using *Tengen*

Toppa Gurren Lagann, Digimon, Fullmetal Alchemist, Tenjou Tenge, and *Azumanga Daioh.* He classifies most of his AMVs as 'action' genre, categorizing the others as comedy, sentimental, or drama (with some overlaps occurring). About his preference for creating action AMV, Maguma says: 'I really enjoy making action AMVs due to the rush one can get from it; I like that feeling in the back of my head that just goes "Woah..."' He also enjoys making drama AMVs 'cus with it you can try to express a storyline or bring out a trait of a character that not many notice or get to see'.

Maguma's best-known AMV, 'Konoha Memory Book', is set to Nickleback's song, 'Photograph'. It features video clips taken from across the first season of *Naruto*. The lyrics speak of someone looking through a photograph album and how the photos jog long-forgotten memories about growing up poor, skipping out on school, getting into trouble with the law, hanging out with friends, first love, and the like. The narrator is leaving his hometown. Despite all that's happened, he's leaving reluctantly and with fond memories. Maguma uses this basic thread to follow Naruto – the principal protagonist in the series – through a range of adventures.

The first verse of the song is accompanied by clips presenting the main characters – Naruto Uzumaki, Sasuke Uchiha, Sakura Haruno, and their ninja *sensei*, Kakashi Hatake – and conveys a sense of some of the mischief and danger Naruto and his fellow ninjas-in-training enact and encounter while developing their skills and characters, e.g., playing truant from school (synchronized clips show students escaping through a school window and running outside), and getting in trouble with the law (clips show someone holding up a record sheet to a sheepish Naruto). The initial segue to the chorus moves from bright yellow and red colours – matching the singer's comment that life is better now than it was back then – to darker, more muted images emphasizing bittersweet memories recounted in the song. At this point the video includes many close-ups that show an individual standing at a remove from others, often with text (e.g., 'Time to say it' and 'Good-bye') superimposed over images and aligning with the lyrics as they're sung. The initial chorus closes with scenes from a beloved elder's funeral. 'Good-bye' does double work here, syncing with the song and farewelling the master *sensei*.

The remainder of the song follows a similar pattern. At times there is a literal syncing between lyrics and images (e.g., mention of cops in the lyrics is matched with images of law keepers in *Naruto*). At other times the 'sync' between lyrics and images has a kind of frisson to it, like the image of Naruto kissing Sasuke (a boy) as the singer recalls *his* first kiss. This particular 'move' references the corpus of Naruto/Sasuke relationship fiction and music videos made by anime fans. Sometimes, the sync between lyrics and images in this remix is more conceptual – as when the lyrics speak of missing the sound and faces of childhood friends, while the clip sequence emphasizes how Naruto, Sasuke, Sakura, and their *sensei*, Kakashi, have formed a close bond over the course of living and training together. Second time around the chorus ups the visual tempo with a bricolage of images that suggests time passing. This bricolage includes pages of the original print-based *Naruto* manga series superimposed over images from the *Naruto* anime series. This speaks directly to *Naruto* having both manga and anime forms, and links to the concept of the photo album at the heart of the song. An image of Naruto running away from the reader is superimposed over other clips, again emphasizing the sense of time passing. This same animation of Naruto is repeated in the closing bars of the song as the singer explains that it's time to leave his hometown and move on.

Maguma first uploaded 'Konoha Memory Book' to AnimeMusicVideos. org (see Tsugasa 2005) in late 2005. AMV fans found it and subsequently uploaded it to YouTube for others to view. 'Konoha Memory Book' attracted close to two million views across these accounts until it was removed by YouTube for infringing the song's copyright. Before its removal, many fans on YouTube identified it as their 'all-time favorite AMV', with some even revealing it moved them to tears while watching it. Maguma worked especially hard on this particular AMV for submission to the 2007 Anime Expo in Los Angeles where it won all sections, although contest rules permitted just one official prize: the Popular Vote Award. It has spawned numerous copy-cat videos using the same song and *Naruto* video clips. An anime fan saw it at the expo and declared on a cosplay discussion board: 'I loved it! My little sister loved it! Our friend loved it and she's not even a fan! It really brought out the highlights of the beginning of the series and reminded us of why we first got into it......'. Possibly, though, the stand-out fan tribute of this remix was a *karaoke* version of 'Konoha Memory Book' that also was uploaded to YouTube for a while. As a mark of its enduring popularity, at the time of writing, copies of his video are currently hosted on websites whose interface is in Belgian, Russian, and French, as well as English, and on many different file downloading service and mirror sites (e.g., Megaupload.com, Accuratefiles.com) located on servers around the world.

Maguma has pursued a deep understanding of what needs to be done to create what other AMV remixers consider a 'good' AMV. This includes avoiding as far as possible using clips with subtitles or series end-credits (because the printed text in these clips rarely matches what's happening in the song), ensuring high-quality clip resolution across the entire video (e.g., clips downloaded from YouTube can have a much fuzzier resolution than clips taken from a DVD), ensuring a seamless 'sync' between the video and the music/song, and paying attention to the mood and meaning of a song, and matching this with the colours and action in the accompanying video clips. That said, Maguma accepts that he has to work with what he has available, and often includes clips with subtitles, downloaded clips, and title and credit sequences.

Non-fans of anime can enjoy and appreciate the stories Maguma tells, but anime fans see many additional layers of meaning actively built into his videos that non-fans inevitably miss. If the viewer doesn't understand the tense relationship between Naruto and Sasuke in the original anime they will only interpret the closing scene in 'Before We Were Men' as two youths fighting in the rain, rather than Maguma's intended exploration of a possible deep connection between the two.

Maguma is sensitive to anime fans watching his videos and regularly posts 'spoiler' alerts alongside his AMVs to warn viewers that key plot points will be given away. He uses alphabetic text in other interesting ways, like superimposing text or other devices within the AMV to help viewers interpret his work. He identifies this as a 'fan service' (e.g., in one video, words like 'passion' and 'angst' appear at specific points in the video to help convey his meaning).

His notes for each video uploaded to AMV.org specify the genre, identify the song and band used, provide some additional background details on each, and invite users to leave comments and to rate his videos. These requests for comments bespeak Maguma's investment in his AMV making and his interest in being recognized for his work. Requests for comments include statements such as, 'Please leave a comment if you watch this! I love hearing what you all have to say' and 'Well I hope you all enjoy it. Please **please PLEASE** leave an opinion.' Part of the motivation behind requests for comments is that this kind of feedback is highly valued on AMV.org as a marker of influence. Maguma also recognizes his friends who are interested in anime and/or AMV. His 'liner notes' for his AMV on AMV. org sometimes include 'shout outs' to specific friends and a dedication to a teacher who gave him an anime DVD. Maguma also uses terms familiar to anime and Japanese pop culture in his contextual notes, too. For example, the information text Maguma wrote for one AMV concludes with the full-caps text: 'WARNING YAOI-ESQUE ENDING!!!' 'Yaoi' is a term used outside Japan by fans of Japanese manga and anime to describe a genre of manga and anime that focuses on male/male love (Wikipedia 2010g). Yaoi texts are not necessarily sexual in nature, nor are they considered to be gay texts *per se*. Maguma explains that he described this particular

AMV as yaoi because '[t]he AMV overall has that kind of passionate feeling of the two [Naruto and Sasuke] longing for each other kind of sense. And in the end they're just practically face to face in the rain, and with the lack of a visual and the rain still running it leaves you to think what might happen.'

Maguma is an avid artist and his profile page on DeviantArt.com shows how he draws on many of the characters from his favourite anime series, remixing them in various ways (e.g., making shorter, more childlike 'chibi' versions of characters). He also focuses on drawing original takes on established manga characters, like Naruto and Ryuiko. DeviantArt.com is a site for serious artists – with many professional artists showcasing their work here and providing important insights into their own creative process, not to mention important feedback on new artists' work. This is not a network for the faint-hearted or easily intimidated. Feedback can be brutally honest and searingly evaluative. A good deal of his uploaded work is in-process, and Maguma regularly invites viewer feedback on this work and seeks advice on directions to take his drawings in. He also writes and draws original manga comics and posts these for feedback. A review of a recent first page for a new manga comic includes:

> panel 1: nicely done i can see the stance perfectly as it was supposed to be depicted though i didn't notice the monkey or what he was doing. (i suppose you can blame the scanner for that)

> panel 2: The tail has to have a little more wiggle motion if there is any, it must be the scanner.

> panels 3, 4, 5: I can scarcely tell what is going on, focus on it using concentration lines.

The review ends on a positive note, and Maguma responds to each suggestion, agreeing with some of the critique and elaborating on what he was trying to achieve. This pattern is repeated elsewhere throughout his online gallery.

Maguma's AMV remixing has led to an avid interest in anime cosplaying, and he devotes considerable spare time to designing costumes, making accessories and other costume bits and pieces, role playing narratives with others on weekends, attending anime and manga conventions in character, organizing events such as weekend meet-ups and convention competitions. He also posts reviews of recently read manga novels. He mostly documents his cosplay in photographs uploaded to his Cosplay.com and Flickr.com profiles, as well as to his Livejournal blog – which is especially active.

Maguma uses it to alert his network to upcoming conventions and events, to organize groups of cosplayers to get together, and to seek help with creating particular costumes. He's currently creating his first costume entirely from scratch, and a recent blog post sought advice on what kind of material would be best for a Pokémon Ranger cape. In an extended conversation between Maguma and five others, cotton twill emerged as the favoured option. He attended Anime Expo 2010 as Charlie Nash, a character from the *Streetfighter Alpha 3* video game. On his Cosplay.com profile, Maguma lists owning 23 different costumes, and has posted several hundred photos of himself in character. His characters are drawn from a wide range of anime and manga resources, including video and card games (e.g., Pokémon), manga (e.g., *One Piece, Dragon Ball Z*), and anime movies and television series (e.g., *Tengen Toppa Gurren Lagann*).

Maguma is a good example of someone who set out from what we have called a 'projective' orientation to AMV creation and has progressively morphed into a full-fledged fan deeply immersed in a participatory culture of anime/manga fan practices. Jacobson (2010: 31) notes that for many people 'creative remix is one way to see what they can achieve with the technology they have'. This was a key motif in Maguma's early interest and activity in AMV, along with seeing how AMVs are put together. Several

---

Reflection and discussion

To what extent and in what ways does the case of Maguma convey a sense of engaging in new literacies, with respect to the following?

- new technical aspects
- a new ethos
- Discourse memberships
- making, communicating, and negotiating meanings
- contexts of social practice
- encoded texts

To what extent and in what ways is the account enriched by visiting Maguma's online spaces: AnimeMusicVideos.org; Dynamite breakdown.DeviantArt.com; Youtube.com/user/maguma; Cosplay.com/member/48130; Maguma-sama.livejournal.com?

years later he remains proud of what he was able to do using *Windows Movie Maker* to edit his remixes. These days his fan involvement is diverse, rich, and highly dedicated to helping build and resource, in the company of others, the fan practices and communities he is passionate about.

This chapter has focused on writing as media remix. Chapter 5 focuses more centrally on conventional alphabetic texts, as we turn our attention to participating in blogs, wikis, and other online collaborative writing spaces and practices.

Appendix: Some popular everyday remix practices

Kinds of remixes	Kinds of involvement	Some literacy dimensions	Some online spaces, sites, and examples
Making machinima videos	Expressing a fan identity	Narrative development skills using a set range of pre-established resources (e.g., setting, the 'look' of characters)	• Halomachinima.wikia.com
	Expressing enjoyment of a game, etc.	Video editing skills – being able to use editing software to splice together different stretches of recorded action to create a cohesive whole	• Warcraftmovies.com
	Exploring new ways of conveying narratives or social commentaries	Understanding how to use video clip transitions and video effects in ways valued by other machinimists	• Wiki.secondlife.com/wiki/Machinima
	Experimenting with becoming a short film director	Using audio recording and editing software to create a soundtrack; including voices for dialogue and music	• Machinimart.com
	To maintain social relationships with friends and others	Understanding how to create a soundtrack that doesn't sound 'tinny'	• Machinimafordummies.com
		Understanding how to manipulate game resources to suit narrative purposes (e.g., changing character point of view by changing 'camera angles')	• Koinup.com/on-videos
		Player character manipulation skills – how to move player-controlled characters, how to have characters look like they're interacting with one another	

(continued)

Appendix (continued)

Kinds of remixes	Kinds of involvement	Some literacy dimensions	Some online spaces, sites, and examples
		Writing programming scripts that 'run' inside the game and manage character movements in real-time (not a necessary skill)	
		Understanding how non-player characters work within a game and within a machinima movie	
		Syncing screen capture software with in-game action	
		Understanding how to leverage the original game story for maximizing the machinima narrative (this narrative may have very little to do with the original game storyline or characters, as in *Red vs. Blue*)	
		May include an affectionate parody of the original game	
		May be a 'bragging' video about a clan's online game playing strategy	
	Exploring the medium as artistic, social commentary and/or political expression	All of the above, plus perhaps experimenting with different video effects to really push the definition of machinima to the extreme edge	• Friedrich Kirschner's work. See, for example: Person2184.com • *War of Internet Addiction* by Oil Tiger Machinima Team

	For commercial entertainment purposes	As with making machinima in general, but with close attention paid to television-quality production values	• Season 10, Episode 8 of the television show, *South Park* (titled: *Make Love not Warcraft*)
		Understanding of the culture of machinima making when tied to a popular multiplayer game (like *World of Warcraft*)	• *Red Dead Redemption* machinima movie short (30 mins.) directed by John Hillcoat. Aired 26 May 2010, on the Fox network in the USA
	For commercial marketing purposes	As with making machinima in general, along with a strong sense of how to create a 30-sec. video that has a marketing spin	• Volvo's 'Game On' commercial, which mixes 'real life' video with *Grand Theft Auto*-like machinima footage
			• Coca-Cola's *Grand Theft Auto*-style 'Coke Side of Life' commercial
Making movie trailers	Expressing a fan identity	Knowing how to access original movie footage to use in the remixed trailer (e.g., downloading relevant clips; ripping a DVD)	• Fanfiction movie trailers that remix, for example, *Harry Potter* and *Star Wars* video clips to 'map out' a 'new' movie (see Thomas 2007b). Or – alt-universe-style – *Harry Potter* mixed with *Pride and Prejudice*
	Expressing enjoyment of a movie, series, book, etc.	Understanding the importance of 'saming' resolution and screen sizes of different clips used for continuity purposes	
	Translating an enjoyed narrative from one medium to another	Knowing how to convert video files if needed (not all file types are compatible with all video editing software)	• See, for example, *Twilight/New Moon/Eclipse* fanfiction movie trailers on YouTube.com
	Expressing a movie director or movie maker identity	Paying attention to original movie storylines and leveraging them where possible in creating a new movie storyline	• See *Harry Potter* fanfiction movie trailers on YouTube.com

(continued)

Kinds of remixes	Kinds of involvement	Some literacy dimensions	Some online spaces, sites, and examples
		May involve knowing how to include written text in the remixed video to help convey the new storyline	• See *Batman* fan films on YouTube.com
		Using video and audio editing techniques to create a sense of 'wholeness' out of disparate clips	
		Paying attention to spoken language in the clips and using this to full effect, or muting it to make the visual clip 'work' within the new trailer	
	For humorous, entertainment and/or spoofing purposes (e.g., creating a 'new' trailer for an existing movie that shows it to be the exact opposite of what it really is, or something else altogether). Sometimes referred to as a 'recut'	Having access to key scenes from the movie that match one's purpose (e.g., finding clips online to download)	• *Mary Poppins* edited into a horror movie trailer
		Can include shooting live action footage and setting it to the movie soundtrack (e.g., *Twilight* trilogy movies set to live action scenes that spoof the vampires and werewolves). This involves understanding the importance of multiple camera angles, shooting distances, framing, etc.	• *The Shining* edited into a feel-good movie trailer
			• *Sleepless in Seattle* as a horror movie trailer
		Selecting clips judiciously, based on the spoof to be achieved	• *Crocodile Dundee* as a horror movie trailer
			• *American Pie* as a horror movie trailer
			• *Rain Man* as a thriller movie trailer

Fanfiction short movies	Expressing a fan identity	Selecting relevant music for the new soundtrack to help convey the new intended movie genre	• Thehuntforgollum.com
	Expressing enjoyment of a book, series, movie, etc.	Using video editing techniques (e.g., cutting, splicing, transitioning) to create a seamless whole	• *Buffy vs. Edward: Twilight Remixed* by Jonathan McIntosh
	Experimenting with becoming a short film director	Locating/creating and importing suitable soundtrack into video editing software, and syncing movie trailer and music appropriately	• *Transformers* fanfiction movies
	For artistic purposes; it may involve a retelling or original interpretation of a favourite book or other non-movie narrative	May involve using machinima techniques and editable resources, such as Second Life, to provide settings and characters for new storylines	• *Dracula's Guest* by Alessandro Cima
		May involve taking clips from an original movie and re-editing them to create a new movie narrative that extends or adds to the original movie(s)	• Theforce.net/fanfilms
		Including 'opening credits', such as a clip from a real movie production company credit (e.g., the Dreamworks company credit sequence), or a faux company credit sequence created especially for the fan film to give it a stamp of authenticity	

(continued)

Appendix (continued)

Kinds of remixes	Kinds of involvement	Some literacy dimensions	Some online spaces, sites, and examples
Making music videos A music video in this sense centralizes the song, rather than uses songs to simply accompany a series of slides or clips, such as those created to celebrate someone's birthday or wedding anniversary	Expressing a fan identity (e.g., of a band, of anime, of rap music) Expressing enjoyment of a particular song or music track Expressing support for indie music, or for music that is controversial in certain circles Expressing support for an issue or injustice Expressing a music video editor identity	Locating the target song file and ensuring it's in a file-type compatible with the video editing software to be used. This might include understanding digital rights management codes added to songs that limit the ways in which they can be used Locating or generating (e.g., via machinima, via stop-motion animation) video clips to splice together to create the video portion of the music video Understanding that there needs to be some logical connection between the song and the visual images – this doesn't mean a literal match, but that there's at least something being told that's 'understandable' Understanding how to sync video and audio and how to fine-tune this using digital video editing software Understanding that the meaning of songs operates on a number of levels, and how this can be leveraged within a video in terms of dominant colours used, the pacing of action within or across clips, etc.	• AnimeMusicVideos.org (see, for example, *Konoha Memory Book*, *Narutrix, Euphoria*) • Search YouTube.com for 'machinima music video' or for *Still Seeing Breen*) • The Grey Video (by Laurent Fauchere and Antoine Tinguely to support Danger Mouse's 'Encore' song from his *Grey Album* music remix)

Creating fanfiction			
	Expressing a fan identity	Understanding the structure and purpose of narratives and using this to guide writing	• FanFiction.net
	Expressing enjoyment of a book, series, movie, etc.	Paying attention to the source narratives and characters	• Thequidditchpitch.org
	Expressing or developing a writer's identity	Crafting an engaging plotline that remains 'believable' despite the new twists given to characters and extant storylines	• Patronuscharm.net
	To become a proficient fiction writer	May include writing contextualizing notes to known and unknown readers about the story	• Fanfiction.mugglenet.com
	To maintain social relationships with friends and others	May include understanding how chapters 'work' in fanfiction writing and making use of them	• Harrypotterfanfiction.com
	Promoting the fan space	May include knowing how to post narratives online – which includes deciding on the best forum, and how to categorize one's story within the forum	• Trekfanfiction.net
		May include writing reviews and providing feedback on others' narratives	• Fanfiction.wikia.com
		Using good grammar and spelling; or using bad grammar and bad spelling for developing characters, etc.	• Halo.bungie.org/fanfic
		Responding to feedback either in 'author notes' (see Black 2009) or by incorporating feedback into revisions	• Theforce.net/fanfiction
			• Starwars.wikia.com/wiki/Fan_fiction
			• Twilighted.net
			• http://www.free-ebooks.net/?category=Fan+Fiction (examples)
			• Fictionalley.org
			• Wikihow.com/Write-a-Fanfiction
			• Halcyon-shift.net/gift-shop/squeebook
			• Expressions.populli.net/dictionary.html

(continued)

Appendix (continued)

Kinds of remixes	Kinds of involvement	Some literacy dimensions	Some online spaces, sites, and examples
		Signalling one's knowledge of the universe of the original stories drawn on in the fanfiction (e.g., demonstrating you are a fan of the *Harry Potter* books and movies, and are closely familiar with all the characters and storylines)	• Fanfiction.net/s/5294551/1/A_TenStep_Guide_to_Writing_Twilight_Fan_Fiction • Booksie.com/editorial_and_opinion/article/pocketxfullxofxdreams/a-writers-guide:-writing-ocs-and-original-characters-in-fanfiction
Photoshopping	Humorous purposes – to make others laugh, or simply to entertain oneself or close friends	Knowing how to import an image into an image editor	• KnowYourMeme.com
	Expressing an artistic identity	Understanding how to use a range of tools within the image editing software to crop, blur, smudge, erase, colour match, etc.	• Worth1000.com
	Expressing a photography-related identity	Being able to match camera angle, colours and resolution, etc. when adding cropped photographic elements to a base image	• Fark.com/contests
	Participating in a competition (e.g., Worth1000.com)	May include knowing how to upload final photoshopped photos to an online space	• Somethingawful.com/d/photoshop-phriday
	Participating in a meme (e.g., Lostfrog.org)	Understanding how to create a recognizably meaningful juxtaposition of images	• Propagandaremix.com
	Social commentary purposes, or to make political points	Contributing guides and how-tos via You Tube.com, dedicated forums, etc.	• Adbusters.org • Photoshopfacelift.com • Photochopz.com • PSdisasters.com • Photoshopdisasters.com

Creating fan art	Expressing an identity as an artist	Being able to draw/paint, etc.	• TheOtaku.com/fanart
	Expressing a fan identity	Understanding how perspective, shadows and shading, etc. work in 2D drawings	• Artisticalley.org
	Developing drawing/artistic skills	Knowing that simply tracing images is not valued as fan art	• Fanart.lionking.org
		Developing a personal 'style' that is nonetheless in keeping with the original texts/images	• Blizzard Entertainment fan art (us.blizzard.com/en-us/community/fanart/index.html)
		Knowing how far to modify/tweak/remix original images while having them remain recognizable	• Search DeviantArt.com for 'anime' or 'manga'
		May involve asking for or sharing drawing tips with others in forums (e.g., how to draw shine on hair)	
		May include constructively reviewing others' fan art	
		May include responding to and incorporating feedback from others into one's own artwork	
		May involve knowing how to draw using a digital tablet and stylus	
		May include knowing how to scan an image for uploading to an online space	

(continued)

Appendix *(continued)*

Kinds of remixes	Kinds of involvement	Some literacy dimensions	Some online spaces, sites, and examples
Political remix (video, images, etc.)	Expressing a political or social commentary or critique	Requires being up to date with current news events, or familiar with significant social issues	• Knowyourmeme.com • Politicalremixvideo.com
	Expressing a journalistic identity	Having something to say that appeals to others	• Feministfrequency.com/2010/08/ remixing-pop-culture-event- videos/
		Identifying how to convey a lot of meaning in a limited amount of space or time	• Rebelliouspixels.com
		Knowing how to edit digital video or photo- shop or create audio tracks	• Video24-7.org/video/political_ remix.html
		Being skilful with juxtaposition – of images, text and images, soundtrack and video clips, voicetrack and video clips, etc.	• Youtube.com/view_play_ list?p=D52BD242C8855525; see also: Horwatt (2010). A Taxonomy of Digital Video Remixing @Www.scope. nottingham.ac.uk /cultborr/ chapter.php?id=8
		Knowing how to tap into spaces where the remix is likely to attract widespread atten- tion	
		Perhaps understanding how to anonymize the origin of the upload of the political remix	

Remixing music	Expressing being a fan of particular songs/musicians or of a particular TV show or movie's soundtrack	Identifying music, songs, or samples that can be remixed to form a coherent new song or music track	*The Grey Album* (DJ Danger Mouse), which remixes Jay-Z's *Black Album* and the Beatles' *White Album*
		Paying attention to rhythm and music genres	Bed Intruder Song by Autotune the News
	Exploring new music creation possibilities without necessarily being a singer or musician	Understanding the importance of seamless transitions between music samples	*Doctor Who* theme song remixes at whomix.trilete.net
		Knowing how multiple tracks work within a remixed music project when using music editing software	*Harry Potter* movie soundtrack remixes
	Remixing original lyrics as a response to a popular song for personal or friends' entertainment purposes. May celebrate the original song, or may be a social commentary on the song itself	Identifying a receptive online space for sharing remix with others	Overclocked Remix (remixed video game soundtracks; Ocremix.org)
		Knowing how to use audio editing software to splice together different music elements into a cohesive whole	ccMixter.org
			Remixfight.org
		May include writing new lyrics or generating voice-overs for certain sections of the remix	See live remixes by popular DJs like: Armin van Buuren, DJ Rap, Lisa Lashes, Tiësto, David Guetta
	Remixing news and other events as songs	May include a public performance dimension	The album, *The Score* (The Fugees), which remixes folk and rap music
	For commercial artistic or entertainment purposes	Identifying music, songs, or samples that can be remixed to form a new song or music track	The song, 'Tengo un Sentimiento' by Calor Norteño (remix of Black Eyed Peas' 'I Gotta Feeling,' and traditional narcocorrido themes and lyrics)
		May pay close attention to dance rhythms	
		Includes a public performance dimension	

(continued)

Kinds of remixes	Kinds of involvement	Some literacy dimensions	Some online spaces, sites, and examples
Mashing up web applications	To facilitate some activity, interest, or pursuit To inform others for personal or professional use To reuse/repurpose existing content for specific purposes May serve commercial purposes (e.g., selling items, encouraging consumption of a service, a single upfront user fee)	Involves knowing about APIs Knowing what databases to access and how (e.g., indexed, cartographic, aggregated) Knowing what existing service or database will mash up successfully with which other(s) Having access to how-to guides Sharing created services with others, and knowing how to do so Understanding the difference between desktop/webtop and apps-based mashups In some cases, be able to put together a user interface for the mashup (e.g., using HTML, CSS, Javascript) Have access to server space for hosting the mashup application, and knowing how to load it to the server and make it available to others	• Twittervision.com (combines Twitter with Google Maps) • Wikipediavision (combines Wikipedia's recent changes feed with Google Maps; lkozma.net/wpv/index.html) • Causeworld.com • Myfavbands.com • Google.com/enterprise/ marketplace • PandaApp.com • Programmableweb.com • Apigee.com • Openmashup.org
Cosplaying/ Live action role playing	To express a fan identity To express solidarity and friendship	Knowing the character being played very closely – including the larger storyline of the series or movie from which the character comes	• Cosplay.com • Cosspace.com • Acparadise.com

Enjoying developing ad-libbed narratives during cosplay		Designing a costume that recognizably 'belongs' to the character being played	• Search YouTube for 'cosplay' • Larpers.wordpress.com
		Coordinating with other people and their characters within a cosplay session	
		Knowing how to sew, fashion realistic-looking accessories (from cloth, wood, even metal, etc.), or knowing someone willing to do it for you	
		Accessing costume patterns, how-tos and ideas online	
		Knowing how to locate and purchase difficult to make items (e.g., wigs, shoes)	
		Being able to ad lib and enact a collaborative storyline during cosplay	
		May include attending conventions in character	
		May including blogging about costumes and cosplay sessions	
		May include establishing an active profile on a cosplay website and posting photos and videos of cosplay, along with commenting on others' posted items	
Modding video games	To express a fan identity	Understanding the logic of a game's system (how different objects typically work within the game, how characters interact, how the storyline plays out, etc.)	• *Counter Strike*, originally a mod of *Half Life*

(continued)

Appendix (continued)

Kinds of remixes	Kinds of involvement	Some literacy dimensions	Some online spaces, sites, and examples
	To extend the enjoyment of a game for self and others	Deciding whether to extend the original game in some way, or simply using the game as a resource to create an entirely new game	• Wikihow.com/Make-a-Simple-Mod-of-a-Game
	To hone skills as a video game developer	Likely to involve lots of trial and error and retrial, etc.	• Theprohack.com/2010/05/game-modding-tools-collection.html
		Paying attention to design, layout, what can and cannot be done within the terms of the original game to make the mod workable or user friendly, etc.	• Psx-scene.com/forums/ps3-game-modding/
		Using online tutorials and help spaces to assist with a mod	
		Using tool sets or level editors for modifying games (these often ship with PC games now)	
		May involve sharing tips and problem-solving advice on forums	
		Deciding to what degree to modify the game (e.g., adding a new weapon through to adding an entire new level or map to a game)	
		Can include identifying ways of sharing mods with others. This, in turn, includes finding space to host the mod for download, etc.	

CHAPTER 5

Blogs and wikis
Participatory and collaborative literacy practices

In this chapter we explore some typical examples of everyday practices involving blogs and wikis. We are especially interested in some of the different forms participation takes within these contexts, and in what it means to think of contributors *collaborating*.

Blogs and blogging

Background

Forerunners to blogging (or weblogging), as we have come to know it, began in the early 1990s, as websites listing annotated hyperlinks to other websites. When someone with a website found other sites they thought contained interesting, curious, hilarious, and/or generally newsworthy content, they would create a link to that material, annotate it briefly, and publish it on their website (see RebeccaBlood.com for a sense of what these first blogs looked like). Readers could decide on the basis of the description whether it was worth a click to check the link out. It was an early form of insider generosity: 'I've found this stuff that I think is interesting and you might like it too. Here is a brief description. If it sounds interesting just click here.'

These early 'bloggers' tended to be computing insiders, for at least two reasons. First, you needed access to internet server space and some knowledge of webpage and hyperlink markup language in order to be able to post material to the internet. Second, you needed a certain kind of cultural understanding of the web to see it as a place where you could actually publish information relatively painlessly, rather than just 'surfing' to see what you could find, or searching to try to locate specific kinds of information. Well-known early blogs of this original kind include *ScriptingNews* (Scripting.com), the no-longer-maintained *Camworld* (Camworld.org), and *Infosift* (Jjg.net/retired/infosift) (Blood 2002).

The diverse social practices collectively known to us now as blogging emerged from the late 1990s with the introduction of easy-to-use publishing tools and blog hosting services through Pitas.com and Blogger.com (owned initially by Pyra Labs). This made it relatively easy for internet users who were unfamiliar or uncomfortable with using hypertext markup language and the principles of web design, and/or with getting web hosting, to start blogging. Setting up a blog now simply involved going to a website, signing up for a blog account, following a few fairly straightforward instructions, and in less than 30 minutes one would have some 'copy' up on the web that was automatically formatted and laid out to the tune of your choice by means of whichever off-the-shelf template you had chosen. As websites, blogs had a different look and feel from traditional personal homepages, and they offered a built-in interactive dimension with readers through the 'comments' function – where readers could respond to a blog post – that was not available on conventional websites.

The quantum simplification of web publishing quickly spawned a new mass generation of bloggers. This new generation was much more diverse than the original blogging generation. Many began using weblogs as a medium more like regularly updated journals than indices of hyperlinks, and posts could document anything and everything from what the blogger had for lunch that day to movie, book, and music reviews, to descriptions of shopping trips, through to latest illustrations completed by the blogger for offline texts and all manner of draft texts made available for commenting upon; and the like. Technorati.com, a popular blog search service, was tracking around 30 million blogs in the first week of March 2006 (up from 2.7 million blogs in June 2004, and 24.2 million in December 2005). By the end of 2007, after which Technorati adopted a more qualitative approach to tracking, it was tracking 112 million blogs.

From the outset, blogging has been a dynamic phenomenon. The kinds of things bloggers want to do have stimulated and in turn been stimulated by developments in blogging tools. In addition, the kinds of things bloggers want to do, and how they want to do them, have been influenced by everyday events and changes in social practices in their wider lives – which they 'blog out of' – as well as by technological developments in bandwidth, mobile devices, networking applications, and the like. This dynamism persists. In its latest state of the blogosphere report, Technorati (November 2010) observes the extent to which the lines between blogging, microblogging (think: Twitter, Jaiku), and social networking are disappearing in conjunction with bloggers engaging increasingly with various social media sites and platforms. 'As the blogosphere converges with social media, sharing of blog posts is increasingly done through social networks – even while blogs remain significantly more influential on blog content than social networks are' (ibid.: n.p.). At the same time, mobile blogging is growing rapidly. Already, 25% of the respondents to Technorati's 2010 survey of bloggers engage in mobile blogging from devices like smartphones and tablets, and 40% of these say it has changed their blogging behaviour, 'encouraging shorter and more spontaneous posts' (ibid.). Clearly, such dynamism cautions against making definitive claims about blogs and blogging, and we will tread carefully here.

Blogs as medium and blogging as practices

In 'A blogger's blog: exploring the definition of a medium', dana boyd (2006) argues that discussion of blogs and blogging has largely focused on understanding and evaluating blogs by means of analysing blogger 'output' in 'content and structure terms' (ibid.: n.p.). This is because blogs have often been defined by tool developers, media, and researchers in these terms.

The *content* orientation to blogs and blogging reflects a tendency to see blogs as 'a genre of computer-mediated communication' (ibid.). From this standpoint, 'variations on styles are viewed as sub-genres', and sub-genres in turn are usually identified 'by drawing parallels to pre-existing genres of textual production such as diaries and journalism' (ibid.). *Structural* features include such aspects as: the logic of bloggers making posts that are sequenced in reverse chronological order; the comments feature; ease of hyperlinking; tools for collecting 'feeds' and for 'syndicating' a blog, and so on.

Using this framework, researchers have been able to tell us a lot about the textual qualities of blogs, their dissemination and reach – including mapping blog networks – regularity and persistence of blogs, popularity, and so on. At the same time, however, this kind of focus 'obfuscates the efficacy of the practice and the acts of the practitioners' (ibid.). Accordingly, and consistently with the approach we are taking in this book, boyd 'invites scholars to conceptualize blogging as a diverse set of practices that result in the production of diverse content on top of a medium that we call blogs' (ibid.). This involves seeing blogs as both a *medium* and *product* of practices.

By a medium of/for practice, boyd means in the sense of an extension of ourselves by and through which we can express ourselves: 'a medium is the channel through which people can communicate or extend their expressions to others' (ibid.). As a medium, says boyd, blogs are more like *paper* than they are like diaries or journals (genre/content). Just as we can use paper to 'write out of' any and all dimensions and facets of our lives, in all kinds of (generic) expressions and forms – lists, notes, instructions, theses, letters (to friends, family, editors, etc.), birthday wishes, condolences, recipes, inspirational thoughts, etc. – so blogs are 'a flexible medium, allowing all kinds of expression and constantly evolving' (ibid.).

In the terms we are using here, people take up or come to the medium of blogs as all kinds of people (Discourse memberships, affiliations), with all kinds of interests, affinities, and purposes, and varying kinds and degrees of knowledge and skills, and so on. They engage in a practice we can refer to generally as blogging, from the standpoint of the social practices, Discourses, roles, relationships, interests, etc., in their respective lives, and they 'blog out of' these. What and how they blog become their particular blogging practices (which may evolve over time). The fact that bloggers can be, and *are*, so different from one another on so many dimensions underpins the wisdom of understanding blogging as 'a diverse set of practices that result in the production of diverse content' (ibid.). To engage in *blogging* can simultaneously be to engage in some aspect of, say, being a parent, fan (of something or other), teacher (of one kind or another), gadget buff, activist or supporter of causes (of different kinds), an employee, corporate executive, advertiser, steam punker, sci-fi author, gardener, and so on.

To do this with a 'medium that we call blogs' means that bloggers use in different degrees and ways and combinations the various affordances of blogging tools and platforms. Depending on what kind of blogging work they want to do, the kind of audience they want to reach, the kind of image they want to project, their degree of computing proficiency, and so forth, they may prefer one blogging service to another; they may click on image posting icons a lot to upload photos to their blog, or rarely do so; they may disable the comments function (or leave it enabled), or set comments preferences so they can moderate comments or exclude anonymous comments; they may or may not embed home-grown or found videos into their blog post; they may or may not enable syndication of their blog so that new posts are collated by a blog 'feed reader' service; they may (or may not) include functions/applications that enable readers to 'like' a post to their Facebook page or 'tweet' it to Twitter, or 'digg' rate it. As discussed in the following section, blog reading practices vary according to whether readers comment or not, how they comment, whether they 'like' or 'tweet' a post, or re-post or link to their own blog (if they have one), and so on. Some readers manually visit particular blogs as part of their daily routines, while others might prefer to use 'feeds' that send new posts on a nominated blog directly to their feed readers or, alternatively, confine their blog content reading to what they access through their social networks. Other readers may 'surf' blogs somewhat randomly and follow leads and links as they go along or, alternatively, search out blog posts using a generic search engine like Google or a more specialized blog searching tool like Technorati.com.

Reflection and discussion

Identify a small range of blogs using a search engine like Technorati. com, Blogpulse.com or Blogsearch.google.com. Document examples of evidence for and against the view that blogs are more like paper than they are like diaries or journals (see boyd 2006).

Blogs and blogging from the standpoint of readers

The diversity inherent in blogs and blogging conceived as practice is greatly enlarged when we factor the diversity of blog readers and blog reader practices and perspectives into the equation. Eric Baumer, Mark Sueyoshi, and Bill Tomlinson (2008) begin their account of a small-scale ($n = 15$) qualitative study of 'ways' of blog reading by noting that 'most research on blogs focuses on either the blog itself or the blogger, rarely, if at all focusing on the reader's impact' (n.p.) – despite the interactive nature of blogs as a medium. Based on data collected from each participant by means of two semi-structured interviews, logging software, and a short survey, the authors document considerable diversity of blog reading practices within what is a relatively homogeneous study population, most of whom had been active blog readers (and most of them bloggers as well) for three to seven years. Most readers associated their blog reading with 'chilling', 'brain candy', 'doing nothing' and, even, 'wasting time', and described their blog reading as routinized, if not habitual – albeit in different ways. They read in varying degrees and ways for 'information', 'inspiration', 'entertainment' and 'because it's something they've always done'. Notwithstanding such broad similarities across respondents, the authors found very different responses to questions like 'what is a blog?' and 'what does it mean to be part of a blog?' Overall, they found many interesting variations among their subjects in their manners of reading and interacting with blogs, along such dimensions as 'the content of the blog, the intent of the reader, the perceived intent of the blogger, and the relationship of the reader to the blogger' (ibid.: n.p.).

In relation to the approach we take here, following boyd, of blogging as practice, Baumer and colleagues argue that their findings dispute the genre–content–structure approach. They claim:

> our findings align more closely with boyd's (2006) argument that blogs are a medium, and that a variety of different activities and interactions can occur in and through the medium. Furthermore, drawing on reader-response theory (Lewis 1992), we argue that in order to distinguish among different types of blogs it may be less useful to look at the structure or content of the blog and more informative to follow the ways that readers read and interact with the blog.
>
> (ibid.)

So, for example, some respondents felt that a good post deserves a reply, and commenting is a courtesy; others felt differently, believing that merely reading a blog is sufficient for participating. One respondent said she could only respond *positively*. She would not comment on a post if she could not do so positively, and would not respond contrarily to comments even if she disagreed with them. Some readers did not expect responses to their comments to 'big blogs', but did expect responses to comments made on friends' blogs. For some respondents, 'feeling connected' meant feeling connected to the blogger, and they appreciated experiences where the blogger–reader relationship felt like 1:1 rather than 1:Many. Others felt more connected in terms of content. Changes may occur over time, as when a reader initially relates to a blog because of its content, but subsequently begins relating to the blogger. Across all such differences, most respondents valued blogs/bloggers conveying a sense of 'authenticity' – e.g., in the sense of getting an inside glimpse of a blogger's life, and/or recognizing that posts are 'opinion' or 'personal narrative'.

Overall, Baumer and colleagues found that 'the activity of blogging, of which readers are an integral part, is far more heterogeneous and multifaceted than previously suggested' (2008: n.p.). Despite the relative homogeneity of their study population, they found that the ways in which

they read blogs, and even their definitions of what constitutes a blog, are dramatically different … [and that] rather than using structure or content-based features … to classify blogs, it may be more informative to consider them in terms of interactional features and readers' experiences.

(ibid.: n.p.)

Reflection and discussion

Identify one or more blogs where you would regard yourself as 'part of' or 'included in' what's being blogged about, or how it's being blogged about, etc. If you're new to the blog, spend some time reading through it in order to become familiar with the overall purpose or intent of the blog and to develop a sense of who the blogger 'is' within this particular blog. Consider the following:

- To what extent do you believe you can be part of a blog as 'just a reader'?

- If you can be 'just a reader', what is it about your practice of being a reader that makes you part of the blog?

- If being part of a blog requires more than simply 'being a reader', what is it about your overall interactive practice concerning the blog that makes you a part of it?

Blogging *Project Runway*: an evolving multiblogger blog

Multiblogger blogs – where more than one person is responsible for generating posts to a blog – throw interesting light on what it means to 'write' and 'read' a blog. There are many such blogs – including high-profile ones like BoingBoing.net (which has four regular bloggers and a revolving cast of invited guest bloggers), CrookedTimber.org (blogged by a large group of academics interested in world politics), and DailyKos.com (an open, left-oriented political blog that lets any user register as a poster to the blog), to name a few.

Blogging Project Runway (Bloggingprojectrunway.blogspot.com) is a multiblogger fan blog devoted to dissecting, commenting upon, and extending the enjoyment to be had from the long-running TV series *Project Runway* – a 'reality' television show that runs as a serialized competition focusing on fashion design. Each episode, contestants are given a design challenge, e.g., creating an outfit out of scrap paper, or for someone who has lost a lot of weight. Each week a winner is selected by a panel of judges based on how well the designers met that week's challenge – which typically accrues the winner some special bonuses (e.g., they can't be judged off in the next week's competition, they get first choice of resources in the next challenge). Likewise, each week, a contestant is 'voted out' of the competition by the judging panel – intensifying the competition amongst the remaining contenders – until a final winner is selected at the end of the season. The competition also includes up-and-coming models who wear the designers' clothes on the runway. Each week the model for that week's losing designer is eliminated along with the designer.

The designers are collectively mentored by Tim Gunn, who was Chair of Fashion Design at Parsons The New School for Design in New York City before joining an American fashion label in 2007 as its chief creative officer. The judging panel comprises a high-profile model (Heidi Klum), who also hosts the show, a well-regarded magazine editor (Nina Garcia) and a famous American designer (Michael Kors), along with a different guest judge each week (e.g., famous designers, celebrities, or people well known in a related fashion design field). The stakes are high. At the end of the most recent season, the winner received US$100,000 to help fund her own clothing line, 'an editorial feature in *Marie Claire* magazine, the opportunity to sell a fashion line on Piperlime.com, [and] a $50,000 technology suite from Hewlett-Packard' (Wikipedia 2010h: n.p.). The winning runway model received US$25,000 and featured in a full fashion spread in *Marie Claire* magazine. *Project Runway* first aired in December 2004, and had run for eight seasons by 2010.

According to Alexa.com, a website impact evaluation service, more than 300 other blogs were linking to *Blogging Project Runway* (*BPR*) in November 2010. The blog was popular in Greece, Japan, Canada, and the USA, having mustered around 14 million page views. Syndicated feed subscription services (e.g., Google.com/reader) indicate that over 1100 people have subscribed directly to automatic updates from this blog. *BPR* remains fiercely proud of its status as a 'fanblog'; the disclaimer at the bottom of the blog's front page reads:

Legal Mumbo Jumbo: This site is an unofficial Project Runway blog.

It is not owned or operated by Bravo, Lifetime,
Full Picture, Magical Elves, Bunim/Murray
Productions or The Weinstein Company.

And that's exactly how we like it.

Currently, a team of three regular writers – Laura K, TBone, and The Scarlett – generate or oversee content posted to the blog. *BPR* is hosted on Blogger. com and has a relatively straightforward interface. Text is white on a black background, and the format comprises three columns of content. The first column includes hyperlinks to the profiles of the blogging team, and links related to all contestants from all eight seasons, along with direct links to the websites and Facebook pages of the most recent season's contestants. The middle and largest column is where blog posts appear, and the third column lists links for contacting the *Blogging Project Runway* team, along with links to the blog's syndication feed and for joining the *BPR*'s emailing list. Two icons in this same column invite readers to join the blog's Twitter feed and Facebook page. A blurb encourages readers to visit the official site for *Project Runway*: 'Visit myLifetime.com for full episodes, Rate the Runway photos, blogs and more!' Beneath this is a list of additional websites and blogs related to the show, or to clothing design and the like. This column also includes a long list of site endorsements as a go-to place for fans of *Project Runway*. The blog hosts various ads that help generate revenue to support the blog.

Readers of the blog and self-professed fans of the show regularly submit material for posting, such as candid photos of themselves meeting up with key figures from the show (photos with the designers' mentor, Tim Gunn, are especially well received by other readers) or with current and past contestants; animated short films commenting on some aspect of a season, episode, or contestant; trailers for imagined movies about a particular contestant using clips from across a season; fan photoshops of key figures from the show; their own summaries and recaps of a given episode they've posted to their own personal blogs and to which *Blogging Project Runway* then links; information about seeing a contestant's clothes for sale in a shop somewhere; video summaries of an episode or fashion show they've edited themselves and submitted to the blog; news about local charity events featuring past contestants; newspaper and magazine articles about some aspect of the show; interesting tidbits they've dug up about the contestants, and so on. Readers comment regularly on posts and vote in polls run by the blog. Poll results can be read as an indicator of reader interest, and provide a sense of blog reader numbers. A recent poll asking who should really have won the (controversial) eighth season generated 7,700 votes.

This fan blog began inauspiciously. In early January 2005, a blogger named Laura K made a modest initial posting on a new blog called *Blogging Project Runway*. Under the post title 'I Miss Project Runway', Laura entered:

> Okay, this might be a bit obsessive but I miss Project Runway [season 1] and I want to be totally prepared for next season [airing December 7]. I intend to blog away after every episode and I hope others will join me with fascinating comments. In fact ... bring on the comments now if you'd like! I'd appreciate any help I can get. Please pass on any PR news or information – thanks.
>
> Also, I'd like to keep this Rated G for ALL audiences – I have five children who enjoy reading my blogs. Thanks for your consideration.
>
> *Posted by Laura K at 9:59 PM* 0 comments

Assuming the comments count in the archives is correct, during the first month of the blog's operation only two comments were posted (by Barb and Bathany). Both endorsed Laura's dislike of a particular contestant in the past season's line-up of competing designers. During the second month most of Laura K's posts received comments, mainly from Barb, the only person to make comments during August 2005. In September there was only one comment (anonymous) and one comment had been removed by the blog administrator. During September and October 2005 there were more posts – one of which prompted seven comments. Laura's posts focused on the up-coming new season and where auditions for the show were being held, along with updates on the first season's contestants. Barb was absent during these two months, but showed up again in November. She was house sitting and had access to Bravo TV – and the show – again. Laura K responded to some of the comments, expressing delight – 'How great. Another fan' – when one reader described *Project Runway* as her life. There were six posts that November, and a total of six comments. Two of these comments were in response to a post that contained a photo of one of the final three contestants – a somewhat controversial designer – from the previous season.

Reader comments increased dramatically in December 2005, when season two of *Project Runway* began. Mention of *Blogging Project Runway* on a widely read shoe blog (blogger Manolo's Shoeblogs.com) helped with drawing attention to the blog at this time, too. Laura K's posts were becoming more regular and more complex. Posts included extra details about each contestant, links to current contestants' blogs and MySpace profiles, and links to interviews with contestants conducted by magazines and high-profile websites were also posted. Laura K began using a high proportion of photographs in her posts as well. Posts were made on 19 days that month, which attracted around 140 comments in total.

By February 2006, The Scarlett and TBone had joined Laura K to form a blogging team. Both had been regular and entertaining commenters on the blog for some time previously. February's posts alone attracted 3,600 comments from readers. Then, as the season unfolded, TBone began to 'live blog' the show for those fans unable to watch it due to work or other commitments. This enabled fans – including those watching live – to follow along on the blog. Live blogging occurred within the comments section of the blog and readers were discouraged from commenting during shows to avoid interrupting the flow of TBone's updates. A separate weekly post was dedicated to readers as a space where they, too, could remark on the show, as well as on what they were doing while the episode was playing – e.g., playing drinking games using key phrases uttered during the show, hosting viewing parties. They regularly commented on the ads played during the show, too, and often made fun of these (not to mention the obvious product placements within the show itself). Typically, in what fast became more like a set of discussion threads or even a chat space than a series of comments on a blog post, different participants in the 'live' blog discussions proposed and discussed who would be that night's challenge winner and who would be voted off, and why; or discussed behaviour in the cutting and sewing rooms, the designers' material and design choices, their methods for approaching a task, and so on. While different commenters favoured different contestants, the feeling overall was that everyone was welcome and differences of opinion were given voice and often warmly debated. Spoiler alerts were attached to this set of particular blog events – TBone's live blogging and fans 'live' commenting – so that readers living in later time zones across the USA would not accidentally have the show spoiled by inadvertently reading about outcomes.

In June 2006, the blog migrated to a new format (blog post archives prior to this are no longer available on the blog). With growing popularity the blog began to include display ads to help support the blog financially. The blog now has a much more sophisticated interface that enables readers to access a plethora of information about all contestants in each season of the show since its inception, to follow links to current contestants' websites and Facebook profiles, to access photo collections of all past contestants' formal shows at New York Fashion Week (these are the contestants who made the final cut for the season – plus one decoy occasioned by the show's scheduling and the timing of Fashion Week), and to archived blog posts. Posts include a significant number of official videos hosted on the show's dedicated website, as well as videos from YouTube uploaded by fans and others. The blog also links to related fan blogs (based on a strong policy of a fan blog being well established and the blog owner also being an active participant on *Blogging Project Runway*). A new commenting system means that comments attached to a blog post can be nested in more 'threaded' ways (i.e., readers can respond to one another and have this response appear directly beneath the comment it pertains to), and reader comments can be 'liked' by clicking on the 'like' hyperlink beneath each comment. Anonymous readers can post comments, although all comments are moderated by the blogging team. An embedded 'live' multimedia chat feature was added to the blog in August 2009, in time for the start of Season 6.

A 'welcome note' to newcomers in June 2006, spelled out a number of the key terms and conditions entailed in participating in the blog:

> Welcome one and all to the BPR community. This is a fun place where we are not only avid fans of the show, but also are friendly toward one another. We have a very low tolerance for in-fighting amongst each other. Please do not use our comments as a venue to pick a fight or bully other commenters. We are all friends here.
>
> While we tend to have our favorites (ask Jan the Dan Fan!) we do not disparage or criticize any of the designers or personalities on the show. There are other sites where this is perfectly acceptable and we enjoy those sites very much, but we are trying to present something different here at BPR. This is a place where all of the designers are supported whether they are first 'auf' [Heidi Klum, the host, says 'auf Wiedersehen' to the contestant voted off the show each week] or Grand Prize Winners. Please be polite. No name-calling. Thank you.
>
> (June 2006 http://bloggingprojectrunway.
> blogspot.com/2006/06/welcome-newbies.html)

Other guidelines for participating include a ban on posting links in comments (following problems with spammers in the comments section). Commenters were advised not to post gossip, innuendo, or downright slander about contestants in their comments. Profanity is banned – the blog presents itself as 'family-friendly' and open to a wide range of readers. Readers are explicitly encouraged to submit materials for the blog to the blogging team, while keeping in mind that *BPR* does have a particular orientation and 'point of view' (ibid.) and not everything will be posted. Commenters are also advised to stay on topic: posts featuring kind words directed to a particular contestant (e.g., one voted off that week), shouldn't be hijacked by unsupportive comments or comments mainly about a different contestant.

The social universe of *Blogging Project Runway* participants and participation is rich, complex, and interesting. The blog has many people beyond the formal blogging team actively contributing to it. During Season 8 (14 episodes), the most recent at time of writing, 392 posts were made and 5261 comments posted. There were also 14 live chat sessions, each lasting around 1.5 hours.

One post – a recap of the final episode of Season 8 – attracted 1575 comments (see: http://bloggingprojectrunway.blogspot.com/2010/10/reactions-to-season-8-finale.html). Commenters on the whole felt 'cheated' by the final decision by the show's two principal judges, which sparked an outpouring of written responses posted to the blog. Many of these comments responded directly to comments left by other readers. Readers' comments across this particular set tend to be more than a single sentence, and include reasons for their dismay with the outcome of this season. Readers clearly felt 'at home' openly sharing their disappointment with (and critiques of) Season 8 overall, and the final outcome in particular. This comment set shows the extent of diverging viewpoints, and that these are responded to thoughtfully, or with requests for elaboration. Critiques include commentaries on fashion, clothing design, wearability, innovation, and fair treatment. As just one example among hundreds, 'Deb in CA' writes:

Deb in CA

It is time for Michael Kors and Nina Garcia [judges for all 8 seasons] to go. Mondo [a Season 8 contestant] so clearly should have won. He created work that was fresh, original and high fashion. Gretchen [the Season 8 contestant who won] is commercial, perhaps wearable, but mundane. Her palette was so dreary and fabric so repetitive. It makes me think that it was the influence of the advertisers wanting more commercial designers. I can't believe Heidi [host and judge] didn't have more tie breaking clout (or Tim [mentor to the contestants]).

I thought the concept of the show was to discover truly original talent. It felt like both Nina and Michael were being vindictive because Mondo followed his own impulses instead of slavishly conforming to their snide comments.

Now reading this blog I find it telling that the embarrassing dress that was so horribly unflattering on Jessica [Simpson, celebrity judge for the finale episode] was a Kors design. I can never stand his stuff I see in stores.

I predict that like many runners-up on American Idol [a show similar in concept but that focuses on singers], Mondo will have the true career. I would wear his dresses in a heartbeat.

11/03/2010, 04:29:08 – Like – Reply

Comments in this same set also critique and discuss changes made to the format of the show in this particular season, along with the 'production' and editing of the show overall. In the following example the indented comments are replying directly to Legoean's 'parent' comment.

Legoean

Many of you are saying that your favorite designer is 'out'.....so...... make the show fire its [judges] who didn't decide the way you wanted them to? How does that make sense. If nothing else EVERYONE will be watching the next 'Project Runway' to see what all this fuss is about. Don't you see how the show will be even more watched now. Think about it. I will always watch Project Runway. Art is something that produces 'emotion' in the viewer. This program has just entered the level of 'great' programs.

10/31/2010, 08:53:21 – Like – Reply   Liked by Guest

Becky

Yep, you are probably right. The show was suffering from its move to Lifetime (which can't even be found in HD, BTW). Project Runway's sponsor/viewer problems weren't a secret so how better to get more attention than stir up some major controversy to get all this PR for PR [Project Runway]? We're just fueling it. Big Time. Falling right into their game plan. Offer Gretchen the "win" to be the fall guy and play it out to the end for a major payoff. Easily worth $100,000 to PR to improve ratings for next season.

10/31/2010, 11:56:03 – Like – Reply   Liked by SunnyV

Guest

hmm - I don't know. The extended program time showed too much of the judges. We know Kors and Garcia too well now. We can see right through them. Their contradictions, their fickle decisions, their self absorption, their cruelty. I think we're just sick of these people. Does anybody outside the PR circle know about any controversy? Doesn't an enticing controversy need publicity and a strong argument for both sides? I haven't heard a strong argument for Kors and Nina. Is the controversy 91% of the PR fans agree the judges are incompetent? Will this controversy draw enough new viewers to replace the fans they lost? Will it draw any viewers? If this was a scheme to create controversy, it's bu[ll]sh** they bit the hand that feeds them. If it's not a scheme, if they really thought Gretchen was better, they're bu[ll]sh** and we're all justified to not watch any more. Either way, I'm done with this show.

10/31/2010, 16:42:00 – Like – Reply

Guest

Maybe Not!! If I wanted to see no talent drama I could watch Housewife's of 'insert city.' PR fans want to see talent... something special – like Mondo, Seth, or Christian. There is no shortage of crappy, cheap, no talent drama. PR fans have come to expect better.

10/31/2010, 20:07:22 – Like – Reply

These two examples suggest that readers feel that what they have to say is worth posting, and that in saying it – even if it does go against the tide of most comments – they will have the chance to spark some interesting dialogue and maybe find people who see things as they do. Interestingly, for the first time in the history of *BPR*, Laura K summarized readers' complaints in an letter to the producers of *Project Runway* (and which she also posted to the blog), advising how to improve their approach to and delivery of the next season of the show (see: http://bloggingprojectrunway.blogspot.com/2010/11/dear-lifetime.html). Because *Blogging Project Runway* has a relationship with the show – it is granted permission to re-post content, the blogging team is sent press releases, etc. – there is a genuine chance this letter will be read by the show's producers. Readers appear to take this possibility seriously, and continue to add suggestions to the blog as to how next season's show could be improved.

Across the life of Season 8, posts to *Blogging Project Runway* included: readers indicating who would be hosting a Season 8 premiere viewing party in their home, and inviting others nearby to get in touch; readers' 'field reports' from related events they attended (e.g., local charity fashion event featuring designers from past seasons); links to recaps of that week's episode on up to 15 other blogs (with this particular post always titled 'Recapalooza'); regular 'From the Mailbox' updates based on material submitted to the blogging team by readers, contestants, and other figures relevant to the show; reader-submitted links to magazine interviews with key figures from the series; photos of attendees at the premiere party for the season hosted by the Lifetime channel; podcast phone interviews with contestants and key figures from the show – including interview questions submitted by readers; posts inviting readers to vote in a range of polls; posts setting up trivia quizzes or mini-challenges for readers to solve; and links to fans' blog posts commenting on the show; various kinds of contests – including using contestants' names in a poem about them, or analysing some dimension of the show (e.g., Reader-Blogger KCortez's post on her own blog about contestant Mondo Guerra's outfits each week; see, for example: http://passmederemote.blogspot.com/2010/09/what-mondo-wore.html). Readers are referred to by a number of 'insider' terms, including 'BPRers' or 'Beepers'.

During the season, *Project Runway*'s official website (MyLifetime.com/ projectrunway) ran a sequence of video blogs made by Tim Gunn that included behind-the-scenes insights, stories, and Tim's commentary on the judging process. Dedicated fans spent hours transcribing these and sending transcriptions to *Blogging Project Runway* to post, so that others who had trouble accessing the vlog could read what Tim had to say. Readers also submitted transcripts of *BPR*'s interview podcasts with contestants. Furthermore, during Season 8 contestants-as-readers (models and designers alike) also sent emails – published with their permission – to the blog. These typically responded to questions asked by the blogging team, brought readers up to date with what the contestant was doing after appearing in the show, or were used to let the bloggers and readers know about events featuring their designs or media appearances, and the like.

Any full-fledged cultural practice account of *Blogging Project Runway* would involve a massive ethnographic undertaking. Sampling reader practices and perspectives along the lines recommended by Baumer and colleagues would, on its own, support many studies. Nonetheless, from the kind of new literacies as social practice standpoint taken here, it is possible to map some significant aspects of this blog as a bounded instance of blogging practice.

It is clear that *Blogging Project Runway* is no single blogging practice. It has evolved massively over time: from a static, post facto, monomodal medium to a multi-temporal, multimodal medium which, during seasons, functions as a real-time mediator of the TV show – but still with the original purpose of enriching fans' experience of the show. Blogger subjectivities and practices have likewise evolved. Laura K, for example, has run the full gamut of blogging experience, from relative novice to sophisticated expert, and has taken on new roles – e.g., as a kind of journalist, as a complaint mediator between fans and the show's producers. The blog's reader 'rights' and contributions have evolved – from commenters-only, in the early days, to potential providers of diverse content in multiple media. Readers participate out of different positions and Discourse memberships: as fans of particular contestants; as critics enacting their personal versions of an appreciative system for fashion design; as providers of fan services, such as when they provide transcripts of video or podcast material; as fashion followers; as many kinds of 'life-stylers', and so on. The blog currently deploys and supports a diverse range of specific literacy practices – currently ranging from 'polling' to movie trailer remixing – which are constantly evolving. Moreover, commenting practice on *BPR* emerges as complex, such as on occasions during the seasons of the show when 'commenting' seems to function more like real-time chat and/or conversations, as well as more conventional comments. Indeed, live blogging within the blog has 'messed' considerably with a default understanding of 'commenting'.

Reflection and discussion

Identify two or more blogs that attract large numbers of comments on a regular basis (Webbyawards.com is a good place to start looking if need be). In light of these, discuss the claim that commenting is not a single practice but, rather, can take many different forms.

Using these same blogs, discuss the view that posting to a blog is not a single practice, but, rather, can take many different forms.

Wikis

A wiki is a collection of webpages whose content is typically organized around a particular purpose, topic, or theme. Content can be collaboratively written, added to, deleted, or modified by users. Wikis are not like static webpages whose content is controlled by a website owner or webmaster. They are more like a shared, online writing space supporting embedded links to other pages internal or external to the wiki. Along with text and hyperlinks, wiki pages may include embedded image, audio, and video files. Many wikis also have built-in discussion space for each page, where users can discuss content and presentation. Because wikis are fully searchable they are ideal go-to spaces for accessing useful and current resources. The 'linkable' qualities of a wiki also mean it can easily become a portal of sorts for special-interest groups, drawing together online materials and useful resources into one easily accessed and easily navigated space.

The best-known example of a wiki is, of course, the massively collaborative online encyclopedia Wikipedia.org, identified by Will Richardson (2010: 55) as the most important site on the web. On Wikipedia, registered users are free to create new entries, edit existing entries, add or update information as things change over time, and flag entries for deletion (e.g., because they are more like product advertisements than 'information'). Beyond Wikipedia, wikis are widely used to support fans' shared knowledge of their common interest and to extend the pleasure of fan practices and everyday interests and routines. The elaborate wiki created by fans of the now-defunct television series *Lost* lives on, and contains character biographies, plot summaries, location details, and discussions of the series and the wiki content itself (see: Lostpedia.com). Similarly, there are countless wikis supporting video and massively multiplayer games. They contain information about solving particular quests or completing particular tasks, detailed descriptions of player characters and non-player characters, procedures for smithing items in-game, game play hints and tips, and the like (see, for example, Wowwiki.com and Nwn.wikia.com). A quick search of Wikia.com reveals wikis at various stages and levels of development under categories like 'Lifestyle', 'Gaming', and 'Entertainment', dedicated to such varying interests as coffee, vintage sewing machines, knitting, cocktails, rest stops and service plazas for travellers, firefighting, Scrabble, motorcycles, the television sitcom *Two and a Half Men*, iPods, android phones, baseball, and much, much more. A further indication of the current reach and scale of wikis is provided by a popular wiki service, Wikispaces.com, which was claiming around 6 million members and 2.75 million wikis in November 2010.

As a number of authors (e.g., Bruns 2008; Davies and Merchant 2009; Knobel and Lankshear 2009; Richardson 2010) have noted, wikis have great potential within education for promoting online and offline collaboration among educators and students within and across classrooms and institutions, as well as for disseminating research and practical resources in accessible ways. Wikis likewise have considerable potential as a professional development medium for educators, as tools, resource hosts, and shared interest spaces. Setting up and contributing to a wiki is not as straightforward as setting up and posting to a blog. However, a range of user-friendly services like Wikispaces.com and the development of What You See Is What You Get (WYSIWYG) editors – where what you see on the screen is very close to the final product, rather than containing lots of html code – mean that wiki use is becoming increasingly common within formal school and higher education learning in countries with efficient computer networking infrastructure (see, for example, Honegger 2005; Beach 2006; Wheeler and Wheeler 2009; Richardson 2010).

Outside of locating entries on Wikipedia for rapid information purposes, wikis remain less commonly subscribed to and are less familiar to readers at large than are blogs, and are more complex – partly on account of their intensely collaborative purpose. Perhaps the easiest way for anyone unfamiliar with wikis to get a rapid initiation is to go to the Wikipedia entry on 'wiki' (at http://en.wikipedia.org/wiki/Wiki) and quickly skim the content of the entry to get an initial sense of its look and feel. Then explore the tabs across the top of the page. There will be three tabs across the top for anyone who does not have a Wikipedia account: 'Discussion', 'View Source' and 'History'. Once someone has registered with Wikipedia they will see additional tabs on each Wikipedia page they visit: namely, 'Edit this page', 'Move' and 'Watch'. Once one has registered with Wikipedia, one has the right to create new entries and/or edit existing ones, as well as to move content to some other location within Wikipedia, and to be kept informed (Watch) whenever a page that one is watching is edited.

Clicking on the History tab leads to a record of all the editing changes that have been made to that entry, including information about the time and date an edit was made and who made it. Clicking on the 'View source' tab provides a sample of some typical 'source code', which shows the kind of 'writing' to be negotiated when someone wants to edit an entry. The actual Wikipedia entry on 'Wiki' contains some information about wiki code compared to standard hypertext markup language, and different wiki services employ different coding protocols; so collaborating on a wiki involves getting up to speed with the relevant coding protocol (Wikipedia's protocols can be found here: en.wikipedia.org/wiki/Help:Contents/Editing_ Wikipedia). Clicking on the Discussion tab leads to discussion lying behind many of the changes that contributors have made to that particular page/ entry. It mentions the kinds of reasons and considerations that contributors have taken into account and regard as important in order to make the entry the best it can be.

This simple procedure reveals – at least superficially – the heart of the collaborative potential of wikis, as well as illustrating many of the features most commonly associated with wikis. That is, the fact that one can go to the URL and read information about 'Wiki' is a consequence of the further fact that many (in this case) English-speaking people all over the world have registered with Wikipedia, mastered the coding protocols, edited the page by making substantive or minor changes, discussed with their immediate 'community' – the other collaborators contributing to developing an evolving 'Wiki' entry with a view to making it the best it can be – the things they believe important for the entry, and continued to keep up with the state of the entry and the state of available information elsewhere about 'Wiki', updating and otherwise improving the entry as best they can. We can speak of collaboration here because multiple people come together around a common interest – making the best 'Wiki' entry they collectively can make – and interact with one another, sharing information and reasons and considerations, in pursuit of their shared, common interest. Moreover, they do this not simply for their own satisfaction but also in order to make the best resource possible available to people at large. Their contributions are part of what Lessig (2008) describes as 'the sharing economy', which exists alongside 'the commercial economy'.

More generally, the procedure provides an initial understanding of features commonly associated with what wikis are. Julia Davies and Guy Merchant (2009: 97–8) provide one such list, as follows:

- The text can be edited by anyone who is registered on the site.
- Individuals who set up the site can set out specific rubrics, guidelines and community values for others to follow.
- Authorship is shared and distributed.
- Editing discussions and histories can be archived and consulted.
- Openness is valued.
- Collaboration is valued and individualism is less valued.
- Wikis are in a constant state of flux.
- Text can easily incorporate links to other sites, to entries on its own site and to profiles of contributors.
- Referencing is highly valued.
- Incorporation of text and items from other sources is endorsed – as long as legally adopted and sources are cited.

While not every wiki will have all of these features, most wikis will exhibit the majority of them in varying ways and to different degrees.

With Wikipedia as the paradigm example, wikis have been researched and discussed from many angles and in relation to various contexts of use. Frequently cited studies address use of wikis within corporate/private enterprises, public-sector organizations, not-for-profit organizations and networks, and learning institutions (including libraries), among others. Within such settings, studies have addressed the use of wikis by health and clinical practitioners, language professionals, research groups and collaborative knowledge-building communities, decision- and policymakers, etc.

The annual Wikisym conference for wiki-oriented researchers invites submissions under such categories as 'Learning and social context', 'Quality and credibility', 'Visualization', 'Understanding Wikipedia', 'Interface tools', and 'Programming and analysis tools'. A quick search on Amazon reveals a mass of books providing guides to using wikis, uses of wikis, wiki programming, leveraging collective knowledge to enhance business performance, and ways to get children excited about learning. Much of the literature has a 'how to' and 'tips for' approach, as well as addressing accounts of issues and problems associated with using wikis, and how to overcome them.

Relative to our focus here, two points stand out from a survey of this burgeoning literature. First, across the variety of topics and themes in the overall academic literature on wikis, the association between the use of wikis as a tool or medium and the idea of users being involved in collaboration of one kind or another – or, participation in collaborative endeavours – is almost universal. Indeed, wikis are widely identified as *collaborative software*. Unfortunately, references to collaboration are often longer on rhetoric and impression than they are on providing empirical detail and developing analytic descriptions and categories of collaboration. It is common for 'collaboration' to mean little more than the idea of people working together in some context. Very often it is difficult to see how participants working on the same wiki are collaborating as distinct, say, from contributing, co-operating or, more simply, just working 'additively'. Apart from a general adherence to the broad, shared 'community rules' assigned to a wiki, it is often even difficult to see how the collective involvement constitutes a community beyond the vague sense in which, say, Toronto may be referred to as a community. Yet, if we are wanting to understand wikis in terms of new literacies, it is crucial that we get a good sense of how roles and relationships, and intersecting knowledges and understandings and Discourse affiliations, and skills, etc., come together to *carry* a practice (as a kind of *system* of activity – that can in a reasonably clear sense be understood as *shared*; as constituting a 'moment' of culture in which people are, indeed, bound together as collective cultural producers and members. *Collaborators* provide a particular kind of 'glue' and perform distinctive kinds of mediating roles within the development and maintenance of a practice, that is qualitatively different from, say, 'contributors' and other 'participants' – although collaborators certainly *do* contribute and participate.

An especially illuminating antidote to self-evident and impressionistic attributions of collaboration is provided by Susan Bryant, Andrea Forte, and Amy Bruckman (2005) in 'Becoming Wikipedian: transformation of participation in a collaborative online encyclopedia'. The authors recruited a small study population whose experience spanned the range from relative novice or newcomer (a few months of involvement) to full-fledged 'Wikipedians' (some of whom had been active from Wikipedia's early days). They informed their study theoretically and conceptually by reference to work on apprenticeship into communities of practice and evolution of participation within activity systems (from activity theory). From the former they looked at participation in Wikipedia in terms of moving from being a novice engaged in 'legitimate peripheral participation' toward becoming 'full participants'. From the standpoint of viewing Wikipedia as a socio-technical activity system, they looked at how subjects (participants) engaged with and understood and interacted differently with the tools, the rules of participation, and other participants, and how they took on different roles and tasks within an overall division of labour, as their perception of the 'object' – the overall objective, purpose, or mission of Wikipedia – evolved.

So, for example, they found that their novice participants began interacting with Wikipedia as *consumers*, who went there in search of information and found errors and omissions that they could edit. As consumers interested in better-quality information that could contribute toward serving that interest, they edited what they knew. Gradually, as they spent more time in the 'space' they moved from becoming occasional editors of individual entries to becoming *'caretakers'* of collections of entries/articles (by becoming 'watchers'). This, of course, involves a transformation of tool use (e.g., the 'watch' function), and changes in tasks and roles within the activity system. This eventually morphed into a growing sense of the community as a whole – as a system – and of commitment to it along lines that involved ways of doing and being in the light of the functioning of the system as a whole. At this point they truly understand the Wikipedia community as a *community* and, indeed, as a (community of) practice. Their growing commitment to this community-system means that they can now take on roles and tasks and tool use and modes of interaction that are informed by a 'systems' perspective – like a bird's-eye view of the 'project'. At this point they become *collaborators* in a very strong sense of the word – the full sense of the word – because they understand parts in relation to a whole, and know how to integrate their activity with the activity of others and, moreover, how to play an integrative or coordinating role in relation to the activity of others. There is, then, an important sense in which the capacity to *collaborate* presupposes an overall conception of a community of practice such that one can act and respond in the light of a system as a whole – or, at least, from a larger perspective than simply contributing 'pieces'. Bryant and colleagues (2005) document aspects of this transformation as seen through the eyes of insiders, and it illuminates the 'new ethos stuff' of engaging in a new literacy in a distinctive way. It sharpens our qualitative understanding of involvement/participation, bespeaking a continuum of transformation in involvements within spaces of participatory cultures:

> We see concrete examples of how participation is transformed in an online collaborative project. As their participation becomes more central and frequent, participants in Wikipedia adopt new goals, new roles, and use different tools although they are doing so in the same 'place.' Their perceptions of Wikipedia change. They identify the site, not as a random collection of articles, but as a community of co-authors who play distinct roles and have distinct talents as they build a resource. They move from a local focus on individual articles to a concern for the quality of the Wikipedia content as a whole and the health of the community. As Wikipedia users move from legitimate peripheral participation to full community involvement, the activities and structures that mediate them necessarily become more complex.
>
> (Bryant et al. 2005: 9)

The second point of interest here to emerge from a survey of the literature on wikis builds on the first and runs parallel to the case of blogs. It is that many studies privilege content and structural aspects of wikis, and relatively few focus in any depth and intricacy on the cultural richness and diversity of wiki-mediated social practices, and on the respective orientations of readers, writers, and reader-writers.

Some interesting clues for how practice-focused investigation might proceed are provided by a recent study by Iassen Halatchliyski, Joachim Kimmerle, Johannes Moskaliuk, and Ulrich Cress (2010) on who integrates the networks of knowledge in the German-language Wikipedia. This is a hypothesis-driven, statistics-based quantitative study of a corpus of articles/ entries. Consequently, it does not address practice in depth. Rather, it points to a very interesting form of reading and writing practice within contexts of building knowledge in wiki spaces, in a way that nicely complements our discussion of Wikipedians as collaborators, and indicates a potentially fruitful focus for in-depth qualitative investigation.

Halatchliyski and colleagues approach wikis as a medium for social practices of knowledge building in the sense of communities of people successfully creating new knowledge. They identify three dimensions of wikis as a medium for knowledge building:

- A *content* dimension comprising the content of the wiki as an 'epistemic artifact' and 'basis for further elaboration and extension of knowledge' (Halatchliyski et al. 2010: n.p.).
- A *discursive* dimension, whereby the wiki platform is seen as 'scaffolding' communication and guiding discourse, such that 'different opinions, disagreements, and conflicts become salient in the wiki text' (ibid.).
- A *network* dimension consisting in the affordances of wikis to 'encourage the integration of different aspects, contradictory statements, and the merging of theories at the level of the whole network' (ibid.). Links within the wiki enable readers/contributors to follow connections in ways that help direct or guide knowledge building.

The authors focus on the network dimension of knowledge building. Analysis of this dimension of wiki-mediated knowledge building involves a macro perspective that addresses the question of how 'different opinions – often resulting from different sub-communities – are brought together in a shared understanding of a broader topic or domain' (ibid.). This pertains to what Halatchliyski and colleagues call 'emergent knowledge'. If we think of wiki-mediated knowledge building in terms of concepts like 'collective intelligence' or 'the wisdom of crowds', they say, the network dimension of wikis is fundamental to the *emergence* of knowledge. Emergent knowledge is produced at 'the level of the community' and is 'more than the sum of the knowledge of all the individuals' in the community. The main goal of knowledge-building practices is to create knowledge that was not necessarily part of the individuals' knowledge before, 'but arises during collaboration' (ibid.). And it arises during collaboration with the assistance of a very distinctive kind of contribution to the wiki, which the authors identify as 'integrative articles' produced by 'boundary spanners'.

For present purposes, the relevant aspect of Halatchliyski and colleagues' work is that they looked at knowledge building in De.wikipedia.org in relation to the two fields of physiology and pharmacology, and the intersection between these fields. From a mid-2009 corpus of almost 5000 articles within and across the two fields, they differentiated initially between authors who contributed (to) articles within one or other field only and authors who contributed (to) articles in both fields – the 'boundary spanners'. They then distinguished between those boundary spanners who contributed (to) 'integrative' or 'intersection' articles and those who did not. They formulated hypotheses related to each category of author, but were especially interested in the authors of 'integrative' and 'intersecting' articles.

Taking Halatchliyski and colleagues' category of integrative/intersecting article authors, we can say that they engage in a particular kind of (new) literacy practice within a larger social practice of knowledge-building in relation to physiology and pharmacology. Within the *collaborative* practices that generate *emergent* knowledge from 'collective intelligence' and 'the wisdom of crowds' – such as new kinds of merged theory and ways of resolving contradictions and apparent incompatibilities – this sub-category of boundary spanners act as a kind of catalyst and a kind of collaborative 'glue'. They make particular kinds of meanings out of the collective corpus of 'intelligence' and advance these for negotiation and subsequent development by others (and themselves).

It is important to make our purpose and meaning absolutely clear here. We do not want to be read as saying that this kind of role and literacy practice within knowledge-building practices is most important, or the most valuable, or the kind researchers in this area should be most interested in. Rather, we are saying that this is one kind of role and practice that could be taken up within fine-grained investigations of *collaborative* practices in wikis. There are all kinds of other options, but this is a reasonably clear example of what a useful option might look like. It helps us understand better the nature and logic of collaboration within knowledge building. It constitutes a particular kind of participation. For educators, of course, it calls attention to a kind of participation well worth keeping in mind if we want our uses of wikis to go beyond 'classroom business as usual' and to issue in full fruits of collaboration: in a meaningful sense of generating 'wholes' that are greater than the sum of their parts. This is an *epistemological* role that will have high status in a bona fide knowledge society. In some ways it is a kind of *mashing up*. Most importantly, perhaps, the role and practice of this kind of boundary spanner can *mentor* as well as mediate the knowledge contributory efforts of others. It models a form of practice – a *literacy* – that can be more easily emulated by others when it is visibly there to be seen and (with support) emulated. Wikis provide a remarkable medium within which this kind of mentoring can occur.

Of course, it can rightly be said that this kind of integrative work far pre-dates the internet, let alone wikis. Print media contain a lot of such writing. Sometimes it is generated by manageable-sized groups of people working together and gets incorporated into jointly written reports. But in such cases not all the information can be 'there' for an extended community of interested people to be able to participate in, such that they can be 'present' when mentoring goes on. It is not possible for an extended community to track the 'frozen' dialogue archived in a 'history', such that they can reflect on what has been going on. The capacity of wikis to enable these things is truly *new* and educationally priceless.

Moreover, in cases like Wikipedia the leverage and value-adding integration are owned by all members and are available to anyone who wants to access it. By contrast, most Western universities are now almost fully implicated in a proprietary ethos based on a particular kind of business model. This means that spaces like Wikipedia present a genuine alternative possibility for 'knowledge professionals' employed by teaching and research corporations to participate in 'the sharing economy' as well as in the 'commercial economy' and, perhaps, to prefigure participation in the hybrid (remix) economy envisaged by people like Lessig (2008).

To conclude our discussion of wikis we turn now to a context of popular cultural activity in a gaming wiki.

Kingdom of Loathing and the KoL wiki

About the game

Kingdom of Loathing (Kingdomofloathing.com) is a free, massively multiplayer role-playing online game developed by Zack Johnson and Josh Nite, and launched online in 2003. The overall goal of the game is to defeat the Naughty Sorceress. To do so, the player's character must complete numerous quests and advance sufficient levels in order to be both powerful enough and to have the necessary skills, items, and know-how needed to defeat her. Once the Sorceress has been defeated, the player 'ascends' and is able to choose a new character class and 'replay' the game.

Kingdom of Loathing is an hilarious, quirky, darkly ironic spoof of role-playing games. The characters and landscape of *Kingdom of Loathing* are rudimentary stick figure and outline drawings. Navigation within the game is mediated by a map and hyperlinks to different gaming areas (e.g., Spookyraven Manor, Mysterious Island of Mystery). Game play is carried by written text, which is filled with popular culture references and spoofs, in-game jokes, and lots of word play.

The *Kingdom of Loathing* universe includes an official live chat feature and a dedicated discussion forum. In 2004, fans launched a web-based radio station called 'Radio KOL' (see: Radio-kol.net). A *Kingdom of Loathing* wiki was established by fans in 2005. The aim of the wiki is to 'create a comprehensive and comprehensible source of spoilerific KoL documentation and analysis. Our hope is that KoL players will come here and add new information, making this wiki as useful and usable as possible' (Thraeryn n.d.).

About the wiki

Due to the complexity of the game and the multiple 'paths' through it, a wiki is an ideal medium for a guide to game play. While the wiki can be used in any way, we typically use it as a just-in-time, just-in-place resource for when we get stuck in a particular quest, or can't defeat a particular monster. There is no real index to the wiki, and information is found via the wiki's search function. Typically, a search for a given game space or item returns a page that has a brief description and perhaps some mention of a relevant quirk. For example, the page for the 'Obligatory Pirate Cove' contains the explanation: 'It be full of pirates of every description', and a hint about 'descriptions that starrrt with s and end in y' (see: Kol.coldfront.net/thekolwiki/index.php/The_obligatory_pirate_cove). Pirates encountered within this game space are variously smarmy, sassy, swarthy, shady, etc. The 'arrr' associated with 'pirate speak' appears in the items listed as 'drops' garnered from defeating each pirate (e.g., arrrgyle socks, crowbarrr, charrrm bracelet).

With respect to pages about particular game spaces, a detailed listing of the 'monsters' encountered (in this case, the various pirates) is typically included, along with which items are dropped, the amount of meat likely to be gained from winning the fight ('meat' is the in-game currency), the number of attribute points that can be gained, and additional relevant details about the monsters' resistance to things like stench or spookiness (and which requires players to don equipment to overcome such resistance). Each monster and item mentioned on the page is linked to a separate page that describes it in more detail.

Additional pages within the wiki include documentation of all the food and cocktail recipes within the game, their needed ingredients, and their effects (e.g., an increase in adventures that can be used that day, an increase in stats); and all the items and equipment that can be made within the game (smithed, crafted, etc.). Sets of pages are also available that document the various quests in the game and how to complete them. Suggestions also are given for how to effectively increase one's meat hoard (which then lets you purchase needed items or pay for certain game turns), how to move quickly through each iteration of the game, how to discover the effects of certain items, and so on.

Writing in the wiki

This wiki is an intensely active participatory space – most pages have a long history of edits and a substantial set of postings to their associated discussion pages (it's not unusual for these wiki pages to have recorded tens of thousands of views). Of particular interest to us here is the way this wiki, like any wiki, reflects certain kinds of reading and writing practices. To begin, we'll take the case of editing the descriptions for gameplay within a recently revamped area of the game: The Bat Hole.

The discussion tab for the Bat Hole wiki page provides a useful behind-the-scenes glimpse of what fans are doing on – and with – the wiki, and how they're reacting to changes made to the game. On 9 November 2010, a number of changes were made to the Bat Hole game space. Players were notified of the change via a brief message on the game's main page. The history tab for the Bat Hole wiki page shows 21 edits by 14 different users made to this page since 2005. Six changes had been made in 2010, with half dating from the space's recent revamp. Edits to the original Bat Hole page include reformatted tables, corrected hyperlinks, inclusion of a new image of the game space's map, various edits to the actual written wiki text (e.g., grammatical corrections), changed image dimensions, and the like. One user, Flargen, first contributed something to the Bat Hole wiki page in December 2006 and then again in November 2010. This included reformatting a table and updating an image.

Flargen's profile page within the wiki and the Talk page attached to his profile show him to be a dedicated and active contributor to the wiki. Flargen describes himself as 'simply a more-or-less typical player who sometimes moonlights as a snarky wiki editor and spader' (source: Kol.coldfront.net/thekolwiki/index.php/User:Flargen). 'Spading' is a term used within the wiki to describe the time and effort many devote to 'figuring out' game mechanics (source: Kol.coldfront.net/thekolwiki/index.php/Spading). Spading (or digging down) 'begins with a hunch' that the user follows; for example, realizing over time that the random numbers returned on fortune cookies within the game aren't so random after all, and how this affects game play (ibid.). Effective spading requires the user to be good at maths, and able to calculate probability as well as error margins.

Flargen lists 'slimeling disgorging' as one of his current spading projects. A slimeling is a familiar who 'drops' (or disgorges) additional items at the end of a successful monster fight. Flargen appears to be interested in documenting exactly what is dropped under which conditions. The history for the Slimeling entry in the wiki shows a significant number of edits and additions by Flargen. On the Talk page for this entry, Flargen has posted a tabulated summary of what the slimeling disgorges. He has added a note concerning his experimental controls as well: 'Some preliminary disgorging data. All of this was collected at -150% items with a 10 pound slimeling, so there was a 0% chance that any of these items could be obtained from any other method (no vivala mask or other pickpocketing sources, either). – Flargen 13:18, 13 July 2009' (source: Kol.coldfront.net/thekolwiki/index. php/Talk:Slimeling). In addition, another user – GoldenS – contributed a similar table, but this time with the familiar's contact lenses equipped, which changes the game play and disgorged items.

Flargen has a list of things he plans to work on within the wiki that he believes need tidying up or fixing. For example, he writes:

Fix the Oyster Egg messes. Most of the egg drop lists use redirect pages instead of direct links.

- Mostly fixed. Related mess to be fixed:

  1 "Obtained From" sections for most oyster eggs is an ugly, unreadable mess.
  (source: http://kol.coldfront.net/thekolwiki/index.php/User:Flargen)

Flargen doesn't seem to hesitate when it comes to editing others' work, either. For example (and taken from the Discussion page attached to his profile):

Hey why did you undo my revision to the Shivering Timbers page? – **Lemon-claw** 03:09, 11 December 2009

- It's not useful. It's not a script. It's a javascript code sniplet used for url manipulations, in order to exploit holes in the game that let you access things you normally wouldn't. And it has long since lost its relevance, and was a short-lived bug that was quickly fixed. It has no place on the wiki. The only time it does is when it is content intentionally made accessible only through such means. – **Flargen** 03:12, 11 December 2009
  (source: http://kol.coldfront.net/
  thekolwiki/index.php/User_talk:Flargen)

This kind of sampling of wiki users, wiki content and page editing histories indicates how the wiki is embedded in all kinds of discussions around game mechanics, the 'look' of the wiki itself and its usability, coding and understanding online game programming, probability mathematics and suchlike, and 'getting the jokes' embedded within the game itself. Looking at this in terms of the overall framework employed in this book, we can see a cumulative commitment to resourcing a shared and distributed game space by keeping the wiki relevant and up to date for all users. Page edit histories and discussion pages strongly suggest the wiki is indeed a joint collaborative writing project. Users engage with one another's edits and additions via the discussion pages, and clearly feel free to add to and negotiate meaningful content created by others.

In Flargen's case, it can be argued that he is reading and writing out of spaces or Discourses associated with computer and web programming (e.g., 'it's a java code sniplet used for url manipulations'), out of gamer Discourses (e.g., his interest in game mechanics), and Discourses associated with being an effective wiki editor (e.g., paying attention to both the 'look' and functionality of wikis). Flargen's contributions to the wiki are impressive and speak to his commitment to helping to generate a resource for the *Kingdom of Loathing* gaming community. Similarly, the almost immediate changes made to the Bat Hole wiki pages suggest a shared commitment among users to keeping the wiki relevant and up to date.

Reflection and discussion

In light of the discussion in this chapter and other relevant sources, and with reference to a selection of blogs, wikis and other online participatory spaces, discuss the relationship between *participation* in an online space and *collaboration* in an online space.

To what extent can you identify different 'shades', 'degrees', or 'forms' of collaborative online literacy practices. What are they?

End note: other online collaborative literacy practices

We have suggested that paradigm instances of collaborative literacy practices presuppose participants having a strong 'systems' sense of an endeavour as a whole, such that contributions can be coordinated and integrated in pursuit of the common end. Distributed writing is not necessarily – and often is *not* – collaborative, at least in this strong sense. Often it is merely cumulative – albeit in ways that might be mobilized for collaborative purposes and integrated in ways that yield new knowledge and other kinds of creations. At the very least it will be useful to recognize varying degrees and shades of collaboration, and that collaborative roles, relationships and tasks will vary. In cases of fanfiction posted online and edited in light of reviewer comments, we might reasonably speak of collaboration, even though the respective participants are not working together on the same artifact in the way that occurs in spaces like Wikipedia. Alternatively, contributions to discussion boards and social news sites where individual contributions cannot be boxed off might be seen as collaborative to the extent that contributors are seeking a common purpose and consciously contributing 'parts' to a recognized 'whole', including advancing contrary viewpoints in order to build perspective and address relevant issues. (By contrast, trolls do *not* collaborate.)

To conclude this chapter we will briefly look at the emergence of online document authoring platforms where multiple contributors to the development of a single text can jointly edit (including simultaneously) an evolving document from wherever they are in the world, and where a history of changes is automatically archived (like in Wikipedia), so that participants can consult or revert to earlier versions as appropriate for advancing the writing. The documents in question might be as elaborate as a research report or as concise as a table, spreadsheet, or figure. It might be as 'creative' as a work of fiction, or as prosaic as a research paper. We are talking here of people using online collaborative document authoring software, of kinds as stripped back as those found at Write.fm or Sync.in or Typewith. me, or as sophisticated as Google Docs (docs.google.com) or ThinkFree. com. In such cases it is easy to find straightforward examples of collaboration because the purposes are often highly specific, understood by all, and the scope and nature of the tasks are typically self-contained and finite.

We will use Google Docs as our example here, since it is a free service that is highly versatile and has expansive potential for educational use (Richardson 2010). Google Docs is an online service that enables users to jointly create word-processed documents, spreadsheets, slide presentations, etc., working together in the same evolving document. Users also are able to upload and store their own documents across a range of file types (e.g., doc, xls, odt, rtf, ppt). There is no client software to be downloaded and installed in order to be able to use this service, and documents created in or uploaded to Google Docs can be accessed from any computer that has an internet connection, using most internet browsers. Users need to create a Google account to use the software and be part of collaborations. Ostensibly free, the service comes with some fine print: notably, while users retain copyright over their work, Google.com claims the right to reproduce any such content for specified purposes. Google Docs is more than just an online text editor. It enables users to share documents with others in two ways: read only, and with editing options enabled. The fact that the document is stored online, rather than on a single computer hard drive, makes it easy to invite others to work collaboratively to produce a text – across distance and time zones.

Briefly, having created an account and accessed the site, users enter a writing space with a similar look and feel to Open Office or MS Office templates. Clicking the 'new' button at the top of the left-hand column opens up a new webpage and a blank document inside a simple word-processing environment. Text can be typed directly into this blank document, or copied and pasted from elsewhere. Formatting changes can be made, too, just as can be done with most word-processing software. Sharing the text with others is straightforward. The user clicks on the 'share' button to the right of the document space, opens a window where collaborators' email addresses are keyed in – once the 'send' button is clicked, they'll receive an email invitation to access the document (collaborators also need to have, or set up, a Google account). As each eddress is entered, the 'owner' of the document can set the degree of access to the document for this particular user (e.g., 'can view', 'can edit'). The default setting for documents is 'private', but other options are available. These include a 'public' option, which means the document can be found and read by anyone online, and an 'anyone with the link' option, which means invitees can access the document without having to set up a Google account.

Because users can see the history of revisions made to a document (including who made revisions), there is always the option of restoring an earlier draft as the current main document. The service automatically saves documents as they're being written or edited to help guard against losing work due to screen/machine freezes, power outages and the like. When the document is finished, it can be downloaded in a number of file formats (e.g., doc, rtf, html) and stored elsewhere and/or put to its intended use. Tutorials for using Google Docs can be found at Google.com/google-d-s/tour1.html. Numerous 'how-to' videos can be found on YouTube.

The types of collaboration afforded by Google Docs – private, semi-private and public – can each play out in different ways. For example, we use private Google Docs with Master's students working in teams, where each document is shared with only a small number of people, and becomes a dynamic space for team-based writing and for us to provide feedback on work in progress (see Chapter 8). These documents cannot be found via a search engine, cannot be accessed without an invitation from the document owner, and cannot be edited without the document owner extending that right.

Google Docs enables all manner of collaborative writing practices, across purposes, styles, duration, size of project, number of participants, and so on. One interesting example arose in April 2010 when the popular social networking site, Ning.com, announced it would begin charging monthly fees for its previously free service and nings that didn't switch to the fee model would be suspended – sending ripples through the education world, which had quickly embraced the Ning platform. A Canadian professor, Alec Couros, saw alternatives being posted to Twitter and elsewhere. He decided to start a collaborative repository of alternative services on Google Docs to which anyone could contribute, and publicized the URL via Twitter (Couros 2010). The document he created was open to the public, and anyone could add to it. Couros sent out the URL to the Google Doc via Twitter 'and within minutes we had several pages of options for both hosted and self-hosted social networking services' (ibid.: n.p.). Within hours hundreds of people had contributed alternatives and edited the site. As we watched the document evolve, it was common to see ten or more people simultaneously adding or editing from Argentina, Australia, Canada, Finland, New Zealand, the USA, and elsewhere. (It was via this collaborative document that we discovered the SocialGo.com service to use with some of our classes.) The final (13-page) document provided hyperlinks to an impressive array of free alternative sites, with annotated comments on services offered (e.g., storage capacity, multimedia hosting), and accounts of users' experiences with the options identified. It is difficult to imagine a more clear-cut instance of a collaborative literacy practice.

CHAPTER **6**

Everyday practices of online social networking

Introduction

This chapter discusses a range of online social networking practices from a perspective we hope speaks to questions like:

- What does it mean to be literate these days?
- What kinds of literacies 'stack up' (best) in terms of terms of meeting people's life purposes and prospects, and in what respects and in what ways do they seem to 'stack up'?
- Why do people like Howard Rheingold talk about 'network awareness' as a twenty-first-century *literacy*, and what might be the educational benefits, as well as the wider life prospect benefits of network awareness?
- To what extent and in what ways might online social networking be relevant to and/or part of educational practices and processes?

After briefly identifying some preliminary matters facing attempts to write about online social networking, we begin by looking at some ideas from social theory, such as the way some theorists have distinguished groups and networks, the significance they attach to this distinction, and how they conceptualize social networks. We then look briefly at social network(ing) sites and services. We use the resulting framework to look at some typical cases of how people engage in social networking, and consider some of the implications of such cases for thinking about new literacy practices, literacy education, and education more generally. This discussion provides a bridge to our focus in the final part of the book on new literacies and social learning.

Some preliminary background issues

Any attempt to think and write about online social networking faces a number of challenges from the outset, three of which seem especially relevant to our discussion in this chapter.

1 How can 'online social networking practices' *per se* best be demarcated from other social practices that include significant components of online social interaction that might be seen as involving participation in social networks? In an age of (online) social media (Bruns and Bahnisch 2009), what kinds of online activity *cannot* be seen in terms of participating in social networks and, to that extent, engaging in online social networking practices? It's almost as if 'social networking' is *everywhere* online these days. For example, Wikipedia's list of social networking websites (Wikipedia 2010i) includes Deviant Art (fan art/visual arts creation), Flickr (photosharing), Indaba Music (online collaborative music creation), LiveJournal (blogging), and Livemocha (foreign language learning). Yet, these are sites that seem primarily to support participation in substantive social practices like blogging, music remixing, fan art, photosharing, and the like. To the extent that we see social networking going on within these services, it would seem to be occurring in an 'embedded' or 'collateral' kind of way, rather than as the 'main game'. By contrast, there are sites and services that 'self-define' first, foremost, and in many cases, solely, in terms of enabling users to engage in social networking/participate in social networks online. Obvious contenders here include Facebook, MySpace, Bebo, Friendster, Hi5, BlackPlanet, MiGente, Academia.edu, LinkedIn, and Orkut, among many others.

When we think of everyday social practices of all kinds across the contexts of daily activity, it is evident that they involve social networks, and that we are interacting with members of our various social networks whenever we are 'in' those practices. It is equally evident, however, that within those contexts of activity we rarely think of ourselves as 'participating in social networks' or 'doing social networking'. Every time we eat a family meal we interact with our most immediate social network, but the thought – let alone the intent – never crosses our minds. Accordingly, we need to keep in mind here a distinction between thinking of social networking/participating in social networks in terms of some kind of discrete social practice – a kind of practice, a domain of practice – and the idea of being able to see engagement in (whatever) social practice as partly falling under the description of participating in social networks if we want or choose (for whatever reason) to see it under that description. In this chapter we will focus mainly on social networking as a more or less discrete kind of activity.

2 To what extent is it helpful or appropriate to approach the task of describing and understanding online social networking practices in the light of formal social network theory derived from established social theory? Alternatively, to what extent might it be preferable to take a more *grounded* theoretical approach to investigating, understanding, and theorizing practices of participation in online social networks – trying to 'see' and understand these practices so far as possible 'on their own terms' – and seeking to build up elements of a theory *from there*, albeit informed (as grounded theorists are) by a broad background appreciation of potentially relevant established theory and research? If we are particularly interested in describing and understanding practices of online social networking from the standpoint of literacy education, how might this shape our preferences or decisions here?

3 How can we best distinguish between participating in social networks as an 'organic' dimension of interacting with others on- and offline, and engaging in social networking in a more 'strategic' sense of trying to extend the reach of one's acquaintances with a view to leveraging value/accruing benefits from a targeted or otherwise enlarged field of social contacts? One way of doing this is to distinguish between social networking as a practice informed by some metalevel ideas about how social networks function and how benefits can be derived from actively building and maintaining certain kinds of networks in certain kinds of ways, and practices of networks that are not informed by some kind of theory and consciously built and maintained in such ways. This distinction resonates with dana boyd and Nicole Ellison's (2007) insistence on distinguishing between 'social network sites' (e.g., MySpace, Facebook, Friendster) and 'networking'. They argue that the verb 'networking' implies forging relationships with strangers, and does not sufficiently capture the extent to which social network sites are used by people to reinforce existing face-to-face social networks (see also boyd 2008).

In this chapter we take a particular position on each of these issues. With respect to the first issue, we focus our attention almost entirely on practices involving the use of social networking services that define themselves as being formally dedicated to facilitating connections between people as their 'core business'. They exist for the express purpose of fostering social ties or relationships of one kind or another among people, based on people as *people* rather than people as 'bearers' of particular *interests* (like, say, practices of photosharing). Hence, for present purposes, services like Facebook are 'in', and services and sites like Flickr are 'out' (even though a good deal of social networking, including 'networking' as described by boyd and Ellison and informed by metalevel understandings of networking as a strategic practice, may – and often does – occur within those services). Moreover, we will organize our account of social practices using dedicated social networking services around a distinction between what might be called 'general social networking services', like Facebook and MySpace, and more 'targeted' or dimension-specific social networking services, like LinkedIn and Academia.edu.

With respect to drawing on formal theory, we believe that some elements of theory and research about social networks are essential for understanding social networking practices of a more 'strategic' nature – e.g., networking as 'leverage' – and, indeed, for understanding the evolving design and architecture of social networking platforms. In addition, elements of formal theory and research speak directly to the contingent link between the flowering of online social media and communications platforms and services and the current 'buzz' – which is near deafening – around social networking practices. Furthermore, social network theory affirms the role and place of the *individual* at the centre of his or her networks, and identifies theoretical advantages for understanding important aspects of social structure and social order that can be derived from focusing on 'social networks' rather than 'social groups' or 'community' (Wellman 2001; Hogan 2009). Focusing on networks with individuals at their centre, and on the kinds of social ties obtaining between members of networks ('nodes'), and on the kinds of relationships entailed by these varying ties, it is possible to obtain rich, deep, and nuanced understandings of how, say, networks 'hang together' and function, rather than the more 'fuzzy' kinds of understandings resulting from emphasis on larger units like groups and communities (Hogan 2009). Concepts and theories generated from this perspective, such as Barry Wellman's (2001; Wellman et al. 2003) account of 'networked individualism', are especially applicable to the current period where individuals are increasingly required to fall back on themselves, their 'own' capacities and resources (including their 'strong' and 'weak' social ties) to make their ways in the world.

Finally, to recognize and identify differences between more 'organic' and more 'strategic' practices involving use of dedicated social networking services, we will present cases of different *kinds* of uses – different kinds of practices – of Facebook, within the context of discussing social practices involving use of a general social networking service. The idea of strategic practices will be expanded with reference to use of what we call 'targeted' social networking services, like Academia.edu and LinkedIn.

Groups, networks, 'networked individualism' and social networking services in everyday life

Groups, networks, social ties, and technological change

Humans have always been involved in and drawn upon social ties of various kinds – kinship, friendship, community, guild, regional, religious, etc. – within everyday routines. Such ties help people to access and distribute various kinds of goods, information, support, reassurances, and services that would be difficult, if not impossible, to manage on their own. While we often think about such sets of social ties in terms of being members of 'groups', some social theorists find it more useful – and particularly in the context of contemporary media – to think of social functioning and 'community' in terms of *networks* (e.g., Granovetter 1973, 1983; Wellman 2001; Wellman et al. 2003, 2006). For example, Wellman (2001: 227) claims that 'we find community in networks, not groups', and that while we 'often view the world in terms of groups', people nonetheless 'function in networks'.

For Wellman, groups describe tightly knit connections between a set of people, and typically involve extended face-to-face interactions, like those found within small villages or small, localized workplaces. Within a group, each member typically knows all the other members directly and the boundaries of the group are fairly well defined. For example, in a small business, the owner and the employees know each other personally, and tend in the main to speak directly to each other about how things operate within this particular workplace. Networks, on the other hand, are typically more loosely knit than groups, and much more readily dispersed over time and space (Wellman 2001; see also, Garton et al. 1997). Within networks, members do not necessarily know each other personally, but are nonetheless connected by any number of means, including a shared interest in something, shared occupations, family ties, shared values, or by the other people in a given network (e.g., a friend-of-a-friend connection), and so on.

While we can think of networks extending far back into human history – since the dawn of trade and exchange – the advent of telephones, trains, air travel, and other communication and transport/travel resources for easily establishing and maintaining ties at distance has resulted in loosely knit and distributed networks becoming increasingly prevalent and important since early industrial times. Under contemporary conditions of globalized post-industrialism, networks 'trump' tightly knit social groups for all but a diminishing range of everyday purposes and interactions. According to Wellman (2001: 228), developments in digital technologies, internet and mobile phone services mean that networks have emerged as 'a dominant form of social organization'. Digitally mediated communication and interaction services have escalated the rise of person-to-person interactions within loosely linked and widely dispersed networks that can operate 'on the go' and 'on the fly'. Increasingly, people are no longer constrained to fixed-in-place communication means like landline phones, or computers tethered to their work desks. They can stay in touch with their various networks regardless of where they are located physically; a person's networks can 'travel' with them rather than needing to be accessed from a designated spot. Digital technologies enable connections to multiple networks simultaneously; access to an 'always on' and always available internet greatly facilitates interactions within one's networks on an any-time-any-place basis. Wellman (ibid.) goes so far as to argue that *community* can be found in digitally mediated 'networks of interpersonal ties that provide sociability, support, information, a sense of belonging, and social identity' (Wellman 2001: 228). While it has always been possible to be part of multiple networks, the networking affordances of digital technologies vastly increase this possibility, and in the short time since Wellman and others began talking about online/electronic social networks in the 1990s we have seen an explosion in the means and practices of online social networking.

Social networks, 'strong' and 'weak' ties, and networked individualism

Social network theorists see networks as composed of individuals ('nodes') who are tied to one another in various kinds of relationships (ties) of varying degrees and types of interdependence. Ties and interdependencies might run along lines of kinship, friendship, economic purpose, emotion, interests, and the like (Feld 1981). Where interdependence is strong, and interaction is regular and intense, network theorists talk of the ties being 'strong'. Strong ties are often, but by no means necessarily, regular face-to-face ties.

Where interdependence is weaker, and contact less regular, ties are said to be 'weak'. Granovetter (1973) also identifies a category of 'absent' ties at the level of mere 'nodding acquaintanceship'. Of course, any given individual will have no ties whatsoever to most other people in the world.

A key idea in social network theory is the idea of the 'strength of weak ties' (Granovetter 1973, 1983), which by now has become practically a cliché – albeit a very powerful and influential one – in discussions of online social networking. In a landmark study of how professionals, managerial, and technical workers heard about job availability, Mark Granovetter (1973) found that almost twice as many heard about the jobs they got being available through their 'weak' ties more so than through strong ties, with the remainder in between. Granovetter's thesis about 'the strength of weak ties' builds on earlier work involving the idea that there is a greater likelihood of overlaps existing among the contacts (ties) of any two individuals who are closely acquainted than there is of overlaps existing among the contacts of any two randomly selected individuals. Granovetter (1973, 1983) argues that an individual's *close friends* are more likely to be socially involved with one another than his or her *acquaintances* (weaker ties) are. The network comprising an individual and his his/her close friends constitutes a more 'densely-knit clump of social structure' (Granovetter 1983: 202) than a network comprising an individual and his/her acquaintances ('low density clumps of social structure'; ibid.). Of course, any of an individual's acquaintances (weak ties) will have their own close friends/strong ties, and these comprise further 'densely knit clumps of social structure'. The link between an individual and an acquaintance – a weak tie – provides a bridge between (two) densely knit clumps of social structure – network segments – that in all likelihood would not otherwise exist. Weak links that provide bridges to network segments offer possibilities for getting information from the edges of the reach of one's social network (ibid.). Granovetter argues that individuals who have more/many weak links have greater prospects for accessing such information than individuals who have fewer/few weak links. Research conducted in the decade 1973–83, while not conclusive, was nonetheless encouraging for the thesis about the strength of weak ties which is often employed in support of networking and other virtual platforms seen as useful for accessing novel information, stimulating innovation, and the like (e.g., Hagel et al. 2010).

Granovetter's work pre-dated the mass internet. Since then, the work of sociologists like Manuel Castells (1996/2000), and Barry Wellman and colleagues (Wellman et al. 2003, 2006), among others, has spawned new ideas about changes in patterns of social organization in the current conjuncture – some of which complement Granovetter's arguments and inform theories and practices of strategic online social networking. One such idea, advanced by Wellman and colleagues (Wellman 2001; Wellman et al. 2003, 2006) is that the rise of internet communications, online social networks, and electronic collaborative platforms across the developed world is associated with a turn toward social systems that are increasingly organized around 'networked individualism', rather than around group-based and local solidarities.

The concept of 'networked individualism' portends a significant shift from societies organized around *groups* – kinship, workplace, local groups, etc. – to societies organized around the *individual* as 'the primary unit of connectivity' (Wellman et al. 2006: 165). This primary unit of connectivity lies at the centre of any number of networks created by means of ties to others, where these ties do not rely on kinship or even friendship and the like, and may be entirely ad hoc or serendipitous in terms of how they are made. People remain connected, but more as individuals who are networked rather than rooted in places and bases. For Wellman and colleagues, this shift 'facilitates personal communities that supply the essentials of community separately to each individual: support, sociability, information, social identities, and a sense of belonging' (Wellman et al. 2003: n.p.). The rise of the always-on internet, easy access to previously unknown others, and mobile ways of communicating with a wide range of people mean that individual networks are often loosely knit and dispersed, especially by comparison with group-based networks, which tend to be densely knit and local (Wellman 2001; Wellman et al. 2003).

Individualized networks are actively established and maintained by the person at their centre by means of 'personal skill, individual motivation and maintaining the right connections' (Wellman et al. 2006: 165). Wellman and colleagues argue that under conditions of networked individualism, the 'loss of group control and reassurance is traded for personal autonomy and agility' (ibid.: 165). At the same time, networked individualism also means 'people must actively network to thrive or even to survive comfortably. More passive or unskilled people may lose out, as the group (village, neighbourhood, household) is no longer taking care of things for them (Kadushin, et al., 2005)' (ibid.). Such arguments are widely used in support of the value of online social networking as a twenty-first-century literacy or skill (e.g., Hagel et al. 2010; Rheingold 2010a, 2010b).

Online social networking services

Online social networking services are best described as digital spaces or platforms formally dedicated to facilitating a range of connections between people. Social networking services are typically 'profile' driven. Members of the service complete a template that elicits personal information, spanning a range from gender and birth date through to favourite music, what they are reading at present, and so on. The template-driven and interactive dimensions of the service are relatively easy to navigate and master, and users require very little computer or internet know-how in order to participate effectively within the site. Indeed, Facebook – the currently pre-eminent online social networking service – has been described as 'training wheels' for the internet because it is attracting so many otherwise hesitant computer users (Huh 2010). The all-about-me profile at the heart of social networking services becomes a launch pad for 'friending' or connecting with others within the site (e.g., family members, friends in physical space, online friends, old school friends, work colleagues, and a host of others). Networks within these services also can be established or built by joining special interest groups that others have made, or creating one and asking others to join (see Knobel and Lankshear 2008).

Formal online networking services require specialized interfaces that help each participant to manage information about themselves, and to facilitate connections with selected others through inbuilt links to their within-network profiles. Online social networking services help participants manage a range of interpersonal interactions with others (e.g., by means of text, image, video and audio messaging systems; testimonial or 'wall' spaces; status updates; news feeds; socially interactive games; quizzes; photosharing and tagging). In short, formal social networking services are organized primarily around the individual and his or her social ties, and somewhat less around shared interests or projects. As boyd and Ellison explain:

> The rise of SNSs [social network sites] indicates a shift in the organization of online communities. While websites dedicated to communities of interest still exist and prosper, SNSs are primarily organized around people, not interests. Early public online communities such as Usenet and public discussion forums were structured by topics or according to topical hierarchies, but social network sites are structured as personal (or 'egocentric') networks, with the individual at the center of their own community. This more accurately mirrors unmediated social structures, where 'the world is composed of networks, not groups' (Wellman, 1988, p. 37).
>
> (boyd and Ellison 2007: 10)

As mentioned earlier, popular, easily recognized examples of social networking services include: Facebook, MySpace, Friendster, along with Cyworld (popular in South Korea and Vietnam), Bebo (popular in the

UK and India), Orkut (popular in India and Brazil), and Hi5 (popular in Mexico), to name only a few. From their inception, social networking services have shared three general, but defining, characteristics:

> [They] allow individuals to (1) construct a public or semi-public profile within a bounded system, (2) articulate a list of other users with whom they share a connection, and (3) view and traverse their list of connections and those made by others within the system.
>
> (boyd and Ellison 2007: 2)

Similar accounts describe social networking services as providing representations of users (e.g., profiles), their social links, means for connecting to others, and some kind of recommendation system to mediate the process of making new contacts.

As noted earlier, when users sign up to a social networking service, they usually complete a template-based form that elicits a range of personal information. Users are also prompted to find people they already know within the networking service, or invite people outside the service to join both the service and their personal network. Personal networks are traversed by either going directly to the profile pages of 'friends', or by commenting on their status updates or other posts as they appear in one's news feed (i.e., an automated summary of what people are doing within the network).

The defining characteristics of social networking services identified above are already beginning to shift, however, as new features get added to different services. For example, formal online social networking services did not originally concern themselves with blogging, the exchange of emails or instant messages, or with posts to discussion boards. Now, however, services like Facebook include a chat function for engaging with people within one's network in real-time text-based conversations. The default page for Facebook accounts no longer opens at a *profile* page but, rather, at a *news feed* page where the Facebook actions of everybody in a user's personal network are listed in chronological order. These actions include their status updates (short statements about anything considered 'postworthy' and which can be 'liked' or commented upon by others within the network), linked-to videos or websites, notes and other information posted by participants to their walls or profiles, changes in profile pictures, game status updates, who has commented on what, who has clicked the 'like' button for what, and so on. This information 'feed' is updated in real time, and closely resembles microblogging in appearance and intention (the main difference here is that a good deal of the information posted to Facebook news feeds is automated by the service itself; for example, the service automatically alerts others to a changed profile image or a new 'friend' addition). Facebook also recently launched a fully embedded email-linked service for members to use to connect with others who do not want to join Facebook.

Formerly, online social networking services were also well-bounded entities; it simply wasn't possible to transfer profile information and social ties across networking services, and each service required its own sign-in account. MySpace – which initially dominated the social networking services used in the USA before being surpassed by Facebook, has now forged a deal with Facebook that lets MySpace users log into their Facebook accounts via their MySpace page. This also enables MySpace users to 'port over their likes and interests listed on Facebook' (Shiels 2010: n.p.). This mashup works both ways – Facebook users can port key elements of their profile into their MySpace profile, too.

Indeed, Facebook is becoming increasingly pervasive online. Interpersonal ties made manifest within Facebook networks are being transported across the web, far beyond the borders of Facebook itself. For example, logging into the *New York Times* news site with one's Facebook account will automatically post a list of which recent articles from this media source friends in one's network have posted to Facebook to share with others (Adams 2010). Similarly, many websites now have automated 'sharing' functions built into them that enable users to post content directly to their social networking service page or to a social media site (see Figure 6.1, for example).

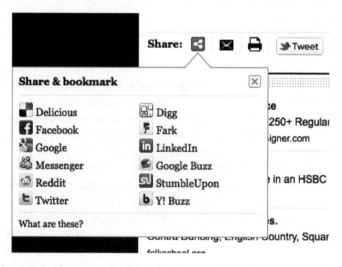

Figure 6.1 Automated sharing functions on the *Telegraph* newspaper online website
Source: Telegraph.co.uk.

Such developments might be seen in terms of social networking platforms enabling the potential for deriving personal strengths from weak ties, as well as enabling social systems to enjoy more rapid and far-reaching diffusion of ideas and trends, which can stimulate innovation and uptake of innovations. Granovetter (1983: 202) argued that his 'strength of weak ties' communication thesis has implications at both the micro- and macroscopic levels:

> [I]ndividuals with few weak ties will be deprived of information from distant parts of the social system and will be confined to the provincial news and views of their close friends. This deprivation will not only insulate them from the latest ideas and fashions but may put them in a disadvantaged position in the labor market, where advancement can depend ... on knowing about appropriate job openings at just the right time ... The macroscopic side of this communications argument is that social systems lacking in weak ties will be fragmented and incoherent. New ideas will spread slowly, scientific endeavors will be handicapped, and [isolated or separated] subgroups ... will have difficulty reaching a *modus vivendi* [accommodating different ideas to allow life to go on].

The kind of 'outreaching' afforded by social networking platforms, along the lines described for Facebook, clearly enables access to and diffusion of information from 'distant parts of the social system' (ibid.). Indeed, the reach is global, and the range and diversity of what can be accessed and diffused become a function of the range and diversity of users' (individually and collectively) weak ties. Of course, much more is involved here than information alone. The same argument applies to what people can become involved in more substantively via communications that can serve to mobilize and organize activity and commitment.

Reflection and discussion

Are dating sites social networking services? (See, for example, OKCupid.com, Gay.com, Match.com, Lavalife.com, eHarmony. com.) On what reasons do you base your decision?

Are Amazon.com and eBay.com social networking services? On what reasons do you base your decision?

Ways with Facebook: the myriad social practices of 'broad-based' online social networking

A decade ago, Howard Rheingold (2002) claimed the new digital 'killer apps' would focus on social relationships rather than information – resonating with Michael Schrage's (2001) assessment of the most powerful impact of computing and communications technologies. Today we might well wonder how it could ever have been thought otherwise. During 2010 it was estimated that Facebook alone had close to 500 million active users, half of whom logged on daily. Perhaps the best way to get a quick sense of the ubiquity of social networking is by surveying Wikipedia's list of social networking sites (Wikipedia 2010i). In terms of registered users, former front-runner, MySpace, is now dwarfed by Twitter's micro-blogging service, and closely challenged by sites like Bebo and Orkut. Wikipedia's list of social networking sites makes it easy to distinguish broad-based or general social networking sites from those that 'specialize' in more targeted user bases, such as people with professional or academic affiliations, or with particular interests around which they wish to interact with kindred spirits. This section focuses on users and uses of Facebook.

Three years after Facebook's launch in 2004, Microsoft paid US$240 million for a meagre 1.6 per cent share in the service (Leidtke 2007), which had an estimated worth of over US$40 billion in 2010 (Schroeder 2010). In December 2010, Facebook remains predominantly privately owned by Facebook, Inc., headed by Mark Zuckerberg.

Originally designed for US university students, Facebook now includes people from all walks of life worldwide. It supports multiple language interfaces and hosts a wide range of 'non-person' nodes in its overall social network (e.g., user-generated groups, merchandising pages of which users can become 'fans', special-interest pages that can be 'liked'). After establishing a Facebook account and providing basic identifying information and other personal details according to the site's profile template, the user logs on to the default opening page. In December 2010 this comprised a horizontal navigational bar and three main columns. The navigational bar includes direct links to 'friend requests', 'messages received', and 'notifications' on the left-hand side, and links to 'home', 'profile', and the user's Facebook account on the right-hand side of the navigational bar. The first column on the default 'home' page lists links to a range of spaces and services available within the Facebook site. Pre-programmed links include those to the 'news feed', and to 'messages', 'events', 'photos', 'notes', Facebook chat, and to 'friends' within one's personal network. These links access a range of services within Facebook that enable users to communicate privately with others, access information about people in their network quickly, view their own and their 'friends' profiles, upload photographs to their album pages, and 'manage' their interpersonal network by accepting new 'friends', deleting no longer wanted 'friends', or limiting what is made public on their profile pages to non-friends. Additional links that users can add to this same column include links to Facebook games, social exchange apps (e.g., Snow Globe gifts, Monty Python gifts), information apps (e.g., world maps showing cities you've visited, birthday calendars), and so on. In short, this column acts as something like a navigational bar as well.

The right-hand column contains summaries of notifications (e.g., event invitations advertised by your friends via Facebook, games-related requests and invitations) and friend requests, prompts to add new friends to your network, and reference to 'Facebook mobile' for accessing your Facebook account while on the go.

The central, and widest, column on the default 'home' page for one's Facebook account contains the news feed for one's entire personal network. 'News' in this case includes status updates (e.g., what someone is doing, eating, thinking about), links to interesting things online (e.g., news stories, political commentaries, humorous things), videos (e.g., music videos on YouTube), posts to a user's 'wall' (a space within Facebook for writing public messages to the profile owner), notice of new additions to users' Facebook photo albums, advice that the user has changed their profile picture or added/changed information about themselves (e.g., no longer in a relationship, now married), news about who has joined or liked what groups or pages on Facebook, and who has added new friends to their network, to name a few.

Many of these 'news' posts are accompanied by the option to 'like' the news (by clicking on the 'like' icon or link) and to add a written comment. This news feed also adds information about when each post/action took place (e.g., 5 minutes ago, three hours ago) and how the update was posted to the news feed – such as via a social media post external to Facebook (so that the same information appears on the user's Twitter/Foursquare/blog and Facebook pages), or via a mobile device (e.g., Android smartphone, Blackberry, iPhone).

A Facebook user's profile page has a very similar layout to the default home page – the most significant difference is the advertisements that appear in the right-hand column, and which are tailored to the user based on their Facebook likes and personal information posted to their profile page. The central column on the profile page only lists what that user has posted to, or done on, Facebook.

As a *platform*, Facebook presents users with a generous range of features and applications which can be used in any number of mixes and measures according to personal interests, purposes, preferences, contacts, sense of 'cool', the kind of image one wants to present, degree of technical knowledge and proficiency, perceptions of self as a writer and communicator, and so on. Consequently, the look and feel of the pages of different Facebook users vary enormously. 'Facebooking', as it were, is no single practice; indeed, there are countless 'ways with Facebook'. The cases presented in the remainder of this section provide the briefest glimpse of the diversity to be found.

Tanya's ways with Facebook

Tanya is a 50-something-year-old woman, living in a small coastal village in eastern Canada, 50km from the nearest town centre. She left school early and mainly has worked short-term jobs ever since. She is currently unemployed, caring full-time for her partner. Tanya now spends most of her days at home and seems to prefer others dropping in to visit more than going to other people's homes. Neither she nor her partner has a car, and her infrequent trips to the city – an hour away – are organized largely around health care.

Tanya's current Facebook profile picture has the words 'A mother's love is a blessing' superimposed over an old image of Tanya and her long-deceased mother. This same image has some purple stars and a teddy bear holding a red heart photoshopped onto it as well. Tanya has 330 'friends' on Facebook. Around 35 per cent of these identify as living locally to Tanya, or as having come from the area. Another 20 per cent identify as coming from further than an hour's drive away, with some living in other Canadian provinces and the USA. The remainder do not identify where they currently live or where they're from. Nevertheless, judging from the relatively small number of surnames shared across the entire set of Tanya's Facebook friends, it would seem that all are known to her personally (Tanya has 'friended' only three 'strangers', popular country-folk musicians from the region). Tanya is one of nine children and many of her Facebook friends include her brothers and sisters, their partners and children, and their children's spouses or significant others. Tanya's partner is one of 14 children, and her Facebook friends include many of his family members. Her network also extends to include the family networks of people who have married into her family network, too, along with local friends – many of whom she had grown up with – and their extended family networks. Tanya's Facebook network, then, largely consists of a set of strong, densely knit ties to people she knows well.

Tanya writes very little on her profile wall. Her news feed typically includes auto-updates from Facebook regarding her 'moves' in a number of social games like *Farmville* and *Treasure Isle* (e.g., 'Tanya just conquered Scale Isles in Treasure Isle!'). Lately, her most common posts comprise links to music videos with titles like: 'A Picture of Me Without You', 'Loving You Makes Me Mine', 'Only Love Like Yours' and 'All That's Left is a Memory'. The bulk of these videos are re-posts of videos found on other people's Facebook pages within her network, although she has also installed the Facebook 'Slide FunSpace' app to help her find videos she likes. Tanya also uses the Facebook search function to track down specific songs and musicians she likes, or that her partner especially likes. These video posts generally attract a number of 'likes' from friends, and every now and then a comment from someone in her network. Her status updates have for the past few months been selected from a Facebook service known as Status Shuffle. Status Shuffle comprises a large set of pre-written statements that can be used to describe how things are in one's life, to make others laugh, and so on. One 'shuffles' through the available statements until an appealing one is found, selected, and automatically added to one's Facebook status line. Tanya seems to use Status Shuffle mostly to express her sadness about her partner's illness. Many of her Status Shuffle updates are 'liked' by a number of others, but few people leave comments. Tanya herself sometimes 'likes' or comments on a video she has posted to her own wall to express how much she appreciates the song.

Tanya also makes use of a number of 'emotional barometers' available on Facebook, some of which take the form of responding to quizzes that calculate how one is feeling that day, or selecting smiling through to crying or angry faces to express a current mood. The items she posts that attract the most attention within her network as judged by 'likes' and comments are photographs of family and friends – many of these images focus on her partner (e.g., taken while visiting some of his favourite places, photos of him with family members). Indeed, posting photographs is a significant part of Tanya's Facebooking practices, and she has uploaded a total of 56 photos in the past three months (as of time of writing in November 2010).

Tanya's news feed has very few contributions from other people on it. In the two weeks preceding this writing someone has sent her a backpack for the *Treasure Isle* game, and she has unlocked three achievements within the same game. She has posted one Status Shuffle update which five people have 'liked' and one person has commented on, saying they plan to copy the message and use it for their own status update. She has one emotional barometer read-out posted, which lists her as feeling: Angry = 19%, Happy = 62%, and Sad = 42%. There is little in her news feed to indicate that Tanya comments on other people's posts within her network. In the past four months, for example, the only comment she posted to any of her friends' walls was in response to a status update about the value of family: 'your very true .100/%'.

Tanya isn't a big fan of reading or television. Her computer is always on, though, and Facebook is always open. Throughout her day, she'll move between whatever it is that needs doing, and checking and being 'on' Facebook. Indeed, Facebook, YouTube and one or two poker (card game) sites seem to dominate the sum of her internet practices. Facebook also seems to play a significant role in keeping her in touch with her outside world. She doesn't have a mobile phone, and doesn't spend much time chatting on the phone. Outside of Facebook Tanya doesn't seem especially 'at home' with her computer or the internet. Recently, she worked out how to access government service sites for printing out forms and the like – although this still typically involves calls to the service centres or to neighbours for help with accessing the correct document and getting it downloaded. Tanya doesn't word process documents, or use communications software like Skype or instant messaging. Neither does she use any email services outside the private messaging service within Facebook, and when she does send messages, they tend to comprise only a short sentence or so (e.g., 'Not doing to good'). She has set up a Facebook profile for her partner, although he's not remotely interested in computers, and his profile comprises mostly messages from nieces and nephews asking how he is. Tanya occasionally logs in and adds Facebook friends to her partner's profile. On a typical day, she spends anywhere from three to five hours on Facebook playing games, looking at people's profiles, uploading photos and linking to music videos.

Corey's ways with Facebook

Corey is a 16-year-old Australian male who has been a member of Facebook for almost two years. He attends a public high school in an area that is rapidly being developed as a dormitory region for a large state-capital and a well-populated and developed nearby coastal region. This area is characterized by demographic extremes with respect to family incomes, housing types and adult occupations.

Corey says he joined Facebook because it was gaining ground in broadcast media reporting and seemed an interesting way to keep in touch with friends. He had used no other social networking service prior to joining Facebook and was interested in 'checking it out'. Corey has 291 'friends' (as of 11 December 2010) who are a mix of family, friends, and others. Most of the people in his network appear to be school mates or local kids he knows personally (judging from the schools they attend and mention of them in Corey's posted photos). Roughly 40 per cent attend the same school as Corey, with 40 per cent more attending other local schools. Only a small number (five in all) explicitly identify as living further afield (e.g., in the west of the state, in Asia, the USA). Family members and family friends comprise the remaining 20 per cent or so of Corey's Facebook network. In the three months preceding this writing, over 50 people in his network have 'liked' something he's posted or commented on it – with around 20 of these doing so more than once. Corey also posts regularly on other people's walls, mostly in response to their status updates, and comments on their uploaded photos, too.

On Facebook, Corey presents himself as someone who is interested in and savvy about cars, likes certain kinds of music, is an avid video gamer, and a particular kind of school student. The bulk of the photos he's used as profile images are of cars, and his Facebook photo albums include pictures of cars or things to do with cars. These include humorous photos, like an image of a car stereo system lying on the ground and on fire, accompanied by his caption 'Valiant stereo upgrade' (implying that destroying the stereo improves its quality). His 'liked' Facebook pages include Pirelli and Super Cheap Auto Racing. His status updates regularly refer to working on his own or a family member's car (e.g., 'adjusting suspension on rc car, pain in the ass'), or otherwise pertain to cars (e.g., 'Lol on ebay pranking people selling cars hahaha').

He is also open about his passion for music. A status update informs his network: 'Just added another 461 songs to my collection of 29,000.' Other updates refer to acquiring Eminem's then-new album – *Recovery* – and how much he's enjoying it; with a subsequent status update comprising a few lines from 'Space Bound' from the same album. Another status update reads: 'Ahhhh, end the day to Nirvana' – referencing the 1990s grunge band. He's apparently *not* a fan of Justin Bieber, and has 'liked' the Facebook page entitled, '"That girl has such a pretty voice!" – "Mom, that's Justin Bieber"'. Music-related interests he has listed on his profile include 40fm (a radio station), LMFAO (an electro/hiphop duo in the USA), and he declares he likes his music LOUD.

Corey is an avid gamer and expresses his interest in video games via his Facebook profile, too. He posts regular status updates about the games he's playing or wants to play – e.g., about watching video advertisements online for the next *Call of Duty* game, commenting that it 'looks great'. Other indicative status updates include count-downs to the release of a new game (e.g., 'Heh heh 6 days till new Need for Speed :D' – a car racing game), or a tally of hours spent playing a new game. Under his set of interests on

Facebook, he has listed The GTA Place – a space dedicated to *Grand Theft Auto* news and fan comments – along with the F.E.A.R. (*First Encounter Assault Recon*) Facebook page, to name two.

Corey is similarly upfront about being a grade 10 high school student. Many of the photographs he's posted to Facebook show him dressed in school uniform – including two of his previous profile pictures (these pictures also appear to have been taken at school, based on the classroom-like backgrounds). His references to school often have a 'students versus teachers' tone to them, or are ironic comments on being a 'typical' student. This includes commenting on something silly a teacher has done in class, or joining in a discussion on someone else's Facebook wall about how boring a book is that they're currently studying. Interestingly, many of his written comments directly pertaining to school appear to have been posted via mobile phones during class. A status update talks about how he and some mates surreptitiously unplugged a teacher's computer mouse, and what happened when the teacher went to try and use it during class. Corey himself doesn't achieve well at school. School reports identify him as barely average in most subjects. He was once briefly suspended from school for a misdemeanour. He relishes every opportunity to miss school in sanctioned ways (e.g., visits to family interstate, family trips to major events that require time off school). Indicative Facebook statements he's 'liked' include: 'Anyone noticed that "studying" is like "student" and "dying" put together?' and 'DON'T YOU HATE SCHOOL INTERNET BLOCKING'.

Corey's news feed is a dynamic space. His status updates and photo posts typically elicit responses from his network members – they either click the 'like' button associated with the post, or write a comment. Corey will generally have ten or more comments attached to a post. These comment sets often take on the feel of a conversation between friends. For example, Corey posted the following as his status at 11pm one school night: 'Bad Company 2 is the shitt.' This elicited the following dialogue:

Julianna:	Do u play on the pc?
Corey:	Yeahh
Julianna:	(: do u play offten b
Corey:	Ohh not really only just started again
Julianna:	Oh ok
Caleb:	What Bad Company 2 is shit, oohhhhh yeah i know aye
Corey:	Ohh, cooz COD is so awesome **cough** i mean overated bullshit
Caleb:	what just because your shit at [playing] it? xD

Corey's updates are regularly 'of the moment' and concern things happening to him at the time. He often posts photos taken with his phone, or updates his Facebook status via his phone. Updates convey a strong sense that staying in touch with others through Facebook is an important part of his daily rhythms. Corey's use of Facebook and phone-based texting merge in interesting ways. Facebook status updates include: 'Someone text me… [phone number]' and another asking for people's numbers to enter into his new phone. A comment posted by Corey on someone else's wall reads: 'Did you get my text???' A status update posted while working on his uncle's farm underscores the importance for Corey of being in touch: 'WOOHOO back in signal [referring to his iPhone], for a little while anyway, havin a ball on the farm though.' Of-the-moment updates often elicit humorous exchanges with his network members, like:

Corey:	Wish I could find my bloody earphones
Uncle:	check on ya head…. LOL
Corey:	Speakin from experiance champ?
Friend:	LOL

Corey's ways of using Facebook include presenting himself as a particular kind of person: one who is interested in cars, music, video gaming, someone who likes to stay in touch with others in multiple ways, as someone who can give and take cheek, and as a rather disaffected school student. These parts of his identity are likely to be well known to others in his network, most of whom he knows offline. Corey is very sociable, adding regularly to his Facebook page. His status updates and photo posts tend to assume an engaged audience, and typically elicit reactions from a range of people, making his Facebook page a dynamic interactive space, albeit one that is largely an extension of his offline life with an extensive set of kindred-spirited peers and family members.

Chris' ways with Facebook

Chris, mid-forties, lives in Los Angeles. He has a Bachelor's degree in sociology, and works in the music industry as a database manager. He is the bassist for the band 'ExDetectives'. A self-professed 'database wrangler and roving Mac Jedi', Chris has had a long and dynamic online presence: personal websites in the 1990s, a highly active blog since the early 2000s (Quartzcity.net), and a pro Flickr account since 2002. He has an active Tumblr account, where he posts curiosities – mainly photos and videos – that don't find a home on his main blog; and active accounts with Delicious, an online bookmarking service; Doppler, a map and photo-based travel documentation site; Twitter; Skype; LibraryThing, a book curating, recommendation and discussion service; Last.fm, a music streaming and playlist sharing site; and Discogs, a social music information, reviews and discussion service, to name just a few. His blog also lists links to his Amazon. com wishlist; his eBay shop; his Google profile; and to the contributions he's made to Wikipedia. His Facebook profile includes direct links to his blog, and to his Twitter and Tumblr accounts. The lines between Chris' online and offline lives are comprehensively blurred – he's always online, accessing multiple internet spaces and services wherever he may be and whatever he is doing, via his omnipresent mobile phone and laptop.

Joining Facebook was an organic extension of what Chris was already doing online. His network of over 300 people (December 2010) includes family and close friends (around 20 per cent of his network, half of whom live close by and half who live quite far away), a set of less strong ties with workmates (8 per cent), and 10 per cent he's not sure how he 'knows' (e.g., some may be fans of his band, people he's met in passing). The remainder – roughly 62 per cent – comprise a loosely tied mix of Facebook friends he has met or come to know via work and his band – such as album cover artists, graphic designers, writers, musicians, and singers, and people working in digital media fields – or online by means of music discussion forums and the like. His network includes two people working for Apple, one for Yahoo! and one for Microsoft. Several work in radio or television. Six identify themselves as freelance writers. Forty identify as belonging to bands (including five in Australia, five in the UK, and one in Poland). Some of these 'friends' are the Facebook pages for the band or for singers, guitarists, drummers within established bands. Almost 20 per cent of his network members identify having a strong interest in music, typically 'indie' or 'alternative' music (e.g., space rock, psychedelic, post-punk), at least half of whom blog regularly about music or work in the music industry (e.g., as session guitarist, DJ, record label employee). Around 75 per cent of Chris' network members include links to their other online spaces within their profiles, too (e.g., to MySpace pages, official band pages, food and music review blogs, record label websites, professional pages, employer or company pages).

In terms of distribution, of those who identify a current location (80 per cent or so), a quarter of Chris' network is located in California (with half of these located in Los Angeles). The second largest grouping – close to 8 per cent – is on the north-east US coast (i.e., New York,

New Jersey, Connecticut, Massachusetts and Pennsylvania). The remainder are widely dispersed across the USA and other countries (e.g., eight in Australia, eight in the UK, and one each in Canada, Austria, Sweden, Germany, Armenia, and Peru).

An active Facebook user, Chris is a strong presence in others' Facebook and in-person networks. Typical updates on his news feed include being tagged in a note written by a friend challenging him and others to name their top 20 favourite guitarists of all time. Chris was the first to respond with his list of 20. He's regularly tagged in videos and photographs posted by others. His birthday prompted 50 congratulatory wall messages from friends. He comments frequently on other people's walls and 'likes' Facebook pages relevant to his interests – including STRATFOR (according to its tagline, the '#1 source for global intelligence'); Psychotronic Netflix, a service recommending forgotten, bizarre, unique movies to be rented from the Netflix video service; Zeising Books, specializing in science fiction, horror, fantasy, small press, art, and mystery books; among others. Chris also makes use of Facebook's event notification pages put in place to help groups advertise events to indicate he will be attending different local live band events. He also updates his Facebook status from his iPhone to say where in the world he is (e.g., 'in NYC'). Chris regularly posts video clips of 'forgotten' or marginal bands to his wall (e.g., a New Zealand 1980s art-noise band, the Pin Group), along with notifications of his own band's show dates and videos from these shows. During October–December 2010 his posts included seven band-related videos (not counting those relating to his own band), three music-related videos (e.g., interviews), eight photos to do with live shows he's attended, four links to articles about television shows or underground films, three links to music articles, two food-related posts, one link to a news article about a toy robot shutting down traffic in a busy city, and one link to a new hybrid jellyfish.

Chris' posts typically generate responses from his network. During this same period 43 different people have 'liked' something he's posted, 15 of whom 'liked' more than one post. In the same period, 25 people commented in response to a post, three of whom commented multiple times. These numbers suggest that his network is loosely knit, more so than built around a small core of strong social ties who regularly interact on his Facebook pages. In reviewing his profile pages, there is a sense that Facebook is something Chris uses to stay in touch with friends, acquaintances and people of whom he is a fan, as well as a space he uses to share with others his often eclectic interests in music, technology, food, photography, and the quirky things in life.

One click writing: networking 'moves' and 'literacy innovation' with the 'like' function

The programmed features of social networking services generally, and Facebook in particular, enable and recruit a range of literacy skills and 'moves' or micro-practices. These include 'friending', sharing photographs, presenting identity 'bits' through images and other texts, sending messages, using applications (apps), managing privacy and self-disclosure, taking part in social gaming, building social relationships (accomplished in myriad ways, such as tagging others in photographs, sending them virtual 'gifts', commenting on their posts, posting on others' walls, adding suggested friends who are 'strangers' to you, etc.), and so on (see, for example, work by: Green and Hannon 2007; boyd 2008; Knobel and Lankshear 2008; Haferkamp and Krämer 2010). If we think of 'facebooking' (or 'bebo-ing', 'orkuting', or 'tweeting') as a literacy dimension of larger social practices of participating in social networks, then friending, tagging, using photos to do identity work, sending virtual gifts, posting to walls, etc., can be seen as elements of 'facebooking' as a ('new') literacy practice.

In the manner of the 'virtuous circles' of appropriation and innovation described by Castells (1996/2000), the interactional affordances of social networking services are taken up, used, extended, and innovated upon by everyday people (see also Wellman 2001; Wellman et al. 2006). Facebook's 'like' function, which is especially popular among its users, provides an interesting case in point. As previously noted, users can '*like*' the posts, notes, photos, status updates, etc., posted by others in their networks by simply clicking the 'like' button or link. When someone 'likes' something on Facebook, an auto-announcement is made within the network's news feed and, if it's a fan page that's liked, a link to this page is embedded within the user's profile as well. This creates text, makes meaning, does identity work, expresses solidarity, sends signals, instantiates one's sense of 'cool' or insiderliness, and so on. It is writing by clicking. It is also an invitation to creative appropriation and extension – for making moves in shaping 'new' literacies.

Since 2009, Facebook's 'like' function has taken on an enlarged life of its own. The function was designed as a means for sharing Facebook content between users (Facebook 2010). In turn, Facebook users have taken advantage of the 'like' function and have created pages devoid of any significant content apart from the actual name of the Facebook page and a list of comments. For example, in December 2010 the Facebook community page entitled 'I have texted lying down and dropped my phone on my face' was 'liked' by 999,249 people and 'Comebacks that make the whole room go "OOOOOHHHHHH"' was liked by 1,693,724. Both pages include comments from people who have 'liked' the page (e.g., '& my nose still hurts lol', 'lets get this to 2 million peoples'), and little else. Countless websites external to Facebook have sprung up that simply list hundreds of statements that can be 'liked' and displayed on Facebook profiles (see, for example, Likeworthy.com, HappyLikes.com, and FBlike.net, Go-likes.info, and Facebook apps such as Apps.facebook.com/likethislikethis and Apps. facebook.com/worthliking). Clicking the 'like' button beside a statement adds it to one's Facebook page. Some of these like-statement services, like FBlike.net and Like This Like This Facebook app, allow users to add their own statements for others to 'like' and post on their Facebook pages. Many of these services also include paid-for like statements that advertise products.

Among the Facebook users we study, Corey is the most regular and avid user of the 'like' function. Between 1 September and 26 November 2010, he posted 39 written status updates, and 139 'like' statements (excluding 'likes' for products, services, and celebrities). He has never contributed to a 'like statement' aggregator, preferring to use what's already available, and typically finds things to 'like' by manually searching Facebook (especially when a new video game comes out, or when he wants to 'like' a particular band), or by spotting a statement on a friend's news feed to 'like' and add automatically to his own profile or, occasionally, by browsing available aggregator lists of 'likes' on Facebook and elsewhere (e.g., Fblike.net). His 'liked' statements even include 'When I'm bored I sit on Facebook and Like stuff...'.

As with his other 'moves' on Facebook, Corey's 'like' statements represent him as someone who loves music, is an avid video gamer, a certain kind of school student, and more. For example, he has liked the following statements:

- '▶Music♪♫♫♬ Volume: _ _ ▬ ■ ■ ■▌ 100 %'
- '"Dude that song is old".... "Well so is ur mom.. but u still listen to her" :P'
- 'Yeah I'll do it in a minute really translates to F*** Off I'm playing COD [Call of Duty]'
- 'Girl: So.. I'm guessing you play COD? Boy: What's COD? :/Girl: Marry me?'
- 'If Facebook were a subject, my parents would be sooo proud. :)'
- 'OK! I am going to get stuck into my homework. *goes to google* OMG PACMAN!'

- '"Would u like to share that with the class?" "No, That's why I whispered it"'
- 'Oh hey life, i didn't see you there behind all that school.'
- 'Teachers call it cheating. We call it teamwork :)'
- '"where's your book?!" "at home." "and what's it doing there?" "having more fun than me."'

While some might aspire to *authoring* like-worthy statements, there is also something to be said for knowing how to *source* and put them to work effectively. To 'get' Corey's 'like' statements is to be well on the way to knowing the real-life Corey, as well as to 'getting' a moment of literacy in flux.

Reflection and discussion

What implications does a practice like Corey's writing-with-one-click have for how we define 'writing'?

Targeted social networking services and 'strategic' social networking practices: the case of Academia.edu

Some social networking services (i.e., sites and services organized in the first instance around putting people together rather than resourcing interests) are more 'targeted' or 'focused' than others. They aim to put people together on a single dimension or in relation to a specific purpose – such as networking people *professionally*, or networking people who share a particular occupational role or passion. Services of this kind include LinkedIn.com, a popular business and professional networking service; LibraryThing. com, which 'connects you to people who read what you do'; Ravelry.com, a network for knitters and yarn workers; Audimated.com, for music artists and fans; Exploroo.com, for travellers to share information, travel tips and photos; and Delicious.com for social bookmarking, to name a few. Each of these services is organized primarily around user profiles; that is, upon signing up for the service, users complete a template that prompts them for information about themselves (e.g., age, gender, location, biographical details) and their relevant interests (e.g., books they've read, music or bands they like), which generates a profile page about the user. Functions embedded within the profile page typically include an automatically updated list of 'friends' or 'fans', methods for finding people, groups, or content to add to your personal network, links to privacy settings, links to spaces where members can add content to the network, and links to collective or collaborative spaces (e.g., a news feed that documents new content, discussion forums). Clearly, lines can get blurred here between 'resourcing personal interaction' and 'resourcing interests'. The distinction cannot be absolute because people cannot be separated from their interests. It is a matter of emphasis.

Writing about the importance of having the wherewithal to access and develop social ties with people who can help shape, direct, and inform interests and passions, John Hagel, John Seely Brown, and Lang Davison (2010) speak to the importance of online social network services for enhancing face-to-face networks and optimizing your 'performance' within an area of passion or interest. Targeted online social networking services can be used to help find and *access* 'people and resources when we need them' (ibid.: 9). Knowing how to access people and resources is increasingly important in a world that is changing so quickly that we often aren't sure 'we even know what we're looking for' (ibid.: 24). According to Hagel and colleagues, social networking services also can facilitate your 'ability to *attract* people and resources to you that are relevant and valuable, even if you were not aware before that they existed' (original emphasis; ibid.). This includes making serendipitous connections between people, ideas, knowledge, and the like that are facilitated by the architecture and the strong and weak social ties created within online networking services. In addition, for Hagel and colleagues, attracting fruitful attention is enhanced by 'findability' (Hagel et al. 2010: 110). Targeted social networking services up the ante in terms of making it easier for someone to be found by others who share similar, if not the same, interests.

Hagel, Brown, and Davison discuss how these kinds of networking services – like LinkedIn.com, for example – can help people tap into what they call 'knowledge flows' or information about developments and innovations 'at the edges' of your sphere of interest. These same networking resources can also help a person to contribute insights, tips, resources, and knowledge to the area in order to help others reach their own full potential. They present an example of a mechanic who is given a stock of knowledge about cars and how they work, upon her initial training, but who needs to be able to tap into flows of knowledge about changes in car maintenance and repair (e.g., pertaining to electronics) in order to maintain a competitive business. Knowledge flows for this mechanic can be tapped and contributed to in myriad in-person and online ways, including active, online specialist discussion boards that discuss developments and new technologies in car manufacturing and maintenance (Hagel et al. 2010: 11).

Hagel and colleagues address social networking within the context of a much wider discussion of a contemporary paradigm shift in approaches to resourcing human endeavours, as we note in the following chapter. Nonetheless, much of what they have to say is directly relevant to discussing targeted social networking services. For example, they distinguish between strong and weak social ties within personal networks established on a targeted social networking service, and argue that both are important. Strong social ties describe people at the core of one's network and who often are known well face-to-face. Strong social ties provide long-term support and encouragement within an area of interest or an endeavour. Weak social ties are created with people who inhabit the 'edges' of a person's network and are included because they are friends of friends, or because they work in the same field, or share something in common with your own area of interest. Interestingly, it is these weak social ties that Hagel and colleagues see as having the most potential to connect a person with new ideas, new resources, new ways of thinking, and insights into the 'new' edges of a practice or 'flow' of knowledge (Hagel et al. 2010: 23). This cross-pollination is at its best when it is cross-institutional, and makes good use of 'super-nodes' or people who can bridge 'groups of people who might not otherwise know each other' (ibid.: 158).

People involved in education at school, community, and university levels have been quite active in establishing targeted social networking services. The education sector has a strong history of using email discussion lists and online forums to discuss education issues, share ideas, and create social ties across geographic distances and time zones (cf., Mason 1998; Schlager et al. 2002; Marshall 2007). One social networking service currently gaining traction within the higher education community is Academia.edu. This is a free social networking service dedicated to 'helping researchers connect to each other and find material that's relevant to their field of study' (Kincaid 2010: n.p.). Academia.edu was launched in September 2008, and two years later (at the time of writing) is recognized as the largest online social networking service for academics (Wikipedia 2010j).

Creating a profile on Academia.edu involves providing your name, some biographic data, and institutional affiliation (university, university department or institute, or independent researcher status). These labels become 'tags' within a member's profile. Clicking on them generates a kind of 'family tree' graphic showing who else from that department/institute or university has an Academia.edu profile. These taxonomies include spaces for faculty, post-doctoral students, graduate students, and other department members. The template spaces for these roles underscore the primary clientele for this networking service. Each profile also includes a set of self-generated tags that describe the member's research interests (for example, 'literacy', 'new literacies', 'new media', 'digital literacies'). Clicking on these tags generates a list of everyone within Academia.edu who has used the same tag or tags to describe their research interests. This enables moving beyond your circle of close professional ties to discover others sharing similar research foci. Each profile on Academia.edu also has provision for uploading conference papers, articles, chapters, book manuscripts, presentation slides, conference and job announcements, and so on. These can also be tagged (e.g., 'adolescent literacy', 'digital media') to be found in within-network searches.

Within Academia.edu social ties are one-way (as in Twitter), rather than two-way (as in Facebook). That is, other users do not need a member's permission to 'follow' them; following someone does not mean they will follow you in turn. The service also suggests people to follow, based on your research interests, institutional affiliations, and existing professional ties within the network. It is also possible to 'follow' a research area within the network. The research area 'New Literacies' had registered 67 'followers' at the time of writing, for example. Browsing through this list of followers enables interested others to explore the work of (potentially) interesting others. Finding someone interesting and clicking through to their profile page to read samples of their work and so on also makes available their lists of departmental colleagues, their followers and who they are following. It thus becomes relatively easy to traverse other people's professional ties along with the resources these ties make available, thereby potentially generating weak ties that tap into new knowledge flows and the new edges of a field of study.

For members, the default front page of Academia.edu contains updates regarding activity associated with your profile and uploaded resources (e.g., who searched for you using Google and the search terms they used, what pages within your profile were viewed or what documents were read) as well as a news feed comprising status updates, documents uploaded, announcements, who is now following whom, and so on, for all the people you yourself are following within the network overall.

While 'findability' isn't a concept used by the developers of Academia. edu, they clearly take it seriously and have actively built it into the service. The search engine internal to the network looks for 'questions, people, research interests'. Entering a question like, say, 'What is literacy?', returns a listing of matched documents available within the network. Searching for 'new literacies' returns a number of people who have listed this as a research interest, along with matched documents also available within the network. Members' names and uploaded content are also indexed to external internet search engines, and a quarter of the traffic to members' pages is currently generated by external searches (Alexa 2010). Furthermore, the external search words used by others to find your Academia.edu profile or documents are listed automatically on your own profile page as 'keywords'. The operative assumption within Academia.edu seems to be that 'findability' matters, and knowing how your work is being 'found' can be used to develop or inform attention-attracting or idea dispersion strategies. The service also documents the number of times your profile or uploaded documents have been viewed by others as a marker of whether others are finding your work useful or worth paying attention to. As explained on the site:

> Keywords are search queries that people have used on Google, and other search engines, to find your pages on Academia.edu.
>
> Tip:
>
> To make your page appear higher up on Google:
>
> • Link to your Academia.edu page from your department website
> • Upload more documents - papers, talks and a CV
>
> You can see statistics on how many views your pages have had by visiting the My Stats link in the page footer.
>
> (Academia.edu 2010: n.p.)

Thus, some of the social practices encouraged by Academia.edu entail sharing your work as widely as possible with others. From a literacy perspective, this calls for understanding how to make the most of tags that will attract a wide viewership; making your work freely available in an easily accessed manner (e.g., easy-to-download and read pdf documents); working out who is useful to follow and why; knowing how to make use of the service to tap into knowledge flows within your field; and knowing how to maintain a dynamic and informative profile that's worth following, to name just a few. For example, in posting (with permission) the page proofs for one of our own books, we found that if no tags were added, only those people following our profiles would be alerted to the uploaded manuscript through an automated notice posted to their respective news feeds. Adding the tags 'new literacies', 'digital literacies', and 'new media' increased that number 40-fold: comprising the larger set of members who had included at least one of these three tags in their listing of research interests and would be most likely to find the document through a tag-based search. Academia. edu's 'findability' provisions have interesting implications for what it might mean to have a 'higher education take' on key drivers from new shifts within business cultures, as described by Hagel and colleagues (2010), with respect to academics marketing or actively promoting themselves and their work within higher education networks.

Explicit encouragement from the Academia.edu developers to upload documents to your profile likewise facilitates cross-pollination and access to ideas. Searching for or browsing tagged research interests pulls up lists of potentially relevant documents that you might not otherwise encounter so easily: including pre-publication and post-publication versions of books, chapters, and articles not available in the libraries you can access, through to conference papers that have flown under your attention radar. For example, running a search for the term 'social network' during the course of

---

Reflection and discussion

- As a professional in your field, how important – or not – is it (or will it be) to deliberately work at attracting attention to your own work and ideas?

- A number of online social networking services include platforms that more or less comprise a set of empty templates which groups of people can use to meet their own goals, needs and interests. These services include sites like Ning.com, BigTent.com, and Grouply.com.

- Sign up to the English Companion Ning (Englishcompanion. ning.com), a well-recognized social network designed expressly for English teachers, and examine the ways in which users themselves contribute to this network via blog posts, group discussions, and forum threads. Compare this social networking service with Academia.edu in terms of access provided to new ideas and knowledge flows, support for or evidence of developing strong and weak social ties, 'findability', and so on. Discuss what your comparative analysis suggests in terms of participating effectively in targeted social networking services.

   If you're not interested in the English Companion Ning, you could alternatively look at:

   o New Media Literacies Community (Newmedialiteracies.org)
   o Digital Arts Education (Digitalartsed.ning.com)
   o Classroom 2.0 (Classroom20.com)

writing this chapter generated a list of around 100 documents on Academia. edu. These provided access to recent research from countries as diverse as Australia, Malaysia, Macedonia, and Singapore, written from varying and interesting theoretical and discipline orientations, and without reference to literacy as a key organizing concept. None was returned in earlier Google Scholar searches and all have helped inform this chapter.

Network awareness as a literacy practice

As noted in Chapter 1, Howard Rheingold identifies 'network awareness' as an important early twenty-first-century literacy. Within an increasingly networked world, network awareness operates on two key axes: understanding network 'architecture' and control, and understanding the social uses of networks (Rheingold 2010a; for similar ideas, see Wellman 2001). The *structure* of digital networks includes such things as: programming code and protocols; government regulations and laws; market ownership and control; and the very architecture of the internet as a complex set of connections, nodes, servers and their physical location, file transfer protocols, and interface displays that 'affect the systems in which and by which humans communicate (e.g., de-centralized or centralized control)' (ibid.: n.p.).

Rheingold uses Reed's Law to link the structural dimensions of online networks with social networks themselves. Reed's Law describes three kinds of value that can accrue from online networks: 'the linear value of services that are aimed at individual users, the "square" value from [networks] facilitating transactions, and the exponential value for facilitating group affiliations' (Rheingold 2010b: 22). Linear connections tend to be organized around moving content from producers to consumers (Rheingold's examples include published stories and consumer goods). As the network increases in scale and reach, 'transactions (e.g., e-mail, voice-mail, securities, services) become central' (ibid.). At the level of groups, value centres on the ways technical and social networks support collaboration and collective action (Rheingold's examples include newsgroups, virtual communities, auctions, and organizing get-out-the-vote campaigns; ibid.).

The importance of network awareness lies partly in understanding the relationship between technical and social networks, and how this affects who has access to, can use or participate in, and have control over key goods, ideas and services both on- and offline. This includes understanding and appreciating freedom. Network awareness includes asking important questions like 'Who will control the freedom to innovate online?' (Rheingold 2010b: 22). This important question resonates with Chris Anderson's (2010) valuing of the 'wide-open Web of peer production' or what he calls the 'generative Web' – where 'everyone is free to create what they want' (n.p.). Generative web space is not confined to apps or heavily template-based and auto-updated driven services. It refers to non-commercial spaces, resources, services, and platforms that thrive under conditions of being 'driven by the nonmonetary incentives of expression, attention, reputation, and the like' (ibid.; see also Berners-Lee 2010). From this perspective, many young people (as well as not so young) display impressive network awareness in the ways they mobilize internet resources and cobble together creative and productive ad hoc online networks of collaborators to pursue shared creative and innovative purposes (see, for example, Leander and Frank 2006; Leander and Lovvorn 2006; Leander and Mills 2007; Thomas 2007a). Understanding how formal, ad hoc and targeted social networks and services 'work' – and who ultimately controls them – is integral to Rheingold's conception of network awareness: such as understanding what members are choosing to endorse by means of, say, their one-click writing (e.g., are they knowingly sharing product advertising messages?; are they celebrating diversity?).

The development of members' profiles within social networking services, what kinds of person they present themselves as, and how they contribute to the network are also important elements of network awareness. Rheingold emphasizes the importance of recognizing that people leave a kind of digital audit trail across the internet, and that others can access and interpret the information left by this trail (the innocuous-seeming 'like' button appended to sites outside Facebook is a good example of how audit trails get made). Accordingly, network awareness includes knowing how to access and manage the privacy settings for a range of social networking services, and paying attention to what one is sharing or divulging online (Rheingold, in interview with Powell 2010: n.p.). Interestingly, recent research suggests that young people are widely aware of online privacy issues and the importance of self-regulation online (see boyd and Hargittai 2010; Ito et al. 2010; Livingstone and Brake 2010), suggesting that they are developing important forms of network awareness that will serve them well across a range of contexts.

Being able to fine-tune one's networks is also important to Rheingold: knowing who to pay attention to in one's networks, who is expert, trustworthy or entertaining, and knowing who to perhaps exclude. This in turn links to understanding the importance of 'reputation' and reciprocity online and how these can also help one effectively participate online (Rheingold 2010b), and how to become 'attention worthy' and be seen by others as someone worth recruiting to their networks. Knowing which social networking services and other internet resources will best suit one's needs is part of this. Understanding which networks focus on social relationships and which focus on professional development and networking, and which can be constructed out of available social media to suit particular collaborative purposes, usefully extends what people can get from being online.

Reflection and discussion

- What might be some of the implications of Rheingold's 'network awareness' for classroom teaching (especially in schools where internet access is heavily filtered)?

- Ito and colleagues (2010) urge educators to engage with young people's interest-based social networking practices and build on these within the classroom. Discuss how this might look in practice.

Examining social networking services and practices of online social networking alerts us to a range of 'new literacies' understandings, dispositions, and proficiencies involved in using networking platforms, services, and other internet resources effectively. These include: knowing how to increase one's 'findability' (if this is a personal goal) through judicious use of tags; knowing which social ties are important and why; joining relevant, high-profile groups within a network; actively contributing ideas and resources to a network; and so on. They also include knowing how to 'read' others' contributions within a network – such contributions may be more about expressing solidarity and identity than useful information. Participating effectively in a social network may also entail knowing how to use social media and resources to work collaboratively with others to achieve shared goals and how to contribute resources, tips, expertise, and the like back to the network for the benefit of its members at large.

Interestingly, as the practices and potential of online social networking services and practices are becoming more widely researched and understood, their significance for learning – formal, non-formal, and informal learning alike – is being recognized and advocated by influential advocates of *social learning* for educational reform. We take up the idea of social learning in the next chapter.

PART 3

New literacies and social learning

Social learning, 'push' and 'pull', and building platforms for collaborative learning

Introduction

This chapter explores three ideas that have recently been associated with each other in discussions of how contemporary internet architecture supports participatory and collaborative approaches to learning within non-formal and formal settings. These are the concept of 'social learning' as developed by John Seely Brown and Richard Adler (2008), the distinction between 'push' and 'pull' paradigms for mobilizing resources in pursuit of human purposes (Hagel and Brown 2005; Brown and Adler 2008), and the idea of building 'collaboration platforms' for social learning (Jarche 2005, 2010; Cross 2006; Brown and Adler 2008). As will become apparent in the course of this chapter, the kinds of new literacies discussed in previous chapters are related to social learning in a dynamic and reflexive way. To a large extent they are acquired via processes of social learning within participatory cultures. At the same time, however, these new literacies are integral to forms of ongoing social learning that will become increasingly important for living well in the foreseeable future. This chapter turns attention to social learning and will provide a framework for discussing some empirical cases in Chapter 8.

Social learning

Multiple versions of social learning

Conceptions and theories of social learning are not new and, despite some 'family resemblances', differ significantly from one another and are used to do substantially different kinds of scholarly, research, and applied work. One broad line of social learning theory is commonly traced origins-wise from work in the late nineteenth century by Cornell Montgomery, and subsequently through the work of Neal Miller and John Dollard (e.g., 1941) in the 1940s, Julian Rotter (e.g., 1954) in the 1950s, and Albert Bandura (e.g., 1977) in the 1970s. This work draws on currents within fields like behavioural psychology, cognitive psychology, social cognition and clinical psychology. It is concerned with understanding modes of learning that build on observation of situated human behaviour rather than on direct involvement and, in some versions, is referred to as observational learning, and in others as imitation, vicarious learning, and modelling. Variants of this theory have been used to study disposition toward aggressive behaviour, social deviance, and criminal inclinations.

By contrast, Mark Reed and colleagues (2010) discuss in recent work social learning as a 'normative goal' within natural resource management and policy in the interests of environmental and ecological sustainability. From this perspective, social learning is understood as involving a change in understanding at the level of 'social units' (such as an organization, an institution, or a community of practice), that occurs through interaction where 'the message is spread from person to person through social networks' (ibid.: n.p.). This is a version of social learning as a process of proactivity for desirable outcomes. Indeed, Reed and colleagues see some of the roots of this version of social learning in Freire's 'conscientization' pedagogy among Latin American peasants where participants collectively became 'critically literate about their circumstances ... through collective reflection and problematization' (ibid.).

The concept of social learning that we are interested in here shares some features with these other versions, but differs significantly from them. It has been developed over the past 20 years by John Seely Brown and colleagues (Brown et al. 1989; Brown and Duguid 2002; Brown and Adler 2008); most recently with particular reference to higher education learning settings. It draws on diverse work done in sociocultural studies of language and learning, social cognition, cognitive science, socio-technical studies, media and communication studies, and other related fields since the 1980s. It also reflects and responds to important social, technical, economic, and institutional changes that have occurred during this same period.

Background to the present view of social learning

In a seminal paper published in the *Educational Researcher* in 1989 – prior to the widespread diffusion of concepts like 'communities of practice', 'cognitive apprenticeship', 'situated learning and cognition', and so on that were realized during the 1990s; and prior to the era of mass access to the internet and the emergence of the World Wide Web – Brown, Allan Collins, and Paul Duguid challenged some key assumptions integral to formal classroom learning on the basis of then emergent research. Foremost among these was the assumption that learning involves transmitting 'abstract, decontextualized formal concepts': treating knowledge as 'theoretically independent of the situations in which it is learned and used', and treating the context and activity in which learning occurs as 'ancillary to learning' rather than inseparable from and integral to what is learned (Brown et al. 1989: 32). Referring to examples like the difference between acquiring vocabulary in the normal course of situated everyday engagements outside of school and learning vocabulary via abstracted dictionary definitions in class (see Miller and Gildea 1987), Brown and colleagues (1989: 32) argued that 'different ideas of appropriate learning activity produce very different results'. They suggested that by separating learning from 'authentic' activity grounded in physical and social contexts and situations, formal education largely defeats its goal of promoting 'useable, robust knowledge'. In place of decontextualized abstracted knowledge transfer, they advocated approaches like cognitive apprenticeship (Lave 1988; Collins et al. 1989; Rogoff 1991) that 'embed learning in activity and make deliberate use of the social and physical context' (Brown et al. 1989: 31).

A key part of this early formulation involved the idea that knowledge is always an outcome of sociocultural practices in which people use mental and material tools, acquire and employ skills, and draw on forms of existing understanding and knowledge and belief, to undertake tasks and pursue particular purposes and goals – including *knowledge-specific* purposes and goals. The goals and tools they use, and the beliefs, understandings and extant knowledge they draw upon are not individual, private possessions but, rather, are social. They have been developed and refined over time by other people pursuing purposes in socially recognized ways. Sometimes these are purposes aimed specifically at producing knowledge to inform wider purposes (e.g., in science or in problem solving or trouble shooting). Sometimes the purposes are routine, and knowledge grows out of them as an accumulation from the wider practice – for example, agricultural knowledge accumulates out of people routinely engaging in agriculture, as well as out of the research activities of people like agronomists and soil scientists. However, the concepts, tools, procedures, skills, beliefs, and so on, vary to a greater or lesser extent across different contexts and situations and groups of 'practitioners'/communities of practice. This means that unless we have some idea of the procedures and variations involved in the particular practices and activities out of which knowledge is generated, we cannot possibly – other than by random coincidence – *have* the knowledge that the practitioners (producers and bearers of knowledge) and their kindred colleagues have. We certainly cannot do the same kinds of things with that knowledge as they do. It cannot *mean* to us what it means to them.

Brown, Collins, and Duguid (1989: 33) make the point with respect to conceptual tools (ideas, concepts, formulae, rules of thumb, interpretive frames, etc.) as follows:

> Conceptual tools similarly reflect the cumulative wisdom of the culture in which they are used and the insights and experience of individuals. Their meaning is not invariant but a product of negotiation within the community. Again, appropriate use is not simply a function of the abstract concept alone. It is a function of the culture and the activities in which the concept has been developed. Just as carpenters and cabinet makers use chisels differently, so physicists and engineers use mathematical formulae differently. Activity, concept, and culture are interdependent. No one can be totally understood without the other two. Learning must involve all three. Teaching methods often try to impart abstracted concepts as fixed, well-defined, independent entities that can be explored in prototypical examples and textbook exercises. But such exemplification cannot provide the important insights into either the culture or the authentic activities of members of that culture that learners need.

If we want to *learn* deeply, we need access to the means, contexts, and tasks that are integral to generating knowledge, not simply to content transmission and abstracted activities of application like 'essay writing'. To be sure, you can write 'history essays' without knowing anything about how historians work; but you cannot write *history*, *do* history, or acquire *historical* knowledge – that is, *know* history. The significance and costs of separating learning from authentic contexts of knowing became increasingly apparent and better understood during the period between the publication of Brown, Collins, and Duguid's paper, and the publication of Brown and Adler's (2008) paper on social learning.

Three related factors are especially pertinent here.

1 During the intervening period rapid and far-reaching advances were made in theory and research relevant to understanding the nature and significance of social learning. This is the period during which concepts and theories of 'situated cognition', 'situated language', 'literacy and learning', 'situated practice', 'social practice', 'communities of practice', 'cognitive and cultural apprenticeship', moving from 'being a novice' to 'becoming an expert', or from being a 'peripheral participant' to a 'full participant' though processes understood in terms of concepts like 'legitimate peripheral participation', 'guided participation', 'participatory appropriation', and the like, became established in research on learning (see, among many other examples, Lave and Wenger 1991; Rogoff 1991; Chaiklin and Lave 1996; Cook and Brown 1999; Wenger 1999; Gee 2003, 2007; Sawyer 2006).

2 At the same time, processes of structural change beginning in the 1960s and 1970s escalated and impacted dramatically on social institutions and economic life in modernized Western societies. As noted in Chapter 1, the downscaling of the welfare state and consequent restructuring of bureaucratic institutions upped the ante for citizens across the social spectrum to develop new 'institutional epistemologies' by learning how restructured organizations function. Keeping up with institutional change was an important catalyst for the related ideals of lifelong learning, learning how to learn, and transferring knowledge and training. The growth of global outsourcing in manufacture and services, the consequent loss of many traditional jobs, the increased significance attached to symbolic analytic work, 'higher order skills' (see Gee et al. 1996, for an overview), and increased skill and knowledge demands on frontline (formerly routine production, 'unskilled', and 'semi-skilled') workers, raised the bar for job-related knowledge and understanding, as 'initiative', 'entrepreneurial spirit', 'troubleshooting ability', and increased demands for 'innovativeness' and 'value-adding capacity' became the order of the day. These new 'requirements' placed intolerable strain on 'low level knowledge' and 'mere information'. Competitive edge and, even, economic viability, within an organization's workforce increasingly called for 'the kinds of thinking skills that allow one to be

an "expert novice" ... expert at continually learning anew and in depth' (ibid.: 164). These requirements transcend learning as 'content', but require learning within contexts, situations, and practices that *ground* processes, procedures, purposes, and tasks.

Similarly, the nature of technological and global changes during the past two decades has greatly increased the complexity of many everyday *systems* – ranging from organizations to more or less routine processes (such as locating stock or arranging delivery). This has upped the ante for 'systems thinking' and 'systems understanding' on the part of employees/participants/members of organizations and for practices. What looks rational from one perspective or standpoint (individual, local, immediate) may be irrational or damaging from the standpoint of a system as a whole. Hence, participants need to understand their places and roles within such systems, and to understand 'the workings of the system as a whole, as well as its interrelations with other complex systems' (ibid.). Unless your knowledge and understanding here is grounded in appropriate kinds of activities and procedures, it is likely to be partial, inaccurate, fragile, and fallible. It is difficult to understand your place and role within a system without the opportunity to take on an identity and engage in activity within the system. Moreover, without such experiences it is difficult to recognize that there are such things as systems thinking and systems understandings to be pursued and mastered. Given the contemporary significance of competent systems thinking within everyday life it is no coincidence that one of the most (in)famous internet memes, Leeroy Jenkins (Wikipedia 2010k), celebrates an individual's gross lapse in acting appropriately as part of a system.

3 Developments in new technologies, and especially in the burgeoning reach, power, and collaborative potential of the internet, have generated diverse contexts and opportunities for situated, activity-based learning of kinds that diverge strikingly from conventional classroom learning approaches. (Of course, new technologies have also been widely appropriated for 'business as usual' approaches to learning.) These include the kinds of non-formal learning within contexts of participation addressed at length in previous chapters. Everyday grounded experience of such learning on the part of many people of all ages and from all walks of life means that there is by now a large, wide, and diverse experiential base from which to refract, understand, and compare varying learning modes to which we are exposed within different cultural contexts. These same developments coincide with frequent policy statements about

requirements for effective participation within an information society and/or a knowledge economy, calling for twenty-first-century skills, enhanced creative and innovative prowess, sensitivity to the importance and role of design, and so on.

Social learning, multiple learning modes, and access to people

In 'Minds on fire: Open education, the long tail and learning 2.0', Brown and Adler recognize that if populations are to thrive in the foreseeable future they will increasingly depend on the availability of 'robust local eco-systems of resources [that support] innovation and productiveness' (2008: 17). Being able to produce in sustainable ways, and to innovate in ways that generate new resources and products from what already exists rather than digging further into scarce resources will be especially important. Ability to supply innovative and efficient creators and producers, and to support their ongoing learning and creative activity is, then, a crucial component of robust resource eco-systems.

To date, societies have depended on formal higher education systems to support such learning. But this option seems to be running out of time. Brown and Adler observe that the sheer demand worldwide for ongoing learning of the kinds required for future viability and sustainability likely cannot be resourced on the conventional bricks and mortar, pre-set courses, teachers and administrators model. Demand and resource availability are in tension. Furthermore, and equally problematically, even if the resources *were* available to meet the numerical demand, current approaches to teaching and learning are out of sync with what is needed to prepare populations for their future lives. Conventional higher education courses and credentials have proved to be poor and inefficient performers in terms of innovation and productiveness. The same emphasis on decontextualized and abstracted content transmission that characterizes formal education at the school level likewise dominates higher education.

By contrast, as we have seen, innovation and productiveness are often conspicuously *present* among participants in popular affinities, who learn and create and innovate in the company of others within grounded contexts of practice (of all kinds). Every single instance of modding a video game, mashing up web services and applications, or designing and creating an artifact for a virtual world is an innovation, and mashups are paradigms of adding value to existing resources. Moreover, the kinds of learning that mediate and accompany such forms of productiveness (think Wikipedia, mobile device apps, serviceware mashups) do not presuppose bricks and mortar and formal courses, although some of them (think Facebook) famously emerge from non-formal activities among campus-based learners. None of this is to imply that innovation and productiveness cannot and do not issue from conventional higher education institutions. A proportion does. But it is often highly resource-intensive, confined to small numbers of people, proprietary, and exclusive. Future living requires a much wider diffusion and at many more diverse levels, since the innovations required for living well are often everyday and 'simple': what is important is nurturing the innovator and creative producer in the every person, as well as in the lab scientist.

Such considerations bespeak the significance and efficacy of social learning as conceived by Brown and Adler, particularly as supported and amplified by collaborative web architecture and platforms. Before outlining their account of social learning, we will briefly mention two important points they make by way of background.

First, Brown and Adler say that because web architecture now provides a sophisticated *participatory* medium that is widely used for purposes of *sharing,* it can support *multiple modes* of learning (2008: 18). For example, many institutions make their course materials and other educational resources available for free use by anyone via initiatives like the Open Educational Resources movement (e.g., Oercommons.org) – thereby supporting learning in non-formal/non-enrolled modes in addition to their formal enrolment mode. More generally, this same architecture means that students enrolled in an institution can often bring their online social networks to study groups, discussion groups, and debates that arise organically on campus (ibid.: 24). Insofar as the 'real' educational goal is to support the kind of learning that enhances innovation and productiveness, it is ultimately of less importance what mode it occurs in than the fact that it occurs at all.

Second, Brown and Adler claim that the kinds of practices supported by Web 2.0 urge us to see the internet more in terms of offering access to other people than (simply) in terms of providing access to information. Today's internet makes it increasingly easy 'for people with common interests to meet, share ideas and collaborate in innovative ways' (ibid.: 18). Of course, the importance of shifting attention toward the way the internet affords access to other people was evident to some commentators prior to the flowering of Web 2.0. For example, Michael Schrage argued that viewing the computing and communications technologies of the internet through an information lens is 'dangerously myopic'. According to Schrage (2001: n.p.):

While it is true that digital technologies have completely transformed the world of information into readily manipulable bits and bytes, it is equally true that the genuine significance of these technologies isn't rooted in the information they process and store.

A dispassionate assessment of the impact of digital technologies on popular culture, financial markets, health care, telecommunications, transportation and organizational management yields a simple observation: The biggest impact these technologies have had, and will have, is on relationships between people and between organizations.

The so-called 'information revolution' itself is actually, and more accurately, a 'relationship revolution'. Anyone trying to get a handle on the dazzling technologies of today and the impact they'll have tomorrow, would be well advised to re-orient their worldview around relationships.

(original emphasis)

Brown and Adler filter this observation through their particular interest in learning. They say that 'the most profound impact of the Internet, an impact that has yet to be fully realized, is its ability to support and expand the various aspects of social learning' (Brown and Adler 2008: 18).

Reflection and discussion

- Using an academic literature search engine, such as Scholar Google or the Web of Science, identify some accounts of 'social learning' that you think are informed by different discipline areas, or that you would describe as different 'paradigms' of social learning.
  - What are they?
  - What discipline or disciplines do you associate them with?
  - What are some of the key differences between them?
  - What do you think are some significant educational implications of these differences?

- Many writers and researchers have drawn a distinction between 'acquisition' and 'learning'.
  - Spell out how you understand this distinction.
  - How would you describe the differences and/or similarities (if any) between 'acquisition' and 'social learning'?

Social learning, participation, and learning to be

By 'social learning', Brown and Adler mean, in the first place, learning based on the assumption that our understanding of concepts and processes is constructed socially in conversations about the matters in question and 'through grounded [and situated] interactions, especially with others, around problems or actions' (2008: 18). From a social learning perspective, the focus is more on *how* we learn than simply on *what* we learn. The emphasis shifts from 'the content of a subject to the learning activities and human interactions around which that content is situated' (ibid.). That is, the emphasis shifts from what Brown and Adler call a 'Cartesian' view of learning as a matter of getting content into heads – on the model of providing private minds with raw materials from which to produce thought and knowledge – to seeing learning as a matter of involving individuals in processes and practices within which knowledge, understanding, and ideas are produced by participants as *social* accomplishments. The social view of learning and knowledge proceeds from the same basis as the practice approach to social theory discussed in Chapter 2. For example, with Wittgenstein, this orientation shares the view that there is no such thing as a private language. Rather, language – and hence mind, and hence 'I', and hence 'knowledge' – is *public*: in the ways that Gee (1992) speaks of 'the social mind'. With Freire (1974/2007: 124), it shares the view that 'it is the "we think" which establishes the "I think" and not the contrary'. It is within and through shared practice that meanings – significance – ideas, categories, evidence, tools, tests, techniques, and all the other things that *constitute* knowledge come into being. And, as mentioned earlier in this chapter, it is only within contextualized activity – learning in context – that we can achieve 'nuanced' understanding and knowledge, since knowledge is constituted in practice. What we learn is a consequence of how we learn, and social learning has a very different 'take' from traditional formal learning on the *how*.

Social learning also puts the emphasis squarely on 'learning to be' (Gee 2007: 172; Brown and Adler 2008: 18). According to Brown and Adler (2008: 19):

> mastering a field of knowledge involves not only 'learning about' the subject matter but also 'learning to be' a full participant in the field. This involves acquiring the practices and the norms of established practitioners in that field or acculturating into a community of practice.

This underpins the efficacy of social learning for promoting an ideal of 'deep learning' (Gee 2007), in contrast to the kinds of surface learning that so often result from formal education approaches based on driving decontextualized content into heads in pre-determined sequences. Like 'social learning', deep learning means different things to different people. The distinction between deep and surface learning is usually traced to a phenomenographic investigation of learning reported by Ference Marton and Roger Säljö (1976) and is often touted as an approach to study or a critical thinking method. In our present context, however, we are more concerned with deep learning as a *qualitative kind* of learning rather than a procedure or approach. That is, we are interested in social learning as a broad approach to learning that has particular efficacy for promoting learning that can be described as 'deep' because it has different kinds of affordances, consequences and potentials when compared to surface learning. This is deep learning in a sense that people like Howard Gardner (1991) identify as all too often missing in cases of 'successful' students. Drawing on extensive research from the 1960s to the 1990s, Gardner provides case after case of school and university students

who exhibit all the overt signs of success – faithful attendance at good schools, high grades and high test scores, accolades from their teachers – [yet] typically do not display an adequate understanding of the materials and concepts with which they have been working; including students who receive honor grades in college-level physics courses [but] are frequently unable to solve basic problems and questions encountered in a form slightly different from that on which they have been formally instructed and tested.

(ibid.: 3)

By 'deep learning', as against the kind of surface learning reflected in the myriad examples of the kind Gardner refers to, Gee means learning that can generate 'real understanding, the ability to apply one's knowledge and even to transform that knowledge for innovation' (Gee 2007: 172). He argues that if we want to encourage deep learning, it is necessary to move beyond 'learning about' and, instead, focus on 'learning *to be*' (ibid.; our emphasis). He claims that deep learning requires that learners be 'willing and able to take on a new identity in the world, to see the world and act on it in new ways' (ibid.). In part, this points to the *materiality* and *situatedness* of deep learning, where ideas and 'content' are grounded in specific tasks, interactions, purposes, actions, outcomes, and the like. In addition, however, if one is learning to be an historian, or a music video creator, it is necessary to see and value things about the world and one's work or activity in the ways that historians and music video creators do. Among other things, this is because in any domain, if knowledge is to be used, the learner must probe the world (act on it with a goal) and then evaluate the result. Is it 'good' or 'bad', 'adequate' or 'inadequate', 'useful' or 'not', 'improvable' or 'not'?

(Gee 2007: 172)

Gee argues that this involves learners developing the kind of value system that Donald Schön (1983) calls an 'appreciative system' as a basis for making such judgements. Appreciative systems

are embedded in the identities, tools, technologies, and worldviews of distinctive groups of people – who share, sustain, and transform them – groups like doctors, carpenters, physicists, graphic artists, teachers, and so forth through a nearly endless list.

(ibid.: 172)

The efficacy of social learning is predicated on the fact that it immerses learners in processes of induction into the 'ways' of becoming 'full practitioners' and acquiring their appreciative systems, as well as getting hands-on practice with their mental and material tools within authentic contexts in which they are employed by successful practitioners from the outset. As Brown and Adler (2008: 20) put it:

In a traditional Cartesian educational system, students may spend years learning about a subject; only after amassing sufficient (explicit) knowledge are they expected to start acquiring the (tacit) knowledge or practice of how to be an active practitioner/professional in a field (Polanyi 1966). But viewing learning as the process of joining a community of practice reverses this pattern and allows new students to engage in 'learning to be' even as they are mastering the content of a field. This encourages the practice of what John Dewey called 'productive inquiry' – that is, the process of seeking the knowledge when it is needed in order to carry out a particular situated task [a.k.a. 'just-in-time-and-just-in-place,' which is a hallmark of non-formal learning in affinity spaces of the kinds discussed in earlier chapters].

By way of contrast, Brown and Adler consider the kind of induction into non-formal social learning available via participation in Wikipedia, which resonates closely with our discussion in Chapter 5. They focus on how the process of becoming 'a trusted contributor' to Wikipedia with administrative access rights to 'higher level editing tools' than those available to rank and file contributors 'involves a process of legitimate peripheral participation that is similar to the process in open source software communities' (Brown and Adler 2008: 19). Within open software communities beginning/novice programmers start working on 'relatively simple, noncritical development projects' (like building or improving printer drivers; ibid.: 19). As and when they have displayed capacity 'to make useful contributions and to work in the distinctive style and sensibilities/taste of the community' they may be invited to participate in 'more central projects', and the best of the best are invited to work on the system's kernel code (ibid.: 19). In the case of Wikipedia, the process of enculturation that can lead to administrative rights is mediated by access – via the History and Discussion functions – to non-formal mentoring, since the openness of the process exposes to anyone who chooses to study and learn from it the process by which content is discussed, contested, negotiated, and so on. This enculturation process enables 'a new kind of critical reading – almost a new form of literacy – that invites the reader to join in the consideration of what information is reliable and/or important' (ibid.: 19) from the very outset of contributing.

Some more everyday examples of social learning

While Brown and Adler foreground the potential of Web 2.0 platforms and services to support social learning, it is important also to consider examples that are primarily face to face, local, and may presuppose little or no internet access whatsoever. These, after all, are the original spaces of social learning.

Social learning in Knowledge Producing Schools
One example of a broad social learning approach within a formal context of school-based learning is presented by the Knowledge Producing Schools (KPS) initiative that has evolved over the past decade in a cluster of Australian schools (Bigum 2004; Lankshear and Knobel 2006; Rowan and Bigum 2010).

This initiative recognized that formal education is based on a model of consuming knowledge – a legacy of the Cartesian view as described by Brown and Adler. To the extent that school-based learning engages in production, in the form of essays, projects, reports, and the like, this is typically of a pseudo or 'fridge door' variety: something written for a teacher to grade or to adorn a fridge door for a day or two in the absence of an authentic audience for an authentic product (Bigum 2004: 63). The Knowledge Producing Schools initiative was conceived on the basis of approaching the use of new media in schools from the standpoint of relationship technologies: means for mediating relationships with a wider community in the manner identified above with reference to Schrage (2001). It was also based in part on the idea that in an age of boundless information, communities need to develop 'point of view' in order to use information well in decision-making, policy development, and building identity. From these ingredients emerged the idea that schools could enter relationships with organizations, groups, and community leadership to produce knowledge artifacts that would be authentically useful for and usable by their end users. Right from the start, the work to be done was negotiated between the schools and the end users. Moreover, the intended recipients were also seen as sources of expertise on matters of quality, usefulness, standards, relevance, etc., that an artifact would have to honour in order for it to be acceptable. Furthermore, the community at large was viewed as a source of relevant expertise to be called upon by the schools in the knowledge production process. Members of the community could provide learning support in matters as various as using specialized tools to industry standards in procedures like video editing and for validating perspectives and material integral to developing an informative point of view.

In a typical example, groups of grade 6 students worked in collaboration with the local cattle sale yards to produce a documentary about the history of the sale yards for a Beef Expo in 2003. They video-interviewed representatives of different sectors in the cattle industry, recorded *in situ* footage of activities, provided voice-overs and bridges between sequences, and edited the components to produce the documentary as a CD-ROM. This CD-ROM was used at an international beef festival and by the local council to promote the region. The work proceeded from a view of education as a 'whole of community responsibility'. It contracted deep and committed relationships between the school and the beef industry 'community'. Moreover, the entree to digital visual media work came via a student teacher with a sibling who was employed in digital video production and who provided free expertise. While the Knowledge Producing Schools projects did not necessarily involve new literacies in the sense we are concerned with here, many of them *did* involve processes of learning to use new media within 'authentic' contexts of productive use. This kind of social learning, grounded in strategic relationships aiming at knowledge production from particular points of view within cultures of participation, and on sharing and building upon distributed expertise and collective intelligence would be enhanced exponentially by access to various collaborative web services and resources.

Passion, persistence, and success through social learning
For reasons that will become apparent a little later when we address the theme of the contemporary paradigm shift from 'push' toward 'pull', *passion* is a recurring theme throughout Brown and Adler's discussion of

how Web 2.0 resources can support multiple learning modes and routes toward (higher) educational experiences that are conducive to building capacity for innovation and productiveness. In relation to non-formal participatory learning settings, they note that many Wikipedia articles begin from the efforts of passionate amateurs. With respect to more formal settings they identify the way that online participatory cultures both respond to and stimulate passion for learning. They affirm that for practically any topic a student may be passionate about 'there is likely to be an online community of practice of others who share that passion' (2008: 28). From the other direction, they argue that finding and joining communities that ignite passion can 'set the stage' for social learning experiences where learners/ students can acquire 'both deep knowledge about a subject ("learning about") and the ability to participate in the practice of a field through productive inquiry and peer-based learning ("learning to be")' (ibid.). Such passion becomes, in effect, an engine for learning under contemporary conditions of rapid change because it no longer makes good sense simply to count on the kind of long-term motivation that inclines people to learn something now on the assumption that it may come in useful later. What is *also* and *increasingly* required is the kind of passion that motivates 'in the now' to pursue mastery of what serves in the 'now' or, at most, will serve 'in the near', and to maintain this passion as the driving force for surfing change and staying in touch.

This theme is taken up and extended in very interesting and important ways by Elisabeth Hayes and James Gee's account of women becoming involved in design, production, and participating in learning communities within the context of *The Sims* gaming affinities (Gee and Hayes 2010). In the context of a much wider and richer discussion they advance cases and arguments highly relevant to the line we are running here – following Brown and colleagues – on social learning, 'push' and 'pull', and building learning platforms to support grounded learning of kinds that can generate and nurture creative applications of knowledge, innovation, and productiveness.

At the heart of Gee and Hayes' discussion is what they see as the significance of 'grit', understood as a disposition that combines 'persistence plus passion' (ibid.: 67) for experiencing success under current and foreseeable social, economic, 'globalizing', and epistemic conditions. Their account of 'grit' is a variation on the view advanced by Angela Duckworth and colleagues (2007) as perseverance and passion for long-term goals. 'Perseverance' has connotations of endurance over the long haul for some long-term benefit, but where intrinsic drive and motivation might not be strong at the time. By contrast, 'persistence' has connotations of sticking at something not simply on account of achieving external goals, but (also) 'because of [one's] passion for the area or domain in which the problems reside' (Gee and Hayes 2010: 67). The argument, in brief, is that the ability to innovate – like creativity more generally – presupposes *mastery* within an area or domain. Getting 'on top of' a practice enables us to see opportunities for new angles; for expanding aspects of the practice in new directions; for creating potentially fruitful 'hybrids' of elements within a practice or with components from other practices; or for doing things that may be similar in most respects to what people already do, but have not yet done. Pursuing mastery requires 'thousands of hours of practice' (ibid.) in addressing issues and problems, in trial and error, learning how others do things, and so on. In short, mastery presupposes 'persistence'. Persistence, in turn, requires passion '[o]therwise people give up' (ibid.: 67).

Gee and Hayes explore in depth a range of cases of girls and women who have learned to become *Sims* designers and who have experienced success within the larger *Sims* community. They possess 'grit' in abundance. Their experiences inform us about some of the ways people become passionate about an interest, and how participating in 'passionate affinity groups' is crucial to growing passion. Their examples are not of lone rangers but, rather, of social learners whose gritty dispositions and successes partly reflect personal idiosyncrasies, but have developed and thrive within spaces and under conditions of participatory cultures. Gee and Hayes draw on cases of 'typically untypical' (ibid.: 79) informants like Tabby Lou, Jade, Izazu, and EarthGoddess to develop new elements of a theory of social learning.

Tabby Lou is a grandmother with a health condition that took her out of the workforce and confined her to home. She learned to play *The Sims* initially in the context of visits by her daughter and grandchildren. One granddaughter said she would like a purple potty to put in her *Sims* houses, and Tabby Lou decided she would create one, even though she knew nothing about the process. Tabby Lou began exploring and found tools available for doing the job, but tools she did not understand and had to learn to use. She then found *Sims* community resources that could help her, but that going forward meant seeing herself as a budding designer, on the periphery of the community, in need of community support to meet her initial goal. This drew her in and 'reconstituted' her as a member of the community, interacting with others and pursuing her goals. But as with the case of Maguma discussed in Chapter 5, Tabby Lou's initial interest began hooking her into a new identity: from the identity space of a grandmother wanting to learn how to create a purple potty from the fringes of a games (design) community, she began to start seeing herself as a designer and a member of a community 'that brought her status, support, and friendship' (Gee and

Hayes 2010: 89). She now wanted to become the designer she could be. This in turn required endless further hard work, but 'grit' prevailed here and, in due course, was reinforced and rewarded by experiencing genuine success and recognition as a *Sims* designer – rewarded with 'millions of downloads and hundreds of thousands of thank-yous' (ibid.: 90).

On the basis of cases like Tabby Lou, Gee and Hayes advance a 'purple potty' theory of how passion emerges and grows, in a trajectory, as part of a larger theory of social learning that can lead to successful innovation and creative appropriations and applications of knowledge. They summarize the trajectory of passion as follows:

> Have a strong desire to do something‡identity and community‡find the needed tools‡gain grit in the service of doing it‡identity and community [a new iteration]‡get hooked on the learning‡transfer grit to the learning itself‡become successful (ibid.: 89; ‡ signifies phases and iterations)

The examples provided by Gee and Hayes' informants go way beyond 'mere participation'. At one level they are examples of *success*: they exemplify the possibilities inherent in non-formal social learning for 'making one's way' in the sense of attaining social goods. While Tabby Lou herself, and many others like her, do not aim to make money from her designs, there is no reason other than personal preference why she could not. Hers is exactly the same process and trajectory that many successful entrepreneurs, apps creators, and others have followed for making a livelihood. It is one way – and an increasingly common one – to build a career. At a different level, however, cases like Tabby Lou's provide examples of full-fledged *collaboration* in learning. As EarthGoddess, another of Gee and Hayes' informants – who may stand in for countless others – puts it with respect to how she learned to create (successful) content:

> Having access to patient people who have been there and done that (and are generous enough to share what they know with me) has ... been instrumental. I think there's always a time when you get hung up [when your own efforts at trial and error and tinkering are not enough] and need to ask someone with the experience.
>
> (ibid.: 101)

Esteem for support provided and a will to reciprocity incline designers like Tabby Lou and EarthGoddess to become mentors, to provide help, and to *lead* within the community, as they continue learning themselves and interacting with those who learn from and with them.

Reflection and discussion

Gee and Hayes (2010) spell out what they call their *theory* of the trajectory of passion (their 'purple potty' theory).

- Why do you think they give it the status of a *theory*?

- What *counts* as a theory? What do theories *do*? When can we reasonably describe something as being a *theory*?

- What *theoretical* work does Gee and Hayes' theory of the trajectory of passion do?

- How could you use this theory in *education*?

Paradigm shift: from 'push' to 'pull'

Having identified the potential of collaborative web architecture to support social learning mediated by participation in online communities of practice, Brown and Adler (2008: 30) conclude their discussion of social learning by arguing that this potential coincides with the need for a new approach to learning that increasingly moves from the familiar 'push' or 'supply' model toward a 'demand' or 'pull' approach. They claim that a demand-pull approach to learning 'shifts the focus' from pushing pre-determined curriculum content contained in (learning) programs to 'enabling participation in flows of action where the focus is both on "learning to be" through "enculturation into a practice" and on collateral (or consequential, "spin off", by-product) learning' (ibid.).

Their argument builds on ongoing work in a complementary area by Brown and colleagues (Hagel and Brown 2005; Hagel et al. 2010). This began with John Hagel and Brown's (2005) original working account of an emerging paradigm shift in our everyday thinking about how to mobilize resources for getting things done, and has latterly evolved into a substantive theory of how to use 'pull' as a strategic approach to achieving innovation, sustainability, and success at both institutional/organizational and personal levels (Hagel et al. 2010). Their work has important implications for thinking about education and learning.

Throughout the twentieth century the dominant common sense model for mobilizing resources was based on a logic of 'push'. Resource needs were anticipated or forecast, budgets drawn up, and resources pushed in advance to sites of anticipated use so they would be in place when wanted. This 'push' approach involved intensive and often large-scale planning and programme development. Indeed, Hagel and Brown see programmes as being integral to the 'push' model. They note, for example, that in education the process of mobilizing resources involves designing standard curricula that 'expose students to codified information in a predetermined sequence of experiences' (2005: 3). Conventional education, in fact, is a paradigm case of the push model at work.

Hagel, Brown, and Davison (2010: 1) speak of a 'big shift' currently in train that is driven by 'new technology infrastructure' and changes in public policy that are responding to rapid social, cultural, and economic transformations occurring on a global scale. Demands for innovation, sustainability, effective responses to rapid changes in knowledge, production, goods and services, etc., are bringing on 'a fundamental reordering of the way we live, learn, socialize, play and work' (ibid.). This 'big shift' entails a move from the familiar 'push' paradigm toward an emergent 'pull' paradigm as the conditions for 'being successful' change.

In an early statement, Hagel and Brown argue that we're beginning to see signs of an emerging 'pull' approach within education, business, technology, media, and elsewhere, that creates *platforms* rather than programmes: platforms 'that help people to mobilize resources when the need arises' (2005: 3). More than this, the kinds of platforms we see emerging are designed to enable individuals and groups to do more with fewer resources, to innovate in ways that actually create new resources where previously there were none, and to otherwise add value to the resources to which we currently have access. Pull approaches respond to uncertainty and the need for sustainability by seeking to expand opportunities for creativity on the part of 'local participants dealing with immediate needs' (ibid.: 4). From this standpoint, uncertainty is seen as creating opportunities to be exploited. According to Hagel and Brown (ibid.: 4):

[Pull models] help people to come together and innovate in response to unanticipated events, drawing upon a growing array of highly specialized and distributed resources. Rather than seeking to constrain the resources available to people, pull models strive to continually expand the choices available while at the same time helping people to find the resources that are most relevant to them. Rather than seeking to dictate the actions that people must take, pull models seek to provide people on the periphery with the tools and resources (including connections to other people) required to take initiative and creatively address opportunities as they arise ... Pull models treat people as networked creators (even when they are customers purchasing goods and services) who are uniquely positioned to transform uncertainty from a problem into an opportunity. Pull models are ultimately designed to accelerate capability building by participants, helping them to learn as well as innovate, by pursuing trajectories of learning that are tailored to their specific needs.

In their most recent statement, Hagel, Brown, and Davison (2010) have described and theorized 'pull' as a strategy in ways resonant with Gee and Hayes' account of learning and success mentioned above. They identify three levels of 'pull': access, attract, and achieve. At the base, 'pull helps us find and *access* people and resources when we need them' in a manner analogous to 'searching' (ibid.: xiv). At the next level, pull involves the ability to *attract* people and resources that are relevant to and important for achieving our goals and purposes – especially people and resources we didn't previously know existed. As mentioned in Chapter 6, this ability is enhanced by the kind of 'serendipity' enabled via weak ties in social networks. The third level of pull is reminiscent of Gee and Hayes' concept of grit, and is 'the ability to pull from within ourselves' the necessary 'insight and performance' needed to 'more effectively *achieve* our potential' (ibid.). When viewed from the standpoint of a journey (or pull) toward achievement or success – e.g., involving innovation, productiveness, viability, competitive edge – 'pull' can be understood in terms of 'trajectory', 'leverage', and 'pace' (ibid.: x). Pull involves creating and putting in place in a systematic way a viable *trajectory* – the direction in which we are heading; passion is crucial here. Hagel, Brown, and Davison advocate making our passions our profession – sufficient *leverage* (mobilizing other people's passions and efforts), and the right kind of *pace* (making progress at the appropriate rate for doing best in prevailing conditions and contexts).

From this perspective, *platforms* can be seen as combinations of components and resources that help us to access, attract, and achieve: to connect with others, optimize the likelihood of serendipity, and persist with our passions (ibid.: xi). As we have seen, Brown and Adler (2008: 30) argue that a pull approach within higher education involves ensuring students have access to rich learning communities established around practices – just as non-formal learners have within spaces of popular cultural participation. A 'pull' approach assumes 'passion-based learning' that is 'motivated by the student either wanting to become a member of a particular community of practice or just wanting to learn about, make, or perform something' (ibid.). Under these conditions, resourcing learning is primarily a matter of building *platforms* to support (collaborative) social learning. Their focus is important for our argument in the final chapter, where we want to move from talking about new literacies and social learning in the kinds of non-formal settings that have dominated our discussion thus far to talking about more formal contexts.

Building platforms for social learning

The idea of a 'pull' approach to learning has been explored from different perspectives. Jay Cross (2006) applies it to informal 'emergent' learning within workplaces in pursuit of value-adding innovation and productivity. In place of 'push' approaches via training programmes, Cross advocates paying greater attention to building and nurturing 'learnscapes' – learning ecologies – 'where workers can easily find the people and information they need' and 'where learning is fluid and new ideas flow easily' (ibid.: 41). This involves creating learning platforms that enable workers to make fast and effective learning responses to needs and challenges as they arise. Within corporate/company contexts such platforms may include 'expertise locators' that map likely go-to people and rich information portals within and beyond the organization; they may build on workplace design decisions to create spaces that encourage 'productive conversation' and establish guidelines for 'conversing productively' (ibid.: 29). More generally, platforms for collaborative learning mobilize 'community, storytelling, simulation, dynamic learning portals, social network analysis, expertise location, presence awareness, workflow integration, search technology, help desks ... mobile learning, and co-creation' (ibid.: 41).

In Cross's account, 'learning to be', 'practice', and 'communities of practice' are largely assumed, because participants share a work culture and are already 'in' a practice. By contrast, Brown and Adler (2008) approach the issue of building learning platforms from the standpoint of social learning possibilities within formal higher education that has long been dominated by content hived off from the kinds of practices in which such content originates and/or finds its natural home.

Consequently, Brown and Adler are interested in the question of how to build platforms for learning that positively enable students to participate in 'flows of action' where they get '[enculturated] into a practice' (2008: 30). Such platforms will involve varying mixes of access to physical and virtual environments, depending on local contingencies, but always on the basis that these environments and resources provide opportunities for learners/ newcomers to participate in authentic practices with access to support and guidance from experienced and expert practitioners – scholars, researchers, and other disciplinary and technical professionals. The resource-intensive nature of this approach entails a special place and significance for access to *virtual* environments and resources available on- and offline. Building the virtual dimension of learning platforms may include mobilizing open courseware made available through initiatives like the Open Educational Resources movement; identifying relevant scholarly websites and networks; enabling online and/or ROM-based access to powerful instruments, simulations, and other kinds of virtual environments; accessing selections from the myriad 'niche communities based around specific areas of interest in virtually every field of endeavour' (ibid.: 31); accessing online technical forums associated with (categories of) products and services; and creating or joining purpose-built collaborative spaces using Web 2.0 resources and services (e.g., wikis, nings, academic social networking sites); providing 'starter directories' or indices of potentially relevant resources on sites like YouTube.com; among many other options.

As exemplars of virtual environments and resources that add community to content, Brown and Adler cite the Faulkes Telescope Project that enables UK students to collaborate with working astronomers (Faulkes-telescope. com), and Brown University's Decameron Web (Brown.edu/Departments/ Italian_Studies/dweb/index.php), which gives students 'the opportunity to observe and emulate scholars at work' (Brown and Adler 2008: 24).

Reflection and discussion

- How would you distinguish between providing *programmes* for learning and providing *platforms* for learning?

- How would you describe the relationship between 'learning' and 'education'?

- Discuss the statement: 'There will always necessarily be some amount of "push" – perhaps, even, quite a lot – involved in educating people/being educated'.

- Discuss the claim that 'some amount of "push" will always be involved in becoming literate'.

In Chapter 8 we describe an impressive initiative that builds social learning approaches into formal education in the USA at the grade 6–12 level, and outline our own attempts to integrate social learning into Master's-level study within teacher education.

Social learning and new literacies in formal education

Introduction

This chapter presents two empirical cases of social learning and new literacies within formal education programmes as examples of current efforts to develop approaches to learning within formal settings informed by the kinds of ideas discussed in Chapter 7.

The first describes some of our own work with off-campus cohorts of teacher education students in a coursework Master's programme. It shows how we introduce them to basic principles and procedures of field-based qualitative research by engaging them from the outset in the *practice* of academic research – as novice researchers – within a team-based approach to researching their own learning activity as media creators. The second describes an ambitious innovation within the US public education system, which uses a 'gamelike' and 'situated' approach to pursue learning attuned to complex and changing demands of early twenty-first-century life.

Social learning and new literacies in a Master's by coursework teacher education programme

Participants in the courses described here have no previous experience in producing academic research or evaluating formal published research in the ways that trained researchers review research literature. Our approach to getting students – all of whom are classroom teachers – started as research producers creates approximations to the kinds of research contexts and purposes we engage in ourselves within our professional lives. Our strategy is to have groups of novice researchers investigating their own team-based learning within areas of activity where they are literally 'beginning from scratch', that is, collaborating in teams to learn how to create a digital media artifact of a kind they previously knew nothing about. Hence, they learn (together) to *produce research* within contexts of learning (together) to *produce media*, as members of teams.

We work with participants to jointly create 'platforms' for collaborative learning that are as open, extensive, 'light', and flexible as possible. These are 'arrangements' whereby participants can access people, websites, written texts, and any and every kind of helpful support – as and when they need it – in order to make progress in their collaborative endeavour. The same platform works across both kinds of learning purpose involved in the course: learning how to create media artifacts from scratch, and the more formally academic kinds of learning involved in learning how to produce academic knowledge by conducting research and reporting outcomes. The emphasis in what follows is on teams of learners *collaborating* in the reasonably stringent senses of 'collaboration' discussed in earlier chapters; that is, having a sense of their activity as a kind of system or 'whole' within which participants must ensure that their work 'comes together' to produce coherent integrated outcomes.

Our own roles in the process and parts in the platform are shaped by our aim to build as much 'pull' and as little 'push' as possible into the experience. Naturally, there has to be *some* 'push' because this is a component within a Master's degree *programme* that has a curriculum. Students are *enrolled*, and we are employed to ensure they learn what the programme says they will learn. This, however, is presented predominantly in terms of what they will be involved in learning to do and be, rather than what they will be learning about. Within these parameters we try to promote as much immersion as possible in the logic of 'pull', without abdicating responsibility for pursuing sound learning outcomes. We try to stick as close as possible to a learning approach in which learners who are total novices at the outset get as far along the way as possible in learning to become proficient consumers and producers of academic research and proficient practitioners within a range of new literacies. Our main aim is to immerse practising teachers in ways of 'pulling' learning, so that if they wish to ponder them further and explore ways of extending them to their own work in schools, as well as in their own ongoing learning as professional people within a domain of activity, they are better placed to do so than they might otherwise have been.

Participants, the course, and learning contexts

The participants

Cohorts typically comprise 30 to 45 students. Participants have low to (at best) modest levels of 'tech savviness' upon entry. Some arrive with their first personal computers (laptops), not knowing how to turn them on. Until recently most have never previously used wireless networking, or accessed (let alone had their own) blogs. Some have never previously sent an email attachment. To date, the most that any cohort members have had in the way of previous experience of working with media applications involved in the course has been creating short sound files in Audacity, and importing short video clips into Windows Movie Maker or images into Photostory (around 10 per cent of all participants to date). As previously noted, none has had any prior experience of conducting research according to the kinds of criteria that define formal thesis study or professional academic research of the kind reported in peer-reviewed scholarly journals or funded in competitive grant-awarding programmes. None has previously read and evaluated research in the manner required for a proficient academic literature review in a scholarly paper or thesis.

The course

The course described here operates in two modes. One is an intensive-mode block course that runs over four weeks. Weeks 2 and 4 are face to face (six hours a day, five days a week), and Weeks 1 and 3 are 'off site' or non-face to face. There is also a semester-long version which involves three face-to-face sessions of six hours, each a month apart. Between these sessions teams meet face-to-face as often as they need to get the work done, and use collaborative internet resources to stay in touch and post work for our ongoing feedback and guidance. The course has two broad purposes:

1 To address the theme of 'new' literacies/digital literacies/new media in theory and in practice;
2 To provide an introduction to literacy research and to researching literacy – how to *locate* and *use* literacy research effectively as teachers,

and how to *do* research. The goal is to enable teachers taking the course to become informed consumers of research and to have some experience of being producers of research.

The course combines the process of beginning learning to become 'research producers and consumers' with the process of beginning learning to become creators of new media, in conjunction with learning about 'new' literacies and approaches to understanding concepts and theories associated with new literacies. Participants are informed ahead of the course that they will be working in self-selected teams, and are encouraged to organize their teams ahead of the first session – which is usually easily done because groups of cohort members often work at the same schools, come from the same towns, or have worked together previously in the programme. Likewise, the nature and operating principles of the course are made clear well ahead of time. Prior contact is made by group email and a detailed outline of the course logic and tasks is provided, with preliminary reading and details of the learning platform clearly specified. Participants know that from the first face-to-face hour they will be working in their teams to collaboratively create a media artifact, and that they will be collecting data from the outset in order to research their learning and report their research.

Preliminary information and resources are provided to give a broad sense of the media and research tasks. Participants receive in advance texts on media options – including 'how-to' tutorials – on data collection and analysis, and on sociocultural approaches to understanding and researching language and literacy. The syllabus is provided a month or more ahead of time, and includes suggestions about what to bring to help with data collection – such as notebooks, digital recording devices (audio, video, still image), mobile phones with cameras, thumbdrives/external disk storage, etc. Participants are informed that they will be expected to get a sense of what aficionados of the media artifact they elect regard as 'good work', and their reading includes abundant references to concepts of social learning, learning to be, appreciation systems, and the like. In short, participants typically arrive at the course with a broad idea of the kinds of things – components – they will be doing, but with little or no working knowledge of how to do them. They often arrive feeling very apprehensive. At the same time, the preliminary materials include exemplars of work done by previous teams, sending the clear message that if participants have faith and work diligently, then completing the course won't prove impossible. Nonetheless, they often *do* arrive feeling anxious, and our aim is ensure they are immersed in the work so quickly and intensely that they forget their worries.

Learning context and settings

This is scarcely passion-based learning! Participants are completing an advanced degree primarily as an additional or career-advancing qualification. The most we can hope for is that teams build *enthusiasm*. To that end participants are given a generous range of media options to select from, including creating music videos, anime music videos, stop motion animations, photoshopping and photosharing, machinima and other movie making, music remix, podcasts, etc. (Knobel and Lankshear 2010). Almost without exception, considerable enthusiasm does emerge – although typically rather more for the media creation aspect than the research. Within these parameters, the approach is as much as possible an approximation to learning to become a kind of person – a kind of digital media creator, a kind of researcher – by spending some intensive time engaging in an activity in a way that will gradually convey a sense of the *practices* in question *as practices*. It inevitably falls well short of taking on identities and developing passion in the sense described by Gee and Hayes (2010), but by the end of the course the options for doing so are well understood. A key aim, invariably met, is for participants to surrender to 'project time'; the time to be put into the course is the time required to create an artifact they can present with pride to the rest of the cohort, and a research report that is at least as proficient as the exemplars available from previous cohorts.

We have two bottom lines for the learning space. First, there must be ample space that approximates in kind to the types of spaces employed in mature versions of the social practices in question: popular cultural media creation and qualitative research. As Lawrence Lessig (2005) recognizes, an adolescent's bedroom is a typical site of popular cultural media creation. This has less to do with the presence of a bed than with having space to run a computer, having some uninterrupted time in which to work, and so on. It also has to do with enjoying a sense of autonomy, so that one has 'free scope and rein' (ibid.) to be creative – one can spread out a bit, make some mess, leave stuff in place until taking it up the next time, and the like. So far as the research dimension of the work is concerned, anything that approximates to the kind of space and facilities associated with research centres, and research and development spaces, will be suitable. Ideally, this includes 'peripherals' like tea and coffee making facilities, space to lounge around in and shoot the breeze, and so on. The second bottom line, of course, is high-speed, unfettered internet access. Ideally we want to ensure that 30 or more people can simultaneously be using the internet in spaces as different as Google docs, Blogger, YouTube, Zamzar, the university's online library, NewLits.org, Wikipedia, and using Google's search engine at large.

The most 'bounteous' space we have worked in to date has been a ski lodge, with multiple levels of inside/outside open space, equipped with tables and chairs and bar stools, BBQ tables, and so on – although a generously endowed teacher resource centre, and a hotel with full conference facilities and ample breakout spaces run close behind.

The platform for collaborative learning

Participants realize that they can 'pull' on any available resource, from anywhere, and at whatever point they need it, that will help them to discover and use what they need in order to achieve their learning purposes as social learners. The operating principle is 'just-in-time-and-just-in-place', and the platform grows and evolves over the duration of the course as new resources are identified and shared.

On the physical/face-to-face dimension, the platform includes, of course, people. This can include anyone, from members of other teams to children at home. We explain that our own role will be more 'elicitive' than direct or expository: we reiterate that 'Google is your friend', and ask, "Have you tried X?" or "Have you asked Y?", or "Have you read Z?" When anyone anywhere in the cohort solves a problem or becomes 'expert' at a function or application, they are identified as a potential 'go to' person for all teams. Wireless laptops – as many per team as possible – are recommended, and are online continuously during face-to-face sessions. Other physical (or online) resources include the course textbooks, starter directories of potentially useful websites, templates for such things as writing comprehensive fieldnotes, typical components of research reports, questions to ask when reading journal articles from a researcher perspective, criteria for data quality, tips for triangulating data sources (hence, for obtaining them in the first instance), tips sheets, exemplars of work from previous cohorts, and the syllabus.

The online/virtual component of the platform is largely 'Web 2.0' in character and predominantly 'Google' in type. It extends to the whole of the internet, including sources like Wikipedia, fan practice affinity sites, technical forums, how-to tutorials, YouTube videos on data collection, and so on. Its collaborative dimension is 'channelled' to a significant extent through a suite of free and relatively robust Google (or similar) applications. It includes a loosely joined, flexible, ad hoc assemblage of services and applications that can be added to, taken up in whatever proportions, and driven by participants. There are no content filters, no webmasters, no intellectual proprietors, no controls. Since much work has to be done outside of face-to-face sessions we emphasize collaborative writing platforms and communications and virtual meeting media to carry work when teams cannot meet physically. To this end we use combinations of resources and applications like the following, according to need, work rhythms, and participant preferences.

- *Google Docs* (docs.google.com). Each team creates working documents to which we are invited and given the same viewing and editing – contributing – rights as regular team members. Contributors get email notification of updates from within Google Docs, and short messages inviting feedback and explaining changes can be included with the notification. We provide continual ongoing feedback, pose questions, suggest options, recommend potentially useful further reading, and so on, directly within each document. We try to model ways of keeping the writing going, prompt where we think points could be elaborated, and so on, but contribute little or no direct text. So far as possible we are always 'there' to try to help maintain writing flows.
- *Google Sites* (sites.google.com) offers a 'light' website that is very quickly and easily established and updated, and can readily be made into a collaborative resource by sharing a collective username and password. A Google site provides abundant archiving space, and a site established for a cohort can serve as a holding and/or publishing space for the cohort and its entire corpus of work. It is created well in advance of the course, carries the syllabus and all preliminary information and task descriptions, and participants are pointed to it as soon as it is available.
- *Google Scholar* (scholar.google.com) is a specialized search tool for academic sources. It provides bibliographic information, a citation count generated within its database, and can be customized to automatically locate and link to resources inside a specified electronic library archive (see below).
- *Online library access to electronic journals and databases, with Google Scholar preferences activated* (scholar.google.com/scholar_preferences). Activating Google Scholar preferences means that if an electronic resource (e.g., a journal article) located by a search is available through the university library to which participants have online access, they will be able to download the resource simply by clicking on a hyperlink, rather than having to record the details of the resource and then run a separate online library database search.
- *Google Books* (books.google.com) provides useful and considerable online access to book content on a 'hit and miss' basis. Sometimes entire chapters that are exactly what is needed *are* available. An easy search using book title or author name quickly leads to the book being sought.

It is then a matter of whether the available content provides what is sought, but the odds are worth taking a chance on.

- *Gmail* (mail.google.com) provides an easy way to establish a Google account that enables access to Google Sites and Google Docs, and is an abundant and readily searchable email service.

- *A collaborative course blog using Blogger* (blogger.com), which can also be accessed via a Google account. Blogger can be set up to allow posting via email or mobile phone, and a shared username and password means anyone in the cohort can post and comment. Alternatively, the blog can be designed as a collaborative forum, with each user posting under their own name or alias. A cohort blog can be used as an all-purpose site for posting information, requests for feedback, raising issues, and doing any other useful work that invites and enables collaboration. Wikis and social network sites like Socialgo.com or BigTent.com are other options, and can be integrated with wikis and other online resources (e.g., JingProject. com, for creating their own how-to video tutorials).

- We also encourage the use of Skype (Skype.com) free telephony, chat, virtual group spaces, instant messaging services, and so on, for easy communication.

- *The rest of the internet* – that is, anywhere a conventional Google search or a more specialized Google Scholar search may lead to for the purposes of furthering the team's collaborative work. This includes affinity spaces, academic websites, file conversion services, file transfer services, specialist discussion boards, social networking and sharing spaces; in short, anything and anywhere that helps get the job done. Participants have on numerous occasions felt emboldened to communicate directly with scholars and other experts, and join their networks as part of their learning process.

The learning approach

As noted above, participants are required to orient themselves for the course beforehand: to sense its 'look and feel'. To this end the syllabus contains information like:

> The course is partly about mastering the art of 'overcoming anxiety' and learning to trust oneself and one's fellow team members to 'come through'. It is also partly about learning to have faith in a cohort's collective capacity to do things you might not previously have thought possible – and that at many points in the course you will think ARE impossible. But they are not impossible – although you will have to take that on faith!!

and

> It is important for participants to recognize that the instructors know
> perfectly well that they are asking a lot of the participants. It is equally
> important for participants to know that the instructors will not let
> them down. By the end of the first face-to-face week each team *will*
> have managed to create a digital media artifact, even though many
> participants may regard themselves as 'computer illiterate' or as 'digital
> klutzes' at the start of the course.

Courses begin with a whole-group session in which introductions are
made, teams are formalized, and we reiterate the emphasis on social
learning. Active work begins immediately after that. When issues or
problems seem pervasive across groups, rapid-fire full-group sessions are
convened – by us or participants – to tap collective thinking and obtain
solutions as quickly as possible (sometimes a group has found a solution,
so we get them to explain to everyone; our aim is to *elicit* rather than
provide responses). Examples here include additional explication of what
it means to write really detailed fieldnotes that describe what's going
on, rather than summarize it; or having a group demonstrate to everyone
else how to use a file conversion service like Zamzar.com to convert flash
video files to wav files.

As near as possible to points of application, and as appropriate, we
convene short 'walk through' sessions on things like how and why to
activate Google Scholar preferences, how to conduct natural language and
phrase-based searches on Google (along with some Boolean terms), setting
up collaborative Google documents, and so on. We also point the whole
group to key guiding templates for their work as near as possible to their
points of application, and quickly walk through these to explain how we
see them operating, and to emphasize trying to use them first and then seek
feedback or clarification. Interaction between groups is encouraged, and
the course website provides generous exemplars of work done by previous
cohorts. These resources and procedures provide timely assistance with such
things as using concepts and theory to inform and shape data collection and
analysis and, later, to discuss analytic results.

We encourage writing as often and as much as possible from the
outset, and committing material to Google docs as soon as can be. Early
on, we move around the groups frequently, looking for points where quick
interventions might be most effective. We assume that what the groups
will most need from us are productive guides to working as well as possible with theory and with collecting and analysing data and discussing analytic results in conversation with prior research and theory. Hence,

we focus most on looking for points at which feedback and reference to expert resources and exemplars are most needed and will be most useful. Teams quickly find they can make good progress on their media creation and generating data on the processes involved. As we get a sense of their data and their media progress we can point to ways for organizing the data, make suggestions about when and how to begin some preliminary analysis of the data (during the 'at home' week between the two face-to-face components), and the like. We try to stay as close as possible to Gee's (2007: 27, 40) principle of 'performance before competence'. In every cohort we find that performance begets *confidence* and teams quickly produce. From that point our role becomes one largely of trying to help them maximize *quality*. Obviously, it is always easier to do this once something is in place – just in time (at the point of need or application) and just in place.

Some typical outcomes

Typical average media creations from the course are two-minute stop motion animations, three-minute music remixes, two- to three-minute machinima movies, and three- to four-minute music videos. Formal, collaboratively written research reports average 6500–7000 words. We gauge that with a modest amount of mentoring by published academics, the best reports of their research would be publishable in any number of peer reviewed journals. We recall fewer than five occasions where team members have complained of an individual not 'doing their share' – from a total of 750 to 1000 participants over five years. Participants frequently report having worked harder here than in any other academic course, and we regularly find participants logged into Google Docs between 1a.m. and 2a.m. during semester courses ahead of a day's teaching.

Indicative examples of media creations
- Stop motion animation
  - Lego Alliance, available at: http://www.youtube.com/watch?v=9hpJCJb4p0w
  - The Escape, available at: http://www.youtube.com/watch?v=JfqWVqZumiw
- Machinima
  - Bar Room Brawl, available at: http://www.youtube.com/watch?v=Ny_Ek5DpXtI
- AMV
  - Sakura: The Climb, available at: http://www.youtube.com/user/mountainclimbers1#p/a/u/0/XmVtw8QoLbg

- Photoshopped celebrity reporting spoof
  - Caught in Cape Breton, available at: http://www.youtube.com/watch?v=XmVtw8QoLbg

Indicative excerpted examples from the teams' conventional (research report) writing component
- Reviewing literature to develop conceptual and theoretical frames

> Gee (2004) focuses on how learning best takes place when it is a highly motivated engagement with social practices that people value. He discusses communities of practice and how individuals learn from those who are more knowledgeable and how everyone in this community of practice or space is able to share interests and knowledge. He addresses social spaces and how people interact with content and with each other within the context of that space ... Participants learn from interacting and sharing with others. According to Gee, 'In an affinity space people relate with each other primarily in terms of common interests, endeavours, goals, or practices, not primarily in terms of race, gender, age, disability or social class' (Gee, 2004, p. 85). People with different levels of expertise and skill can be found and accommodated in a space and each person can obtain different knowledge from the space. While participation in affinity spaces often occurs online, this is not always the case. The focus is not where the affinity space occurs but rather that sharing, participation and the exchange of specific knowledge have occurred.
>
> (Best-Pinsent et al. 2009)

- An overview statement of data collection approaches

> Data were collected by a group of three participants over a period of five days ... resulting in a total of 30 hours of observations, field notes, head notes, post facto notes taken by team members individually at differing times. Field notes [were especially useful] because they documented specific written details and accounts of what was occurring, what was being created, and the emotions that group members had felt. Field notes [involved] writing legibly, marking the time down regularly, using codes, and developing a shorthand language ... At times, it was difficult to write an observation down as events were taking place, so team members made head notes [mental notes researchers make while systematically watching an event within a context where writing notes in the heat

of the moment is impossible] and would write details as post facto notes which were written as soon as possible after the observed event. Some notes were typed and other notes were written down. Group members copied and pasted the URLs of websites that were useful sources of information and took screen shots of those websites.

(Donovan et al. 2010: 12)

- An overview statement of the data analysis approach employed

  The data analyzed for this project comprised our collective field notes with reference made at certain points to our supplementary photographs and field-based videos whenever something in these notes required additional elaboration. The primary method used was pattern finding ... a process of identifying patterns discernible across pieces of information. In the pattern finding process the researcher begins with a 'mass of undifferentiated ideas and behavior, and then collects pieces of information, comparing, contrasting, and sorting gross categories and minutiae until a discernible pattern of behavior becomes visible' (Fetterman 1989, p. 92). We used four questions based on Fetterman's approach to guide our analysis of data:

  o What's going on here?
  o Who is doing what?
  o Have I seen this particular event or action before? Is it significant? Why or why not?
  o What things are happening or being done more than once? What does this mean or suggest?

  Applying these questions to our data meant that we began to notice similarities in what we had collected. We colour coded and identified patterns as they emerged from the data. Our identification of patterns was guided by our review of the literature; that is, we expected to find certain patterns in our data that corresponded to key characteristics of what constitute *new* literacies (e.g., participation, collaboration, distributed knowledge). At the same time, we remained open to finding additional insights into what constitutes a *new literacy* practice in our data as well.

  (Beck et al. 2009: 11–12)

- Creating a table within the process of developing categories during data analysis

Table 8.1 Sample preliminary fieldnote analysis

Problem Solving through Messing About	Problem Solving through an Affinity Space	Problem Solving through Group Collaboration	Problem Solving through a Search Engine	Problem solving through Other Means
I got back into www.youtube.com to search for Haiti, started with search 'President Obama on Haiti.' Parts of the speech I think we can use so I copy and paste the url into www.zamzar.com. I got an error message 'File has no extension'. I asked Holly and Janice if they got this error. They didn't, so I went back to youtube.com. I repeated the process, opening up a new explorer window and it worked. While waiting for the file to convert I go back to www.youtube.com to search for more speeches (see Ann, 7:31,32,33&34)	Interesting – could not find videos on www.youtube.com so I went to google, put search 'Garth Brooks' 'the change' which brought me to video.google.com (help from the prof on the refined search with quotation marks) & found both songs there, but had to try to convert 2 different versions b/c that error 'File has no extension' but the next 2 worked. I converted them in www.zamzar.com then saved them on thumb drive (see Ann, 9:45)	Holly attempted to video Janice showing how to implement the song into Garageband, but she failed to press the record button so they did it twice (see Ann, 1:3)	Holly did the same thing and found a user-friendly site (in her opinion) which included a step-by-step video. Holly was pleased and went ahead w the download but the website was unavailable (see Ann, 3:13)	Holly clicked on www.media-converter.org and searched 'Interlake for Haiti – Haiti News Clips Collection' in the search, then tried to convert and download. This didn't work, so Holly went through chapter 2 in our DIY Media text. This took a long time and she wasn't finding anything so she tried going through the sign up on the site – found out it costs $4 so went back to the book to look for free software converter, checked index in our book, couldn't find it (see Ann 3:11

Source: Clavaglia et al. (2010); fieldnotes

- An example of a substantive research finding

  As part of one creative activity a team learned to assemble and program a Lego kitset robot to perform a simple task. When they analysed the data they had collected (using fieldnotes, and audio and video recordings of their activity and conversations) during the one week in which they assembled and programmed the robot, they saw, graphically, shifts in their technical language. Within two days they were using technical terms and phrases they had never previously encountered when going about their work (e.g., shifting from 'that sun dial thing' to the more technically accurate 'sensor'). Arriving at the basics of a shared language made their work move more rapidly and effectively, and everybody understood each other because they were acquiring the concepts and phrases and terms within concrete situations linked to material processes mediated by expert language modelling (in the form of manuals, online guides, posts in forums, YouTube talk-throughs and demonstrations, etc.). We pointed them to work by Gee (2004, 2007, 2008b) that they had not previously encountered, to indicate the significance of their original grounded finding regarding shifts in their language, and to suggest a possible approach to theorizing it. This included Gee's ideas about game players acquiring 'lucidly functional language' arising from activity that gives them 'embodied, situated meanings for the language' (2007: 158).

Some general observations

The courses enlist participants from the outset in writing the kinds of research reports that we do in our own work as researchers, along with contributory forms of writing integral to research – writing field notes in the heat of the moment, creating tables to organize, summarize or help reduce data, transcribing verbatim recorded speech for coding, and so on. This kind of writing is much easier to do *in situ*, with models and on demand feedback in place. This ease is augmented by the focus on collaborative writing. Participants tell us, unprompted, that this enables them to produce text that they do not think they would be able to produce individually, and certainly not within such a short time frame. They report experiences of being 'emboldened' to write; they take more risks; and they can produce more fluently, confidently, and rapidly – which means there is something 'there' to respond to. Often we get to 'what is right' by progressively responding to something that is 'not right' – but that something has to be there in the first place.

There is good evidence of situated writing producing results. To repeat, participants begin writing from the outset, but always within material contexts and with tangible artifacts and objects of the kinds that bona fide research teams encounter. Researchers have to *write* like researchers, and this takes many different forms. In data collection for example, they have to know how to generate usable field notes; they have to know how and when to capture verbatim speech; they have to know how to transcribe speech reliably; how to recognize an appropriate opportunity for a screen capture on a computer and to make and store and retrieve it. In data organization they have to know how to label and classify and summarize in order to aid data retrieval at the point of analysis. In data analysis one has to be able to render patterns and categories through use of codes and charts and tables and the like. Writing about triangulation of data, for example, becomes lucidly functional in the presence of data pertaining to a specific event or instance when team members collectively bring spoken and observational data to bear upon it, and when they bring complementary perspectives to bear upon it grounded in what they have seen and heard.

Of course, participants are in no ways experts or well-prepared independent digital media producers or researchers by the end of the course. They have simply had an intensive introduction to academic research Discourse and discourse (Gee 1996). By the same token, as we have tried to show here, it seems fair to say that they make noteworthy entrees into forms of reading and writing that are integral to the postgraduate professional formation of teachers under contemporary conditions, and do so within a tight time frame.

Finally, it is clear that the initiative and approach we have described here are a very limited and partial application of the vision of social learning advanced by people like Brown and Adler, and the conception of platforms integral to the 'pull' approach – and the pull approach itself – advanced by Hagel, Brown, and Davison. As we have noted, it does not proceed from passion. In addition, however, it is basically confined to the *access* level of pull. The course is a 'one-off' within a larger programme. At the same time, it is clear that even within such a course it would be possible to draw on and otherwise encourage attention to a social networking dimension harnessed to building capacity to *attract* that would carry far beyond the course. Furthermore, it is arguable that there are traces of *achieve* as described by Hagel, Brown, and Davison (2010). Participants *do* dig deeply – going into project time to muster insight and performance – with a view to realize as fully as possible within the time available their potential to learn something new and to research and report their learning.

Social learning and new literacies at New York's Quest to Learn (Q2L) school

Background

In *Quest to Learn: Developing the School for Digital Kids*, Katie Salen, Robert Torres, Loretta Wolozin, Rebecca Rufo-Tepper, and Arana Shapiro (2011) spell out the conceptual, theoretical, and research foundations for the design of a grade 6–12 public school in New York City that uses '"gamelike learning" to connect student learning to the demands of the twenty-first century and [support] young people in their learning across digital networks, peer communities, content, careers, and media' (ibid.: 2). The Quest to Learn (Q2L) school opened in autumn 2009 with a grade 6 cohort, and will build over six years to become a grade 6 to 12 small school (Q2L.org). In its second year it has 145 students (selected by district-wide lottery) across grades 6 and 7. The school was designed by the Institute of Play (Instituteofplay.com) in collaboration with New York's largest education-reform organization, New Visions for Public Schools (NewVisions.org). It also has collaborative relationships with Parsons The New School for Design (Newschool.edu/parsons), New York City's Department of Education, and the MacArthur Foundation Digital Media and Learning Network (Macfound.org). These collaborations collectively provide diverse forms of support and expertise, across design and research (e.g., in games-based pedagogy, new media literacies, assessment, games design), outreach to school leaders, teachers and students, and resources, such as a specialized learning laboratory. The school's resourcing and operating costs fall within the parameters of the school's district-approved budget.

We cannot do justice to the scope of the vision and aspirations for Q2L here, and recommend readers to the references and websites identified above. Instead, we will identify those aspects of what the school is trying to do that seem most pertinent to our theme of social learning and new literacies, and how institutions might orient toward building platforms for learning. Neither can we indicate how the ideals are playing out on the ground, since the initiative has just begun. What we *can* do, however, is identify and describe the conception of the school and visions for its work in relation to the concepts, values, and concerns that frame our interest here.

The vision

Q2L was envisaged partly in response to the possibility of school becoming 'a catalyst for activating a network of mentors, partners, peers and leaders ... focused on helping kids figure out how to be inventors, designers, innovators and problem-solvers' (Salen et al. 2011: ix). This is about helping to resource the 'learning to be' dimension of social learning (Gee 2007; Brown and Adler 2008), and realizing the first core practice defining the school from the perspective of its architects: namely, 'taking on identities' (Salen et al. 2011: xvii). The Q2L ideal is that students understand that their identities as learners are 'complex' and evolve with their memberships in communities of practice. Students should see themselves as writers, designers, readers, producers, teachers, students, and gamers. Among other things this means ensuring that in the course of their learning students are 'challenged to teach others how to do the stuff they know how to do' within settings where content is treated as 'an actionable resource rather than something to be memorized' (ibid.: x).

To these ends, learning must be *situated*. Students are asked to take on the identities of designers, scientists, historians, mathematicians, inventors, environmentalists, authors, and the like, and to behave like them, within contexts that are real, meaningful, or *both* to the students. These contexts are organized and structured as protracted Discovery Missions comprising sequences of Quests that extend over weeks, and require teachers and students to collaborate in diverse arrays of complex and demanding tasks and processes. That is, Discovery Missions constitute *situations* of practice. This situated learning is *gamelike*. It involves a learning approach intended to promote deep learning by drawing on the 'intrinsic qualities of games and their design' (Gee 2003, 2007; Salen 2007; Salen et al. 2011: 10). Games are carefully designed systems that are learner-driven. They are dynamic *systems* in which players participate, and which they increasingly understand and master as they 'crack' the design of the game (which, of course, the designers intend them to crack). Games simulate worlds of various kinds 'where players grow, receive instant feedback and develop ways of thinking about and seeing the world' (Salen et al. 2011: 11). Games as systems and simulated worlds – environments for engaging in practices of various kinds – produce meanings, are made up of rules, have various components and goals, and present conflicts, choices and space. These are the very essence of situated practices and, thus, are key ingredients for guiding the design of learning experiences (ibid.).

The point here is not that students are learning by playing games *as such*, although they do engage in considerable game playing. Rather, the learning principles of games are used to create learning environments that are based on the intrinsic features of games, because applying these instantiates contextualized situated learning around the kinds of identities and behaviours Q2L wants learners to take on. According to Salen and colleagues (ibid.: 11–12):

> Q2L aims to create a learning environment for students in which they act within situated learning contexts to solve complex problems in math, science, English language arts (ELA), and social studies in gamelike ways. Integrated learning contexts provide practice space for goal-oriented challenges. Work with models, simulations, and games through an evidence based inquiry curriculum serves as the foundation for the study of dynamic systems and their effects. The curriculum supports students in developing a way of thinking about global dynamics, for example: how world economic, political, technological, environmental, and social systems work and are interdependent across nations and regions. High levels of student engagement and ownership in the learning process are valued as students participate in a rigorous process of research, theory building, hypothesis testing, evaluation, and critique, followed by a public defense of results ... Value is placed on work within cross-functional teams where students contribute specialized practices to solve a problem collaboratively. Game design – for either digital or nondigital contexts – provides a platform for students to explore a range of ideas and to build systems to be experienced by others.

Curriculum and learning

The school's curriculum aligns with state standards, has a strong foundation in math and science, and is integrated (ibid.: 16). The Discovery Missions are undertaken within 'specially designed learning contexts' and comprise 'quest like challenges'. Students (with teacher guidance that is in turn supported by access to relevant expertise) have to 'plan, collect data, create theories, test their results and document outcomes' in the process of analysing, building and modifying various kinds of 'dynamic systems – historical, physical, mathematical, technological, scientific, written and social' (ibid.). There is a lot of interaction among students who share expertise and play together as they build solutions to problems in their own work.

The learning approach has been conceived around five key conditions for learning concerned with sharing, reflecting, responding to and providing feedback, evaluation, and distributing knowledge and understanding. Ensuring regular pretexts and opportunities for productive collaboration is a priority, along with teachers and students creating opportunities for knowledge sharing and peer feedback on work. The gamelike approach to learning, of course, emphasizes building continual and transparent feedback into quest tasks and processes themselves (just as players' moves within good video games evoke immediate and informative feedback). The learning environment includes 'channels' (ibid.: 17) for learners to share their knowledge, skill, and work with peers and a wider external community by means of podcasting, streamed video, public events and portfolios, and the like.

Learning experiences are designed with three competency dimensions in mind: Civic/Social-Emotional Learning, Design, and Content. Key competencies across these dimensions include: learning for well-being and emotional intelligence; design and innovation; complexity (or 'systemic reasoning'); critical thinking, judgement and credibility; learning using a design methodology; and learning using smart tools (ibid.: 46). So, for example, learning for complexity within each knowledge domain involves providing opportunities for students to see aspects of their world in terms of the various kinds of inter-related systems – biological, technological, political, social, etc. – that collectively constitute it. To support learning for design and innovation, opportunities are provided across the curriculum for 'tinkering' and for theory building. With respect to using design methodologies and smart tools, students 'act as sociotechnical engineers' across the various knowledge domains, creating 'playful systems' like games, stories, simulations and models, and learn to build a range of 'tools to think with' (smart tools), such as maps, equations, and online dictionaries (ibid.).

Q2L organizes content area knowledge into five 'situated ways of knowing' called Integrated Domains. This approaches knowledge as active: as outcomes of situated *ways* of knowing, or practices within which knowledge is produced, negotiated, tested, critiqued, and so on. These interdisciplinary domains integrate maths, science, history, and literature into 'practice spaces' where students can work at developing a 'games design and systems perspective' of the world in different situated ways. The domains are: 'The Way Things Work', 'Being, Space and Place', 'Codeworlds', 'Wellness', and 'Sports for the Mind', which deals with media literacy and design. Across these domains, learning activities emphasize five learning practices: systems thinking, play design, intelligent resourcing, meaning production, and tinkering (ibid.: 66). Students have to find and use resources on demand 'with intelligence, judgment and sophistication', thereby acquiring a kind of ecological and aesthetic design sensibility, and to produce creative, expressive and innovative meanings by coding and decoding linguistic, numeric, social, and cultural tokens into rich multimodal creations. They also tinker with systems in the form of games, simulations, models of social systems and ecologies, and small machines, modifying them in 'experimental and directed ways' in order to reveal their underlying models (ibid.).

Learning proceeds by undertaking the integrated quests that make up Missions. Sample Missions for grade 6 can be found on the Q2L website (Q2L.org/downloads), as well as in Salen and colleagues (2011: 125–32). A sample ten-week 6th grade Mission called 'Invisible Pathways' in the integrated domain 'The Way Things Work' (maths/science) provides a context for students to explore science and maths-based methods of building simple machines in the process of addressing the question: 'How do the relationships between elements in a system create a dynamic?' (ibid.: 125). This unit is designed to engage students in using tools like digital cameras and 3D simulation models in a sequence of quests that culminate in small teams of students constructing a pathway for a beam of light to travel to a target via several changes in direction. A typical quest requires learners to develop 'an inventory of behaviors' for a beam of light by pairing it with a range of different materials and observing how it behaves under different conditions. The following quest draws on the inventory information to discover what light colour must be used to create a pathway of light that reveals a hidden message. Digital imaging is used to document findings and the images are annotated online. The mission is designed in a way that requires students throughout to 'propose and test theories, observe and gather evidence of outcomes, and apply this understanding to the development of new theories' (ibid.). En route to completing the mission, students, individually and in teams, address diverse questions about how light travels and responds to different materials, and wrestle with an array of mathematical and scientific concepts like the relationship between complementary and supplementary angles, within concrete tasks and settings intended to narrate a trajectory of scientific conduct and ways of being. Throughout the process, the teacher circulates among groups and individuals, modelling procedures and guiding practice. (For an account of the ideal profile of a Q2L teacher, see ibid.: 25–8.)

Program and platforms

Q2L's learning approach is grounded in a closely specified curricular *programme*. This is practically inevitable for public/state schools under foreseeable circumstances of standards-driven formal education and obligatory standardized testing. Nonetheless, even within these constraints the Q2L blueprint reflects a strong emphasis on platform-oriented thinking, and on creating and using platforms to facilitate student learning and to (further) immerse learners in 'access–attract–achieve' logic and habits.

Game design itself – on which the entire learning approach is based – constitutes a learning platform (Gee 2003, 2007; Squire 2006; Shaffer 2007; Resnick et al. 2009; Gee and Hayes 2010) on multiple dimensions. It can be seen as a platform for exploring a range of ideas and for building systems that can be experienced by others. Alternatively, games can be viewed as authoring systems on multiple levels. Learners can use games as platforms for producing such artifacts as

a game (*Gamestar Mechanic*), a mod (*Starcraft*), a video (machinima in *WOW*, *SimCity*, *Second Life*, etc.), a visual text (*Sims Family Album*), an avatar (*Miis*), a written text (*MiLK*), or a body of code (*Alice, Scratch*).

(ibid.: 86)

Within the 'Codeworlds' integrated domain:

Students use writing as the primary mechanic of game play, whether they are playing text adventures or designing or playing textbased mobile games. The emphasis here is in the use of writing as both a mode of action and a mode of expression. Because writing itself is produced as an artifact of the game play, this writing can be assessed to capture student understanding. There is an opportunity to connect this approach to games with the introduction of a programming curriculum that might use authoring platforms, such as *Scratch* or *Alice*, or virtual worlds that support object creation, such as *Second Life*.

(ibid.: 89)

At another level, Q2L has built a customized closed (confined to members of the Q2L community) social-network platform, 'Being Me', that students use on a daily basis for posting work, maintaining blogs, forming discussion groups, tracking their mood, identifying collaborators, giving and receiving feedback, sharing, reviewing, recording, and for other such purposes that extend their learning. 'Being Me' supports socio-emotional well-being by serving as a student-driven program that enables learners to connect their experiences in and out-of-school in ways that are helpful for thinking about their health and identity formation on multiple dimensions. For example,

What issues do students consider important, worrisome, private, or confusing? How do they choose to express their interests and concerns? What ecologies of resources do they create, share, and seek out?

(ibid.: 63)

As a 'multi-faceted learning tool' the network mediates interactions that increase understanding of issues that students identify as important, enabling feedback and reflection, information-sharing, and so on. It 'multitasks' as a curriculum tool, data repository, and networking space that provides opportunities to access, attract, and achieve within life-like and 'real-life' contexts of social, academic, and cultural participation.

Observations

The promise of social learning is the prospect of becoming full participants in 'mature' versions of social practice, acquiring the deep kinds of learning that bestow mastery of a domain through active involvement in affinity spaces or communities of practice where participants learn to *do* and *be* in the ways of competent insiders to the practice. The key point here with respect to formal education is the need to take a trajectory view of learning and of learners, and of the relationships between learning experiences at different points along trajectories. Learners' lives should be viewed as *trajectories* 'through multiple social practices [and D/discourses] in various institutions' (Gee et al. 1996: 4). The ideal for all learning at every point in time – and which is especially significant when thinking about learning within formal education institutions – is that it be *efficacious*. For learning to be efficacious, 'what a child or adult does *now* [wherever they are along their trajectory] must be connected in meaningful and motivating ways with "mature" [insider] versions of related social practices' (ibid.). The particular significance of a social learning perspective is that it reminds us that the learning Discourse of schools should be as 'onside' as possible with insider versions of related social practices beyond school, which means being connected to them in *meaningful and motivating* ways.

The bottom line here is that they be *situated* and *contextualized* in ways that transcend 'doing school' and 'being a school student' in the forms that prevail. School learning practices *are* practices. But they are practices that often do not comport well to related social practices beyond school or to knowledge and applications of knowledge outside of curriculum. Hence, it is important in formal education, particularly at school level, not simply to transcend decontextualized, abstracted knowledge but, also, as much as possible, to ensure that the 'situatedness' of school-based learning – since it *is* situated – is 'onside' with the kinds of related situated practices students encounter beyond (spatially, temporally, and culturally) school.

This has special significance for 'gamelike' approaches to situated learning of the kinds promoted at Q2L. It is an empirical matter as to what extent the 'gamelike' situated learning practices at Q2L play out as approximations here and now to 'mature' versions of being inventors, historians, engineers, scientists, writers, and the like. That is less important, however, than the fact that they seem very well connected in *meaningful and motivating ways* to diverse practices. There is plenty of tinkering, a lot of hands-on involvement with tools, a good deal of networking, and endless practice at learning what it means to take on different identities. There is an organic connection at every point to grounding information gathering, concept development, and understanding in concrete, purposeful practices. There are many obvious spaces within Missions for practising mashing up, modding, and controlling variables, and pulling 'things' apart and putting them back together in the same and different ways to build a sense of systems and how they function. Sarah Corbett's (2010) snapshots of slices of life inside Q2L plainly bespeak *motivating* connections to related social practices awaiting its learners farther along their trajectories, and *meaningful* links to practices about which they are passionate now and that – as we have seen in the cases described by Gee and Hayes (2010) – are integral to everyday and professional lives at all points on foreseeable trajectories. Above all, the Q2L learning approach is profoundly *participatory* in ways that span the senses and sensibilities we might associate with accounts provided by theorists as diverse as dana boyd, Henry Jenkins, John Seely Brown, Lawrence Lessig, and Tim O'Reilly.

The end

The current 'round' of 'new' literacies simultaneously ups the ante and enriches and enlarges the possibilities for social learning. Of course, social learning approaches do not presuppose mediation by new literacies, by new technologies, or 'new' anything else. They simply call for grounding learning in situated practices where participants learn to do and be in purposeful ways, in the company of others who can resource that learning in ways that lead to becoming competent insiders to those practices – which can be realized under any kind of technological regime or configuration of language and literacy practices. Much of the significance of social learning stems from its efficacy for enabling deep learning, fluent mastery of concepts, tools and skills, and creative and productive applications of knowledge and understanding. Because the 'natural home' of social learning is the everyday world of social practice at large, it maintains points of connection to human lives as trajectories in ways that are often lost by hiving off formal education into contrived spaces, time frames, and idiosyncratic ways of doing things.

At the same time, however, it is clear that right now a complex set of social, technological, economic, and cultural conditions are converging in ways that present interesting and expansive possibilities for extending a social learning approach into formal education in ways that can resist counter-productive forms and effects of 'compartmentalized' curricular learning, and help keep that portion of learning that occurs inside school optimally connected to life trajectories beyond classrooms. Exploring these possibilities will involve taking some risks, venturing into unknown territory, redefining our identities and roles as formal teachers and learners, doing some experimenting, going down some blind alleys and getting some wins, reflecting on our experiences, and sharing what we have done and learned with others, and keeping connected to the wider efforts of kindred spirits. Indeed, it will involve building new practices with fellow travellers in the same kinds of ways that members of popular affinities (as well as of corporate affiliations) are building and refining participatory cultural practices across diverse spaces of engagement, and diverse purposes and interests.

It is a worthy challenge, since the prospects of present and future generations for learning and living as well as they can call for nothing less.

Bibliography

Academia.edu (2010) Keywords. *Academia.edu*. http://montclair.academia.edu/ MicheleKnobel/Keywords (accessed 29 Nov. 2010).

Adams, P. (2010) The Real Life Social Network v2. *Slideshare*. http://www. slideshare.net/padday/the-real-life-social-network-v2 (accessed 5 Dec. 2010).

Alexa (2010) Site information for Academia.edu. *Alexa.com*. Alexa.com/siteinfo/ academia.edu# (accessed 29 Nov. 2010).

Alvermann, D. (2009) Sociocultural constructions of adolescence and young people's literacies. In L. Christenbury, R. Bomer and P. Smagorinsky (eds) *Handbook of Adolescent Literacy Research*. New York: Guilford, pp. 14–28.

Alvermann, D. (ed.) (2010) *Adolescents' Online Literacies: Connecting Classrooms, Digital Media and Popular Culture*. New York: Peter Lang.

Anderson, C. (2010) The Web is dead: long live the internet. Who's to blame?: Us. *Wired.com*, 17 August. http://www.wired.com/magazine/2010/08/ff_webrip/ all/1 (accessed 5 Dec. 2010).

Anderson, C. A. (1966) Literacy and schooling on the development threshold: some historical cases. In C. A. Anderson and M. J. Bowman (eds) *Education and Economic Development*. Chicago: Aldine Publishing Co, pp. 347–62.

Bandura, A. (1977) *Social Learning Theory*. Englewood Cliffs, NJ: Prentice Hall.

Barton, D. (1991) The social nature of writing. In D. Barton and R. Ivanic (eds) *Writing in the Community*. London: Sage, pp. 1–13.

Barton, D. and Hamilton, M. (1998) *Local Literacies: Reading and Writing in One Community*. London: Routledge.

Baumer, E., Sueyoshi, M. and Tomlinson, B. (2008) Exploring the role of the reader in the activity of blogging. ACM *Conference on Human Factors in Computing Systems* (CHI 2008). http://portal.acm.org/citation.cfm?doid=1357054. 1357228 (accessed 5 Dec. 2010).

Bawden, D. (2008) Origins and concepts of digital literacy. In C. Lankshear and M. Knobel (eds) *Digital Literacies: Concepts, Policies and Practices*. New York: Peter Lang, pp. 17–32.

BBC (2007) School literacy scheme attacked. *BBC News* (2 November 2007). http://news.bbc.co.uk/1/ hi/education/7073275.stm (accessed 26 March 2009).

BBC News (2004) 'Virgin Mary' toast fetches $28,000. (23 November 2004). http://news.bbc.co.uk/2/hi/4034787.stm (accessed 23 March 2011).

Beach, R. (2006) *Teachingmedialiteracy.com: A Web-Linked Guide to Resources and Activities*. New York: Teachers College Press.

Beck, S., Coley, C., Conway, K., Hoven, D. and Maynard, P. (2009) From collaboration to affinity space: learning a new literacy. Steady Brook, Newfoundland: Research Report for Summer Program. Mimeo.

Beer, D. (2008) Social network(ing) sites: revisiting the story so far: a response to dana boyd and Nicole Ellison. *Journal of Computer-Mediated Communication*, 13: 516–29.

Berlind, D. (2006) Mashup ecosystem poised to explode. *ZDNet*, 27 January. http://www.zdnet.com/blog/btl/mashup-ecosystem-poised-to-explode/2484 (accessed 5 Dec. 2010).

Berners-Lee, T. (2010) Long live the Web: a call for continued open standards and neutrality. *Scientific American*, 22 November. http://www.scientificamerican.com/article.cfm?id=long-live-the-web (accessed 5 Dec. 2010).

Best-Pinsent, D., Payne, A., Patey, M., Hillier, R., Deely, L. and Dawson, M. (2009) Collaboration: interdependence, partnership and power. Steady Brook, Newfoundland: Research Report for Summer Program. Mimeo.

Bigum, C. (2004) Rethinking schools and community: the knowledge producing school. In S. Marshall, W. Taylor and Xing Huo Yu (eds) *Using Community Informatics to Transform Regions*. Hershey, PA: Idea Group Publishing, pp. 52–66.

Black, R. (2005a) Access and affiliation: the literacy and composition practices of English language learners in an online fanfiction community. *Journal of Adolescent and Adult Literacy*, 49(2): 118–28.

Black, R. (2005b) Digital resources: English language learners reading and reviewing online fanfiction. Paper presented at National Reading Conference, Miami, FL, 30 November.

Black, R. (2006) Not just the OMG standard: reader feedback and language, literacy, and culture in online fanfiction. Paper presented at the Annual Meeting of The American Educational Research Association, San Francisco, 10 April.

Black, R. (2007) Digital design: English language learners and reader reviews in online fiction. In M. Knobel and C. Lankshear (eds) *A New Literacies Sampler*. New York: Peter Lang, pp. 115–36.

Black, R. (2008) *Adolescents and Online Fan Fiction*. New York: Peter Lang.

Black, R. (2009) Adolescents, fan communities, and twenty-first century skills. *Journal of Adolescent and Adult Literacy*, 52(8): 688–97.

Blood, R. (2002) Weblogs: a history and perspective, in Editors of Perseus Publishing (eds) *We've Got Blog: How Weblogs Are Changing Culture*. Cambridge, MA: Perseus Publishing, pp. 7–16.

boyd, d. (2006) A blogger's blog: exploring the definition of a medium. *Reconstruction* 6(4). http://reconstruction.eserver.org/064/boyd.shtml (accessed 5 Dec. 2010).

boyd, d. (2008) Taken out of context: American teen sociality in networked publics. Unpublished doctoral manuscript, Graduate Division, University of California, Berkeley.

boyd, d. and Ellison, N. (2007) Social network sites: Definition, history, and scholarship. *Journal of Computer-Mediated Communication*, 13(1). http://jcmc.indiana.edu/vol13/issue1/boyd.ellison.html (accessed 5 Dec. 2010).

boyd, d. and Hargittai, E. (2010) Facebook privacy settings: who cares? *First Monday*. http://firstmonday.org/htbin/cgiwrap/bin/ojs/index.php/fm/article/view/3086/2589 (accessed 13 Nov. 2010).

Brown, J. S. and Adler, R. (2008) Minds on fire: open education, the long tail and Learning 2.0. *Educause Review*, January/February: 17–32.

Brown, J. S. and Duguid, P. (2002) *The Social Life of Information*, 2nd edn. Boston: Harvard Business School Publishing.

Brown, J. S., Collins, A. and Duguid, P. (1989) Situated cognition and the nature of learning. *Educational Researcher*, 18(1): 32–42.

Bruns, A. (2008) *Blogs, Wikipedia, Second Life and Beyond: From Production to Produsage*. New York: Peter Lang Publishing.

Bruns, A. and Bahnisch, M. (2009) *Social Media: Tools for User-Generated Content*. Vol. 1: *State of the Art*. Eveleigh, NSW: Smart Services CRC.

Bryant, S., Forte, A. and Bruckman, A. (2005) Becoming Wikipedian: transformation of participation in a collaborative online encyclopedia. *Proceedings of GROUP05*. http://citeseerx.ist.psu.edu/viewdoc/download?doi=10.1.1.62.5337.pdf (accessed 5 Dec. 2010).

Burgess, J. and Green, J. (2009) *YouTube: Online Video and Participatory Culture*. Cambridge: Polity.

Castells, M. (1996) *The Rise of the Network Society*. Cambridge, MA: Blackwell.

Castells, M. (2000) *The Rise of the Network Society*, 2nd edn. Cambridge, MA: Blackwell.

Chaiklin, S. and Lave, J. (1996) *Understanding Practice: Perspectives on Activity in Context*. Cambridge: Cambridge University Press.

Chandler-Olcott, K. and Mahar, D. (2003) 'Tech-savviness' meets multiliteracies: exploring adolescent girls' technology-mediated literacy practices. *Reading Research Quarterly*, 38(3): 356–85.

Chao, L. and Ye, J. (2010) China's 'War of Internet Addiction' creator, 'Corndog,' speaks. *Wall Street Journal*, 19 February. http://blogs.wsj.com/digits/2010/02/19/chinas-war-of-internet-addiction-creator-corndog-speaks/?mod=rss_WSJBlog&mod= (accessed 5 Dec. 2010)

Clavaglia, J., Landry, A. and Stone, H. (2010) Breaking down the barriers: participating in new literacies. North Sydney, Nova Scotia: research report for Summer Program. Mimeo.

Collier, L. (2007) The shift to 21st-century literacies. *Council Chronicle*, 17(2): 4–8.

Collins, A., Brown, J. S. and Newman, S. (1989) Cognitive apprenticeship: teaching the craft of reading, writing and mathematics. In L. Resnick (ed.) *Knowing, Learning and Instruction: Essays in Honour of Robert Glaser*. Hillsdale, NJ: Lawrence Erlbaum Associates, pp. 453–94.

Common Core Standards Initiative (2010) http://www.corestandards.org (accessed 5 Dec. 2010).

Cook, S. and Brown, J. S. (1999) Bridging epistemologies: the generative dance between organizational knowledge and organizational knowing. *Organization Science*, 10(4): 381–400.

Cope, B., Kalantzis, M. and Lankshear, C. (2005) A contemporary project: an interview. *E-Learning*, 2(2): 192–207. http://www.wwwords.co.uk/elea/content/pdfs/2/issue2_2.asp#7 (accessed 5 Dec. 2010).

Corbett, S. (2010) Learning by playing: video games in the classroom. *New York Times Magazine*, 19 September. http://www.nytimes.com/2010/09/19/magazine/19video-t.html (accessed 5 Dec. 2010).

Coulombe, S., Tremblay, J.-F. and Marchand, S. (2004) *Literacy Scores, Human Capital and Growth across Fourteen OECD Countries*. Ottawa: Statistics Canada.

Couros, A. (2010) Ning alternatives, collaboration and self-hosting. *Open Thinking: Rants and Resources from an Open Educator*. http://educationaltechnology.ca/couros/1795 (accessed 12 Nov. 2010).

Cross, J. (2006) *Informal Learning: Rediscovering the Natural Pathways that Inspire Innovation and Performance*. San Francisco: Pfeiffer.

Cuban, L. (2003) *Oversold and Underused: Computers in the Classroom*. Cambridge, MA: Harvard University Press.

Davies, J. (2006) Affinities and beyond: developing new ways of seeing in online spaces. *E-Learning*, 3(2): 217–34.

Davies, J. and Merchant, G. (2009) *Web 2.0 for Schools: Learning and Social Participation*. New York: Peter Lang Publishing.

Department of Employment, Education, Training and Youth Affairs, Australia (DEETYA) (1998) *Literacy for All: The Challenge for Australian Schools*. Canberra: DEETYA.

Donovan, S., Hawley, J. and Whitty, S. (2010) Social learning resulting from the production of a media artifact. North Sydney, Nova Scotia: research report for Summer Program. Mimeo.

Drucker, P. (1993) *Post-capitalist Society*. New York: Harper.

Duckworth, E., Peterson, C., Matthews, M. and Kelly, D. (2007) Grit: perseverance and passion for long-term goals. *Journal of Personality and Social Psychology*, 92(6): 1087–101.

Duncombe, S. (1997) *Notes from Underground: Zines and the Politics of Alternative Culture*. London: Verso.

Facebook (2010) Social Plugins: Like Button. http://developers.facebook.com/docs/reference/plugins/like (accessed 26 July 2010).

Fan Fiction: The Force.net (2010) Submission guidelines for TheForce.Net's fan fiction archive. fanfic.theforce.net/authors/subguide.asp (accessed 10 Oct. 2010).

Feld, S. (1981) The focused organization of social ties. *American Journal of Sociology*, 86(5): 1015–35.

Fetterman, D. (1989) *Ethnography: Step by Step*: Thousand Oaks, CA: Sage.

Flickr (2010) Secret life of toys group pool. *Flickr*. http://www.flickr.com/groups/secretlifeoftoys (accessed 25 Dec. 2010).

Freire, P. (1972) *Pedagogy of the Oppressed*. Harmondsworth: Penguin.

Freire, P. (1973) *Cultural Action for Freedom*. Harmondsworth: Penguin.

Freire, P. (1974/2007) *Education for Critical Consciousness*. London: Continuum.

Freire, P. and Macedo, D. (1987) *Literacy: Reading the Word and the World*. South Hadley, MA: Bergin and Garvey.

Gallie, W. B. (1956) Essentially contested concepts. *Proceedings of the Aristotelian Society*, 56: 167–98.

Gardner, H. (1991) *The Unschooled Mind: How Children Think and How Schools Should Teach*. New York: Basic Books.

Garton, L., Haythornewaite, C. and Wellman, B. (1997) Studying online social networks. *Journal of Computer Mediated Communication*, 3(1). http://jcmc.indiana.edu/vol3/issue1/garton.html (accessed 16 Nov. 2010).

Gay, J. (ed.) (2010) *Free Software Free Society: Selected Essays of Richard Stallman*. New York: SoHo Books.

Gee, J. P. (1990) *Social Linguistics and Literacies: Ideology in Discourses*. London: Falmer.

Gee, J. P. (1991) What is literacy? in C. Mitchell and K. Weiler (eds) *Rewriting Literacy: Culture and the Discourse of the Other*. New York: Bergin and Garvey, pp. 159–212.

Gee, J. P. (1992) *The Social Mind: Language, Ideology and Social Practice*. Westport, CT: Bergin and Garvey.

Gee, J. P. (1996) *Social Linguistics and Literacies: Ideology in Discourses*, 2nd edn. London: Falmer.

Gee, J. P. (1997) Foreword: a discourse approach to language and literacy. In C. Lankshear (ed.) *Changing Literacies*. Buckingham: Open University Press, pp. xiii–xix.

Gee, J. P. (2000) Teenagers in new times: a new literacy studies perspective. *Journal of Adolescent and Adult Literacy*, 43(5): 412–23.

Gee, J. P. (2003) *What Video Games Have to Teach Us About Learning and Literacy*. New York: Palgrave.

Gee, J. P. (2004) *Situated Language and Learning: A Critique of Traditional Schooling*. London: Routledge.

Gee, J. P. (2007) *Good Video Games + Good Learning: Collected Essays on Video Games*. New York: Peter Lang.

Gee, J. P. (2008a) *Social Linguistics and Literacies: Ideology in Discourses*, 3rd edn. London: Routledge/Falmer.

Gee, J. P. (2008b) Lucidly functional language. In *New Literacies: A Professional Development Wiki for Educators*. Developed under the aegis of the Improving Teacher Quality Project (ITQP), a federally funded partnership between Montclair State University and East Orange School District, New Jersey. http://newlits.wikispaces.com/Lucidly+Functional+Language (accessed 5 Dec. 2010).

Gee, J. P. and Hayes, E. (2010) *Women and Gaming: The Sims and 21st Century Learning*. New York: Palgrave Press.

Gee, J. P., Hull, G. and Lankshear, C. (1996) *The New Work Order: Behind the Language of the New Capitalism*. Sydney: Allen and Unwin.

Gevers, N. (2001) Future remix: an interview with Ian McDonald. *Interzone #172*. http://www.lysator.liu.se/iunicorn/mcdonald/interviews/Gevers_Interzone172.html (accessed 23 March 2011).

Gilster, P. (1997) *Digital Literacy*. New York: John Wiley & Sons Inc.

Graff, H. (1979) *The Literacy Myth: Literacy and Social Structure in the Nineteenth Century City*. New York: Academic Press.

Granovetter, M. (1973) The strength of weak ties. *American Journal of Sociology*, 78(6): 1360–80.

Granovetter, M. (1983) The strength of weak ties: a network theory revisited. *Sociological Theory*, 1: 201–33.

Green, B. (1988) Subject-specific literacy and school learning: a focus on writing. *Australian Journal of Education*, 30(2): 156–69.

Green, B. (1997) Literacy, information and the learning society. Keynote address to the Joint Conference of the Australian Association for the Teaching of English, the Australian Literacy Educators' Association, and the Australian School Library Association. Darwin: Darwin High School, Northern Territory, Australia, 8–11 July.

Green, H. and Hannon, C. (2007) *Their Space: Education for a Digital Generation*. London: Demos.

Green, J. and Jenkins, H. (2009) The moral economy of Web 2.0: audience research and convergence culture. In J. Holt and A. Perren (eds) *Media Industries: History, Theory and Methods*. New York: Wiley-Blackwell, pp. 213–25.

Greenspan, A. (2008) *Authoritas: One Student's Harvard Admissions and the Founding of the Facebook Era*. Pal. Alto, CA: Think Press.

Haferkamp, N. and Krämer, N. (2010) Creating a digital self: impression management and impression formation of social network sites. In K. Drotner and K. Schrøder (eds) *Digital Content Creation: Perceptions, Practices and Perspectives*. New York: Peter Lang, pp. 129–48.

Hagel, J. and Brown, J.S. (2005) From push to pull: emerging models for mobilizing resources. Unpublished working paper, October. edgeperspectives.com (accessed 21 Jan. 2010).

Hagel, J., Brown, J. S. and Davison, L. (2010) *The Power of Pull: How Small Moves, Smartly Made, Can Set Big Things in Motion*. New York: Basic Books.

Hägerstrand, T. (1966) Quantitative techniques for the analysis of the spread of information and technology. In C. A. Anderson and M. J. Bowman (eds) *Education and Economic Development*. Chicago: Aldine Publishing Co, pp. 237–51.

Halatchliyski, I., Kimmerle, J., Moskaliuk, J. and Cress, U. (2010) Who integrates the networks of knowledge in Wikipedia? *Proceedings of WikiSym'10*. wikisym. org/ws2010/Proceedings (accessed 5 Dec. 2010).

Hancock, H. and Ingram, J. (2007) *Machinima for Dummies*. New York: Wiley.

Hawkins, E. (2004) *The Complete Guide to Remixing: Produce Professional Dance-Floor Hits on Your Home Computer*. Boston: Berklee Press.

Heath, S. (1983) *Ways with Words: Language, Life and Work in Community and Classrooms*. Cambridge: Cambridge University Press.

Hirsch, E. D. Jr. (1987) *Cultural Literacy: What Every American Needs to Know*. Boston, MA: Houghton Mifflin.

Hirst, P. (1974) *Knowledge and the Curriculum*. London: Routledge & Kegan Paul.

Hogan, B. (2009) The networked individual: a profile of Barry Wellman. http://www.semioticon.com/semiotix/semiotix14/sem-14-05.html (accessed 12 Dec. 2010).

Hoggart, R. (1957) *The Uses of Literacy: Aspects of Working Class Life*. London: Chatto.

Honegger, B. (2005) Wikis: a rapidly growing phenomenon in the German-speaking school community. *Proceedings of WikiSym'05*. wikisym.org/ws2005/proceedings/ (accessed 5 Dec. 2010).

Huh, B. (2010) 'Mainstreaming the Web' Panelist. ROFLCon, Boston. 1 May.

Hull, G. and Schultz, K. (2001) Literacy and learning out of school: a review of theory and research. *Review of Educational Research*, 71(4): 575–611.

Ito, M. (2005a) Personal, portable, pedestrian: lessons from Japanese mobile phone use, *Japan Focus*, 30 October. http://www.japanfocus.org/article.asp?id=434 (accessed 16 Feb. 2006).

Ito, M. (2005b) Otaku media literacy. *Mimi Ito*. http://www.itofisher.com/mito/publications/otaku_media_lit.html (accessed 22 June 2006).

Ito, M. (2006) Japanese media mixes and amateur cultural exchange. In D. Buckingham and R. Willett (eds) *Digital Generations: Children, Young People, and New Media*. Mahwah, NJ. Lawrence Erlbaum Associates, pp. 49–66.

Ito, M., Baumer, S., Bittani, M., boyd, d., Cody, R., Herr-Shephardson, B., Horst, H., Lange, A., Mahendran, D., Martinez, K., Pascoe, C., Perkel, D., Robinson, L., Sims, C. and Tripp, L. (2009) *Hanging Out, Messing Around, and Geeking Out: Kids Living and Learning with New Media*. Cambridge, MA: MIT Press.

Jacobson, E. (2010) Music remix in the classroom. In M. Knobel and C. Lankshear (eds) *DIY Media: Creating, Sharing and Learning with New Technologies*. New York: Peter Lang, pp. 27–49.

Jarche, H. (2005) Open source: the sensible learning platform. *Life in Perpetual Beta*. jarche.com/2005/04/OLD500 (accessed 5 Dec. 2010).

Jarche, H. (2010) Identifying a collaboration platform. *Life in Perpetual Beta*. jarche.com/2010/05/identifying-a-collaboration-platform (accessed 5 Dec. 2010).

Jenkins, H. (1988) *Star Trek* rerun, reread, rewritten. *Critical Studies in Mass Communication*, 52(2): 85–107.

Jenkins, H. (1992) *Textual Poachers: Television, Fans, and Participatory Culture*. New York: Routledge.

Jenkins, H. (1998) *From Barbie to Mortal Kombat: Gender and Computer Games*. Cambridge, MA: MIT Press.

Jenkins, H. (2006a) *Convergence Culture: Where Old and New Media Collide*. New York: New York University Press.

Jenkins, H. (2006b) *Fans, Bloggers and Gamers: Exploring Participatory Culture*. New York: New York University Press.

Jenkins, H. (2010) Afterword. In M. Knobel and C. Lankshear (eds) *DIY Media: Creating, Sharing and Learning with New Technologies*. New York: Peter Lang, pp. 231–53.

Jenkins, H., with R. Purushotma, K. Clinton, M. Weigel and A. Robison (2006) *Confronting the Challenge of Participatory Culture: Media Education for the 21st Century*. Occasional Paper. Boston, MA: MIT/MacArthur Foundation.

Kadushin, C., Killworth, P., Bernard, H.R. and Beveridge, A. (2005) Scale-up methods as applied to estimate of heroin use. Working paper, Brandeis University, East Waltham, MA.

Kalantzis, M. and Cope, B. (1997) *Multiliteracies: Rethinking What We Mean by Literacy and What We Teach as Literacy in the Context of Global Cultural Diversity and New Communications Technologies*. Occasional paper no. 21. Haymarket, NSW: Centre for Workplace Communication and Culture.

Kelland, M., Morris, D. and Lloyd, D. (2005) *Machinima: Making Movies in 3D Virtual Environments*. Boston: Thomson Course Technology.

Kincaid, J. (2010) Academia.edu raises $1.6 million to help researchers connect with each other. *TechCrunch*, 28 April. http://techcrunch.com/2010/04/28/

academia-edu-raises-1-6-million-to-help-researchers-connect-with-each-other/ (accessed 1 Dec. 2010).

Knobel, M. and Lankshear, C. (2007) Online memes, affinities and cultural production. In M. Knobel and C. Lankshear (eds) *A New Literacies Sampler*. New York: Peter Lang, pp. 199–227.

Knobel, M. and Lankshear, C. (2008) Digital literacy and participation in online social networking spaces. In C. Lankshear and M. Knobel (eds) *Digital Literacies: Concepts, Policies and Practices*. New York: Peter Lang, pp. 249–78.

Knobel, M. and Lankshear, C. (2009) Wikis, digital literacies, and professional growth. *Journal of Adolescent and Adult Literacy*, 52(7): 631–4.

Knobel, M. and Lankshear, C. (eds) (2010) *DIY Media: Creating, Sharing and Learning with New Technologies*. New York: Peter Lang Publishing.

Knobel, M., Lankshear, C. and Lewis, M. (2010) AMV remix: do-it-yourself anime music videos. In M. Knobel and C. Lankshear (eds) *DIY Media: Creating, Sharing and Learning with New Technologies*. New York: Peter Lang, pp. 205–30.

Know Your Meme (2010a) Iraqi shoe toss. *Know Your Meme*. http://knowyourmeme. com/memes/iraqi-shoe-toss (accessed 25 Sept. 2010).

Know Your Meme (2010b) Keanu is Sad/Sad Keanu. *Know Your Meme*. http:// knowyourmeme.com/memes/keanu-is-sadsad-keanu (accessed 5 Dec. 2010).

Koman, R. (2005) Remixing culture: an interview with Lawrence Lessig. oreilly. net. com/pub/a/policy/2005/02/24/lessig.html (accessed 22 Apr. 2006).

Kozol, J. (1985) *Illiterate America*. New York: Anchor and Doubleday.

Kress, G. (2003) *Literacy in the New Media Age*. London: Routledge.

Lankshear, C. (1999) Literacy studies in education. In M. Peters (ed.) *After the Disciplines: The Emergence of Cultural Studies*. Westport, CT: Bergin and Garvey, pp. 199–227.

Lankshear, C. and Knobel, M. (2003) *New Literacies: Changing Knowledge and Classroom Learning*. Maidenhead: Open University Press.

Lankshear, C. and Knobel, M. (2006) *New Literacies: Everyday Practices and Classroom Learning*, 2nd edn. Maidenhead: Open University Press.

Lave, J. (1988) *Cognition in Practice: Mind, Mathematics and Culture in Everyday Life*. Cambridge: Cambridge University Press.

Lave, J. and Wenger, E. (1991) *Situated Learning: Legitimate Peripheral Participation*. Cambridge: Cambridge University Press.

Leander, K. and Frank, A. (2006) The aesthetic production and distribution of image/subjects among online youth. *E-Learning*, 3(2): 185–206.

Leander, K. and Lovvorn, J. (2006) Literacy networks: following the circulation of texts, bodies, and objects in the schooling and online gaming of one youth. *Cognition & Instruction*, 24(3): 291–340.

Leander, K. and Mills, S. (2007) The transnational development of an online role player game by youth: tracing the flows of literacy, an online game imaginary, and digital resources. In M. Blackburn and C. T. Clark (eds) *Literacy Research for Political Action*. New York: Peter Lang, pp. 177–98.

Leidtke, M. (2007) Microsoft deal values Facebook at 15b. Associated Press. http://ap.google.com/article/ALeqM5hKn0T1IOwng1NE5pvvZLewkJ5aVQ (accessed 13 Nov. 2010).

Lessig, L. (2004) *Free Culture: How Big Media Uses Technology and the Law to Lock Down Culture and Control Creativity*. New York: Penguin.

Lessig, L. (2005) Re:Mix:Me. Plenary address to the annual Network for IT-Research and Competence in Education (ITU) conference, Oslo, Norway. October.

Lessig, L. (2008) *Remix: Making Art and Commerce Thrive in the Hybrid Economy*. New York: The Penguin Press.

Lewis, C. S. (1992) *An Experiment in Criticism*. Cambridge: Cambridge University Press.

Livingstone, S. and Brake, D. (2010) On the rapid rise of social networking sites: new findings and policy implications. *Children & Society*, 24: 75–83.

Luckman, S. and Potanin, R. (2010) Machinima: why think 'games' when thinking film. In M. Knobel and C. Lankshear (eds) *DIY Media: Creating, Sharing and Learning with New Technologies*. New York: Peter Lang, pp. 135–60.

Lyotard, J.-F. (1984) *The Postmodern Condition: A Report on Knowledge*. Trans. G. Bennington and B. Massumi. Minneapolis, MN: University of Minnesota Press.

Lyotard, J.-F. (1993) A svelte appendix to the postmodern condition. In *Political Writings*, trans. B. Readings and K. Geison. Minneapolis, MN: University of Minnesota Press.

Mahiri, J. (ed.) (2001) *What They Don't Learn in School: Literacy in the Lives of Urban Youth*. New York: Peter Lang.

Marshall, J. (2007) *Living on Cybermind: Categories, Communication, and Control*. New York: Peter Lang.

Martin, A. (2008) Digital literacy and the 'digital society'. In C. Lankshear and M. Knobel (eds) *Digital Literacies: Concepts, Policies and Practices*. New York: Peter Lang, pp. 151–76.

Marton, F. and Säljö, R. (1976) On qualitative differences in learning. *British Journal of Educational Psychology*, 46: 4–11, 115–27.

Mason, J. (1998) Groupware, community, and meta-networks: the collaborative framework of EdNA (Education Network Australia). *Community Computing and Support Systems*, 1519: 125–36.

McManus, R. (2004) Tim O'Reilly interview Part 3: eBooks and remix culture. *ReadWriteWeb*. readwriteweb.com/archives/tim_oreilly_int_2.php (accessed 22 April 2006).

Merchant, G. (2010) Visual networks: learning and photosharing. In M. Knobel and C. Lankshear (eds) *DIY Media: Creating, Sharing and Learning with New Technologies*. New York: Peter Lang, pp. 77–102.

Miller, N. and Dollard, J. (1941) *Social Learning and Imitation*. New Haven, CT: Yale University Press.

Miller, G. and Gildea, P. (1987) How children learn words. *Scientific American*, 257(3): 94–9.

Navas, E. (2007) The three basic forms of remix: a point of entry. *Remix Theory*. http://www.remixtheory.net/?p=174 (accessed 5 Dec. 2010).

National Council of Teachers of English (2007) 21st-Century Literacies: A Policy Research Brief. Urbana, IL: NCTE. http://www.ncte.org/21st-century (accessed 12 Sept. 2010).

National Council of Teachers of English (2008) The NCTE definition of 21st century literacies. http://www.ncte.org/positions/statements/21stcentdefinition (accessed 12 Sept. 2010).

NCEE (National Commission on Excellence in Education) (1983) *A Nation at Risk: The Imperative for Educational Reform*. Washington, DC: US Department of Education.

No Child Left Behind Act (2001) http://www2.ed.gov/policy/elsec/leg/esea02/index.html (accessed 5 Dec. 2010).

OECD (1991) *Review of National Policies for Education: Norway*. Paris: OECD.

OECD (2009) *PISA 2009 Assessment Framework*. www.oecd.org/dataoecd/11/40/44455820.pdf (accessed 5 Dec. 2010).

OECD Directorate of Education (2010) Adult literacy. Author. http://www.oecd.org/document/2/0,3343,en_2649_39263294_2670850_1_1_1_1,00.html (accessed 12 Sept. 2010).

OECD and Human Resources Development Canada (1997) *Literacy Skills for the Knowledge Society: Further Results from the International Adult Literacy Survey*. Paris: OECD.

O'Reilly, T. (2005) What is Web 2.0?: Design patterns and business models for the next generation of software. oreillynet.com/pub/a/oreilly/tim/news/2005/09/30/what-is-web–20.html (accessed 4 April 2006).

O'Reilly, T. (2010) The web is dead? A debate (an interview with Chris Anderson and John Battalle). *Wired.com*, 17 August. http://www.wired.com/magazine/2010/08/ff_webrip_debate (accessed 5 Dec. 2010).

Oxenham, J. (1980) *Literacy: Reading, Writing and Social Organization*. London: Routledge & Kegan Paul.

Pahl, K. (2002) Ephemera, mess and miscellaneous piles: texts and practices in families. *Journal of Early Childhood Literacy*, 2(2): 145–66.

Partnership for 21st Century Skills (2010) http://www.p21.org (accessed 5 Dec. 2010).

Plotz, D. (2000) Luke Skywalker is gay? Fan fiction is America's literature of obsession. *Slate*. slate.msn.com/id/80225 (accessed 19 Nov. 2004).

Polanyi, M. (1966) *The Tacit Dimension*. Garden City, NY: Doubleday.

Pool, C. (1997) A conversation with Paul Gilster. *Educational Leadership*, 55: 6–11.

Potter, J. (2010) Photoshopping/photosharing: new media, digital literacies and curatorship. In M. Knobel and C. Lankshear (eds) *DIY Media: Creating, Sharing and Learning with New Technologies*. New York: Peter Lang, pp. 103–32.

Powell, L. (2010) An interview with Howard Rheingold. *eLearn Magazine*, 9 February. http://www.elearnmag.org/subpage.cfm?article=111-1&section=articles (accessed 5 Dec. 2010).

Prinsloo, M. and Breier, M. (eds) (1996) *The Social Uses of Literacy: Theory and Practice in Contemporary South Africa*. Bertsham, South Africa: Sached Books and John Benjamins.

Pugh, S. (2004) The democratic genre: fan fiction in a literary context. *Refractory: A Journal of Entertainment Media*, 5. http://blogs.arts.unimelb.edu.au/refractory/2004/02/03/the-democratic-genre-fan-fiction-in-a-literary-context-sheenagh-pugh (accessed 27 Dec. 2005).

Reckwitz, A. (2002) Toward a theory of social practices: a development in social theorizing. *European Journal of Social Theory*, 5(2): 245–65.

Reed, M., Evely, A., Cundill, G., Fazey, J., Glass, J., Lang, A., Newig, J., Parrish, B., Preett, C., Raymond, C. and Stringer, L. (2010) What is social learning? *Ecology and Society*, 15(4). http://www.ecologyandsociety.org/vol15/iss4/resp1/ (accessed 5 Dec. 2010).

Reich, R. (1992) *The Work of Nations: Preparing Ourselves for 21st Century Capitalism*. New York: Vintage.

Resnick, M., Maloney, J., Monroy-Hernández, A., Rusk, N., Eastmond, E., Brennan, K., Millner, A., Rosenbaum, E., Silver, J., Silverman, B. and Kafai, Y. (2009) Scratch: programming for all. *Communications of the ACM*, 52(11): 60–7.

Rheingold, H. (2002) *Smart Mobs: The Next Social Revolution*. New York: Basic Books.

Rheingold, H. (2009a) 21st century literacies. *Howard Rheingold*. http://vlog.rheingold.com/index.php/site/video/21st-century-literacies (accessed 12 Dec. 2010).

Rheingold, H. (2009b) Mindful infotention: dashboards, radars, filters. *San Francisco Chronicle*, 1 September. http://www.sfgate.com/cgi-bin/blogs/rheingold/detail?entry_id=46677 (accessed 12 Dec. 2010).

Rheingold, H. (2009c) Attention literacy. *San Francisco Chronicle*, 20 April. http://www.sfgate.com/cgi-bin/blogs/rheingold/detail?entry_id=38828 (accessed 12 Sep. 2010).

Rheingold, H. (2009d) Crap detection 101. *San Francisco Chronicle*, 30 June. http://www.sfgate.com/cgi-bin/blogs/rheingold/detail?entry_id=42805 (accessed 12 Sep. 2010).

Rheingold, H. (2009e) Twitter literacy. *San Francisco Chronicle*, 11 May. http://www.sfgate.com/cgi-bin/blogs/rheingold/detail?entry_id=39948 (accessed 12 September 2010).

Rheingold, H. (2010a) Network literacy, part one: how the internet's architecture democratized innovation. *Howard Rheingold.* http://vlog.rheingold.com/index.php/site/video/network-literacy-part-one-how-the-internets-architecture-democratized-innov/ (accessed 29 Nov. 2010).

Rheingold, H. (2010b) Attention, and other 21st-century social media literacies. *Educause,* 45(5): 14–24.

Rheingold, H. (2010c) Network literacy, part two: Sarnoff, Metcalfe, Reed's Laws. *Howard Rheingold.* http://vlog.rheingold.com/index.php/site/video/network-literacy-part-two-sarnoff-metcalfe-reeds-laws (accessed 29 Nov. 2010).

Richardson, W. (2010) *Blogs, Wikis, Podcasts and Other Powerful Web Tools for Classrooms.* Thousand Oaks, CA: Corwin Press.

Rogoff, B. (1991) *Apprenticeship in Thinking.* New York: Oxford University Press.

Rotter, J. (1954) *Social Learning and Clinical Psychology.* New York: Prentice Hall.

Rowan, L. and Bigum, C. (2010) At the hub of it all: Knowledge Producing Schools as sites for educational and social innovation. In D. Clandfield and G. Martell (eds) *The School as Community Hub: Beyond Education's Iron Cage.* Ottawa: Canadian Centre for Policy Alternatives, pp. 185–203.

Salen, K. (2007) Gaming literacies: a game design study in action. *Journal of Educational Multimedia and Hypermedia,* 16(3): 301–22.

Salen, K., Torres, R., Wolozin, L., Rufo-Tepper, R. and Shapiro, A. (2011) *Quest to Learn: Developing the School for Digital Kids.* Cambridge, MA: MIT Press.

Sawyer, R. K. (ed.) (2006) *The Cambridge Handbook of the Learning Sciences.* Cambridge: Cambridge University Press.

Schlager, M., Fusco, J. and Schank, P. (2002) Evolution of an online education community of practice. In K. A. Renninger and W. Shumar (eds) *Building Virtual Communities: Learning and Change in Cyberspace.* New York: Cambridge University Press, pp. 129–58.

Schön, D. (1983) *The Reflective Practitioner.* New York: Basic Books.

Schrage, M. (2001) The relationship revolution. *Technology and Society: Merrill Lynch Forum.* http://web.archive.org/web/20030602025739/http://www.ml.com/woml/forum/relation.htm (accessed 19 Nov. 2010).

Schroeder, S. (2010) Is Facebook worth $41 billion? *Mashable/Business,* November. http://mashable.com/2010/11/15/facebook-41-billion (accessed 25 Nov. 2010).

Scollon, R. and Scollon, S. (1981) *Narrative, Literacy, and Face in Interethnic Communication.* Norwood, NJ: Ablex.

Scribner, S. and Cole, M. (1981) *The Psychology of Literacy.* Cambridge, MA: Harvard University Press.

Shaffer, D. (2007) *How Computer Games Help Children Learn.* New York: Palgrave Macmillan.

Shamburg, C. (2010) DIY podcasting in education. In M. Knobel and C. Lankshear (eds) *DIY Media: Creating, Sharing and Learning with New Technologies.* New York: Peter Lang, pp. 51–75.

Shiels, M. (2010) MySpace deal looks to Facebook to gain and retain users. *BBC News: Technology*, 18 November. http://www.bbc.co.uk/news/technology-11792927 (accessed 21 Nov. 2010).

Sholle, D. and Denski, S. (1993) Reading and writing the media: critical media literacy and postmodernism. In C. Lankshear and P. McLaren (eds) *Critical Literacy: Politics, Praxis and the Postmodern*. Albany, NY: SUNY Press, pp. 297–323.

Somogyi, V. (2002) Complexity of desire: Janeway/Chakotay fan fiction. *Journal of American & Comparative Cultures*, Fall–Winter: 399–405.

Squire, K. (2006) From content to context: video games as designed experiences. *Educational Researcher*, 35(8): 19–29.

Squire, K. (2008) Video-game literacy: a literacy of expertise. In J. Coiro, M. Knobel, C. Lankshear and D. Leu (eds) *A Handbook of Research on New Literacies*. New York: Lawrence Erlbaum Associates, pp. 611–34.

Steinkuehler, C. (2008) Cognition and literacy in massively multiplayer online games. In J. Coiro, M. Knobel, C. Lankshear and D. Leu (eds) *A Handbook of Research on New Literacies*. New York: Lawrence Erlbaum Associates, pp. 635–69.

Street, B. (1984) *Literacy in Theory and Practice*. Cambridge: Cambridge University Press.

Street, B. (ed.) (1993) *Cross-Cultural Approaches to Literacy*. Cambridge: Cambridge University Press.

Street, B. (2001) Introduction. In B. Street (ed.) *Literacy and Development: Ethnographic Perspectives*. London: Routledge, pp. 1–18.

Technology Talks (2010) Farmville earnings: Farmville earned 145m in 2009. *Technology Talks: Tips, Tricks, Gadgets and Tech News*, 13 February. http://www.kokeytechnology.com/free-games/farmville/1239-farmville-earnings-farmville-earned-145m-in-2009 (accessed 25 Sept. 2010).

Technorati (2010) State of the blogosphere 2010. *Technorati*. http://www.technorati.com/blogging/article/state-of-the-blogosphere-2010-introduction/ (accessed 5 Dec. 2010).

Terranova, T. (2004) *Network Culture: Politics for the Information Age*. London: Pluto Press.

Thomas, A. (2006) 'MSN was the next big thing after Beanie Babies': children's virtual experiences as an interface to their everyday lives. *E-Learning*, 3(2): 126–42.

Thomas, A. (2007a) *Youth Online: Identity and Literacy in the Digital Age*. New York: Peter Lang.

Thomas, A. (2007b) Blurring and breaking through the boundaries of narrative, literacy and identity in adolescent fan fiction. In M. Knobel and C. Lankshear (eds) *A New Literacies Sampler*. New York: Peter Lang, pp. 137–66.

Thomas, A. and Tufano, N. (2010) Stop motion animation. In M. Knobel and C. Lankshear (eds) *DIY Media: Creating, Sharing and Learning with New Technologies*. New York: Peter Lang, pp. 161–83.

Thraeryn (n.d.) TheKolWiki: About. *Coldfront Kingdom of Loathing: The KoL Wiki*. http://kol.coldfront.net/thekolwiki/index.php/TheKolWiki:About (accessed 11 Dec. 2010).

Tsugasa (2005) The Konoha Memory Book. *Anime Music Videos*. http://www.animemusicvideos.org/members/members_videoinfo.php?v=101473 (accessed 26 Dec. 2010).

US Department of Education (2001) The Elementary and Secondary Education Act (The *No Child Left Behind Act* of 2001). http://www2.ed.gov/policy/elsec/leg/esea02/index.html (accessed 5 Dec. 2010).

Vale, V. (ed.) (1997) *Zines!* Vol. 2. San Francisco: V/Search.

Webb, R. (1955) *The British Working Class Reader*. London: Allen and Unwin.

Wellman, B. (1997) An electronic group is virtually a social network. In S. Kiesler (ed.) *Culture of the Internet*. Hillsdale, NJ: Lawrence Erlbaum, pp. 179–205.

Wellman, B. (2001) Physical place and cyber space: the rise of personalized networking. http://homes.chass.utoronto.ca/~wellman/publications/individualism/ijurr3a1.htm (accessed 5 Dec. 2010).

Wellman, B., Hogan, B., Berg, K., Boase, J., Carrasco, J., Côté, R., Kayahara, J., Kennedy, T. and Tran, P. (2006) Connected lives: the project. In P. Purcell (ed.) *Networked Neighbourhoods*. New York: Springer, pp. 161–216.

Wellman. B., Quan-Haase, A., Boase, J., Chen, W., Hampron, K., Isla de Diaz, I. and Miyata, K. (2003) The social affordances of the internet for networked individualism. *Journal of Computer-Mediated Communication*, 8(3). http://jcmc.indiana.edu/vol8/issue3/wellman.html (accessed 12 Dec. 2010).

Wenger, E. (1999) *Communities of Practice: Learning, Meaning and Identity*. Cambridge: Cambridge University Press.

Wexler, P. (1988) Curriculum in the closed society. In H. Giroux and P. McLaren (eds) *Critical Pedagogy, the State and Cultural Struggle*. Albany, NY: SUNY Press, pp. 92–104.

Wheeler, S. and Wheeler, D. (2009) Using wikis to promote quality learning in teacher training. *Learning, Media and Technology*, 34(1): 1–10.

Whybark, M. (2004) Hopkin explained, 22 November. *Mike.Whybark.com*. mike.whybark.com/archives/001951.html (accessed 9 March 2005).

Wikipedia (2010a) eBay. *Wikipedia*. http://en.wikipedia.org/wiki/EBay (accessed 10 Dec. 2010).

Wikipedia (2010b) Muntadhar al-Zaidi. *Wikipedia*. http://en.wikipedia.org/wiki/Muntadhar_al-Zaidi (accessed 10 Dec. 2010).

Wikipedia (2010c) Criticism of Facebook. *Wikipedia*. http://en.wikipedia.org/wiki/Criticism_of_Facebook (accessed 10 Dec. 2010).

Wikipedia (2010d) Farmville. *Wikipedia.* http://en.wikipedia.org/wiki/FarmVille (accessed 10 Dec. 2010).

Wikipedia (2010e) Game modding. *Wikipedia.* http://en.wikipedia.org/wiki/Game_modding (accessed 10 Dec. 2010).

Wikipedia (2010f) Fan fiction. *Wikipedia.* http://en.wikipedia.org/wiki/Fan_fiction. (accessed 10 Dec. 2010)

Wikipedia (2010g) Yaoi. *Wikipedia.* http://en.wikipedia.org/wiki/Yaoi (accessed 10 Dec. 2010).

Wikipedia (2010h) Project Runway. *Wikipedia.* http://en.wikipedia.org/wiki/Project_ Runway (accessed 26 Dec. 2010).

Wikipedia (2010i) Social networking websites. *Wikipedia.* http://en.wikipedia.org/wiki/Social_networking_websites (accessed 10 Dec. 2010).

Wikipedia (2010j) Academia.edu. *Wikipedia.* http://en.wikipedia.org/wiki/Academia.edu (accessed 10 Dec. 2010).

Wikipedia (2010k) Leeroy Jenkins. *Wikipedia.* http://en.wikipedia.org/wiki/Leeroy_ Jenkins (accessed 26 Dec. 2010).

Wittgenstein, L. (1953) *Philosophical Investigations.* Oxford: Basil Blackwell.

Yu, F. (2010) The Chinese Matrix and the War of Internet Addiction. *Techcrunch. com*, 18 April. http://techcrunch.com/2010/04/18/the-chinese-matrix-and-the-war-of-internet-addiction/ (accessed 6 Oct. 2010).

Names Index

Subject Index